International
Money Management

International Money Management

Max J. Wasserman
Andreas R. Prindl
Charles C. Townsend, Jr.

The Presidents Association

International standard book number: 0-8144-5285-X
Library of Congress catalog card number: 71-173321

FIRST PRINTING

Preface

THIS book, developed for the American Management Association, attempts to give a practical description of the foreign exchange markets and provide a framework for managerial decisions in the foreign exchange area. It begins with a discussion of theory, particularly that of the international monetary framework, and follows it with a detailed section on foreign exchange markets, export invoicing and collections, and a survey of international money management. Completing the book is a section especially designed for the corporate manager who is entrusted with the financial management of the multinational corporation; it covers the translation of balance sheet data, hedging operations, short-term foreign investments, and other aspects of international financial control.

The book does not concentrate on theoretical aspects of foreign exchange; instead, it encompasses the salient points that a corporate manager in an international division or treasurer's or controller's office should master to inaugurate international financial techniques, systems, and controls for a related group of international entities, particularly in light of the momentous changes in the foreign exchange markets since the summer of 1971. The guidelines, systems, and techniques described are based on the business experience of the authors in corporate and banking areas. Foreign exchange and money management are constantly evolving, and it is the aim of this study to provide a basis from which to approach international finance. A bibliography gives detailed references for further study on the points raised.

Charles C. Townsend, Jr. is primarily responsible for Chapters 1 and 12 to 14, Max J. Wasserman for Chapters 2 to 6, and Andreas R. Prindl for Chapters 7 to 11. Mr. Prindl wishes to acknowledge his indebtedness to colleagues of Morgan Guaranty Trust Company of New York, particularly officers of the foreign exchange department, and to Jean-Louis Masurel, who first coined the phrase "international money management" and instituted the advisory group of that name within Morgan Guaranty.

The Authors

Contents

PART ONE

Introduction

1

The Businessman
and Foreign Exchange

THE businessman who operates in more than one country needs to understand not only the workings of the foreign exchange system but also why changes in monetary values occur and how to cope with them. Foreign exchange is the monetary mechanism by which transactions in two or more currencies are effected. It is the purpose of this book to describe the present international monetary system, the interrelation of that system and the banking system, and the methods and procedures that are applicable to international business transactions. As an introduction, this chapter outlines the international framework within which the multinational corporation operates and the problems that the foreign exchange system presents.

The Need for Foreign Exchange

The development of foreign exchange practices and procedures was similar to that of internal monetary systems. In the beginning, trade took place on a barter basis. That had an obvious disadvantage: each of the parties to a transaction had to have something the other wanted. The basis of the alternative, a monetary exchange system, is a material that has an intrinsic value that is relatively stable and so is wanted by both parties to a transaction. The most common examples of such a material—the medium of exchange—are gold and silver. When both buyer and seller accept a medium of exchange, it becomes possible to dispose of goods and, at a later date and in a different place, purchase other goods or services.

With the development of nations, each with its own monetary system, and international trade, a foreign exchange mechanism became necessary and was developed. By means of foreign exchange, goods produced in one country can be purchased in another country. Regardless of its direction, such an international transaction must be denominated in a currency other than that of either the seller or buyer; that is, one party to the transaction must either buy or sell a foreign currency. He does so through the international banking system, and the result is a foreign exchange transaction. The problem that then arises is convertibility, or the relative values of two different currencies.

The International Monetary System

The international monetary system in use to August 1971 was based on the Bretton Woods agreement of 1944. The effect of the agreement was to restrict fluctuations of the relative values of currencies to narrow limits, and the intent was to stimulate international trade by eliminating the risk of major currency fluctuations. A byproduct of the Bretton Woods system was the substitution of credit between countries for an actual transfer of gold. This was due to the commitment of the United States to sell gold at $35 to the ounce, which was terminated in August 1971. The extension of credit has, however, had internal monetary effects in the countries granting the credits and in the countries receiving them.

Methods and procedures that have been developed by central banks and internal banking systems are the means of effecting actual foreign exchanges. Commercial transactions, in turn, are effected through the banking system. Both the international monetary system and the commercial banking constraints of each country must be thoroughly understood before the flow of financial transactions on a multinational scale can be optimized.

Despite the existence of an international monetary system, changes in the value of one currency in relation to another are common, and they make the management of international business more complex. Changes in monetary values are of two kinds: those that reflect supply and demand in the day-to-day market and those that reflect an imbalance between the economies of countries. The Bretton Woods agreement was intended to limit fluctuations to the day-to-day market variety and give special consideration to the handling of imbalances between countries.

Imbalances

Imbalances are due to the relative rates of exchange of two currencies and what might be considered constant values. An example will indicate what causes the difficulty. Assume that two countries are on a gold standard and that at a particular time, 20 units of country A's currency are equivalent to one ounce of gold and 10 units of country B's currency are also equivalent to one ounce of gold. The result is an official exchange rate of two units of currency A to one unit of currency B. Ignoring transfer costs, then, an article of commerce that costs 20 units of currency A and 10 units of currency B is freely exchangeable between the countries. Now suppose that, over a period of time, costs change in both countries; in country A the item that once cost 20 units of local currency now costs 40, but in country B the same item rose to only 15 units of local currency instead of the former 10. Again leaving out transfer costs, there is now an incentive in country B to ship the particular article to country A and, at the exchange rate of two for one, receive back through the banking system 20 units of currency B instead of the 15 that would be received by selling locally. The effective rate of exchange for this particular article is then $2\frac{2}{3}$ to one, and the result is a drain on the reserves behind currency A.

The example of the preceding paragraph is a simplification of thousands of transactions with the costs going both ways, but the final result is a flow from one country to another that must be coped with sooner or later. Once reserves of gold or other currencies have been used up and creditors are unwilling to grant further extensions, action must be taken to restore equilibrium. In our example one approach would be to change the value of currency A so that, in country A, 30 units of local currency would be equivalent to one ounce of gold. That would make the exchange rate between the two countries three units of currency A to one unit of currency B. In foreign exchange the item shipped from country B would be worth only $13\frac{1}{3}$ units of currency B. An alternative would be to increase the value of currency B to $7\frac{1}{2}$ units to one ounce of gold. That would result in one unit of currency B being equal to $2\frac{2}{3}$ units of currency A, and the shipped item would, in either country, bring 15 units of currency B.

The net result of either remedial action would be to restore the trade equilibrium for the particular article of commerce. Again multiplied by thousands of transactions, a devaluation or revaluation of a currency is an attempt to rectify the flow of funds from one country to another.

Reasons for Imbalances

A principal reason for changes in monetary values between countries is disproportionate differences in internal inflation rates that result in price differentials. In turn, the price differentials result in changes in the flow of goods, services, and capital between countries, which brings about the monetary changes. As prices rise faster in one country than another, imports and exports are affected in both.

Internally, inflationary changes are reflected by economic indicators, such as cost-of-living indices; externally, they are reflected by the change in value of one currency vis-à-vis another. The monetary system that evolved from the Bretton Woods agreement was based on the assumption that governments will take the action necessary to control their domestic situations and thereby keep the relationships of their currencies within the agreed-upon limits. Unfortunately, practical politics often preclude or delay necessary fiscal action. The result is that relationships between currencies, the matter of parity, can and do get out of balance and force a devaluation or revaluation. That also has to be taken into account by the businessman who operates in more than one country. Chapter 4 gives the background of parity changes in detail.

To some extent, values in one country as determined by the fluctuations of the currency of another country are a measure of internal changes. For that reason, many of the foreign exchange measures for protecting against changes in currency value are also useful to the businessman who operates in only one country and must so manage his business as to cope with the effects of internal inflation. Valuations in other currencies do identify problems more clearly, but the same identification could be made by using a local currency index and determining the effect of internal price changes.

For the present purposes, it is pertinent to discuss what happens when a business operates in two or more countries that have different currencies. In order to evaluate operating results, a common denominator must be used; it is usually the currency of the country in which the business is principally located or that in which it is incorporated. By the use of a common denominator, one currency is evaluated in terms of another, and that at once gives rise to problems in foreign exchange. In order to operate a business in several countries, managers must cope with transactions in other currencies and adopt policies and strategies that will maximize their return in relation to whatever standards they adopt. All the aspects of a business—its structure and nature, the countries in which it operates, its products and its goals—have an influence on the relative importance of the various factors involved in foreign exchange decisions.

One important point should be made. The decision to operate a business in a particular country should be based on the business advantages to be obtained. Once it appears that a proper opportunity exists in relation to the potential of the market, the resources available, and the risk, then how to manage any foreign exchange problems can and should be worked out. It would be a mistake to base the business structure principally on foreign exchange advantages or disadvantages, which may very well change.

Changes in Monetary Values

A change in the value of one currency relative to that of another may be large or small, but both possibilities must be considered. The currencies of countries that are members of the International Monetary Fund (IMF or Fund) fluctuate within set percentages of a parity expressed in gold and dollars. Certain countries, such as Switzerland, that are not members of the IMF also control their currency within equivalent limits. Other countries have more than one set of equivalent values and frequently change the limits.

The decision by the United States in August 1971 to stop selling gold at $35 an ounce resulted in a floating of almost all major currencies against the dollar outside the parities and limits called for by the IMF. New parities were agreed upon in December 1971. The wider limits or the elimination of a fixed parity make the management of foreign exchange more difficult and the risk greater.

In general, regardless of how a parity is set, a devaluation or a revaluation occurs when the parity is changed. Fluctuations on either side of parity had the same effect but, of course, generally did not persist and could not exceed set limits. They should, however, be taken into consideration. After all, a $\frac{1}{2}$ percent change over a period of one month amounts to 6 percent on a per annum basis, which can be significant.

Changes in the value of a currency affect a business in two ways. In the first place, such changes have an actual cost that arises from transfers of money between two countries. Depending on the specifics of the transaction, either the seller or the buyer has a change in the value determined by his own currency. That is true of any other transaction involving the payment of funds from one country to another, as for royalties, dividends, services, or loan repayment. The effect of currency changes on the transfer of funds is analyzed in Chapter 13.

In the second place, changes in currency values affect the translation of accounts abroad even when no transfer of funds is immediately involved. As pointed out previously, a multinational business generally uses a common denominator in evaluating results whether or not those results are reported on a consolidated basis. For instance, if a businessman in the United States were using dollars as his base currency, he would not say he made p in dollars, q in francs, and r in pounds. He would report, "We made p dollars in the United States, y dollars in France, and z dollars in the United Kingdom." He would generally receive reports in dollars so that he could evaluate and compare the results and might very well give a total dollar figure for the business as a whole. (There is a pitfall for management in doing that; the tendency is to forget that everything is not actually in dollars but only expressed that way. In the example given, total cash is not dollars alone but dollars, francs, and pounds.)

Translation of Accounts

When a business has assets and liabilities in a country other than its home country that are expressed as or due in the currency of that other country, it must, in order to evaluate them, translate them into the home country currency used as a common denominator. There are certain generally well agreed upon methods for making translations of account. A change in the value of a currency other than that being used for a common denominator results in a change in the value placed upon assets and liabilities in the country of that currency and the net worth of the foreign entity. In turn, that change has an effect on operating results and decisions.

As an example, suppose a business in the United States has a subsidiary operating in the United Kingdom. At month end October 1967 the subsidiary has an inventory worth £100,000, equivalent to $280,000. In November 1967 the pound is devalued. The inventory at month end November is still £100,000, but translated into dollars it is now equivalent to $240,000. Without taking other accounts into consideration, there has been a reduction in value of $40,000. That is purely the result of translation of accounts; for there has not been any transfer of funds from or change in amounts in the United Kingdom. Also, the U.K. subsidiary has had no change whatsoever, since on its books the value of its inventory has remained constant at £100,000.

There are, of course, offsetting effects in other accounts that would have to be taken into consideration in determining the overall effect. The economic effect might be different, depending upon replacement cost and the possibility of increasing prices. That is discussed in detail in Chapter 14.

Summary

To sum up, a change in equivalent currency values affects a business in two ways. First, for transfers of funds, more or less of one currency or the other is required by one party to the transaction. That has an immediate measurable effect in one country or the other. Second, translation of assets and liabilities held abroad under changed rates results in different equivalents of the common currency. In turn, those equivalents reflect a change in the valuation of the business abroad, which must be taken into account in order to report correctly the financial position of the business and review its results over time.

To provide a basic understanding of the foreign exchange field, the following chapters outline in more detail the international monetary system, the relationship of national banking systems to it, and the ways in which the financial and the related foreign exchange activities of an international business can be managed within those systems.

PART TWO

The Theoretical Framework of Foreign Exchange

2

Introducing
Foreign Exchange

THE origins of foreign exchange, like those of money itself, are unknown; there is a lack of written records. It is, however, certain that some types of exchange instruments developed between states, or neighboring political and social groups, even in earliest times. Gold and silver particularly had an "international" value and acceptability in the early ancient world. Hoards that have been unearthed indicate that some collectors amassed the coins of more than one nation, perhaps in the course of primitive foreign exchange transactions.

Primitive bills of exchange arising from trade are known to have existed in Babylonia, and the Code of Hammurabi made provision for them. Early foreign exchange markets consisted of meeting places of money changers and were found in the ancient Middle East, Greece, and Rome. Already during the first millennium B.C., foreign exchange,

13

handled through the money changers, appears to have facilitated the foreign commerce of the period.

Such exchange dealings did not escape the general decline in civilization that characterized the Dark Ages. By the eleventh century, however, money changing had again become an important occupation over much of the then-developed world. The growing importance of trade and industry rendered exchange transactions by means of the manual transfer of coins and bullion increasingly inadequate. Consequently, international payments began to be effected by various forms of paper credit instruments, and that practice grew in importance.

The origin of international bills of exchange is usually ascribed to the Jews, who were expelled from time to time from various countries of Europe, and to the Guelfs, who were forced by the Ghibellines to leave Italy. Members of those two groups attempted to recover at least a part of the value of the property that they were forced to leave behind. They put their goods in the hands of trustworthy friends and later drew bills on them, which they then sold to merchants dealing in the goods involved. In the Middle Ages letters of credit were issued to the Crusaders by Italian merchant-bankers who had branches in the Levant areas that were in Christian hands.

By the end of the fifteenth century a relatively modern system of foreign exchange was already in operation. The principal changes that occurred during the sixteenth to eighteenth centuries were (1) the development of forward exchange, or the purchase and sale of exchange for future delivery, to be used as a cover against changes in spot exchange rates, (2) the growth of international investment, (3) the increase in number of foreign exchange markets, (4) the larger role played by banks, and (5) the increased transferability of bills of exchange.

The nineteenth century was characterized by the use of finance bills, or bills designed to accommodate the international movement of capital. Telegraphic and cable transfers started to replace the slower mail transfers as international communications improved. Banks established closer relations with other banks overseas and displayed a greater degree of interbank cooperation.

Forward exchange continued to grow in importance in the nineteenth century. Arbitrage transactions, or the purchase of one currency against a second and its sale against a third to take advantage of exchange rate differentials among the three, made their appearance. By and large, the nineteenth century was relatively free from government intervention in foreign exchange matters. It is usually characterized as a period of laissez faire, with relatively free foreign exchange movements and markets.

By 1914 and the outbreak of World War I, the world's foreign exchange system was quite developed and formed an efficient system of payment for international economic transactions. In general, as a result of the expansion in international commerce, the twentieth century witnessed substantial growth in all phases of foreign exchange, despite a number of governmental restrictions. More and more foreign exchange business was transacted by the use of telephone, Telex, and telegraph. Instead of formal meeting places where traders gathered to transact business, foreign exchange markets became a multinational structure linked by communication networks.

The Development of Exchange Controls

A number of restrictions on free foreign exchange dealings were inaugurated by many countries during the years of World War I, as well as in those immediately following. Governments began to fear the effect on their economies, or the war effort, of letting capital and reserves move freely among the industrial countries. As the war progressed, intervention in the foreign exchange markets was practiced by many of the belligerents and some of the neutrals, and various systems of exchange controls were adopted. The gold standard was abandoned by several European countries shortly after the outbreak of the war, only to be readopted later by some nations and finally abandoned by all, including the United States, during the Great Depression.

In a country where the gold standard was abandoned, some form of the gold exchange standard was usually installed in its place. Under that standard, paper money is employed as the domestic currency and the country maintains a reserve of gold and convertible foreign exchange (convertible into gold, other currencies, or both) so it can protect its rates of exchange, continue to trade during periods of balance of payments deficits, and instill confidence in its currency. Under the gold exchange standard, foreign exchange transactions are carried out by means of various forms of credit instruments and gold is only rarely employed for that purpose.

After 1918 the currencies of some European countries depreciated rapidly because of rampant monetary inflation, and sometimes little attempt was made to support their rates of exchange. With the advent of the Great Depression and its devastating effects upon the national economies, governments appeared to be at their wit's end to discover and apply remedies. Country after country devalued its currency.

The devaluing countries hoped that lower exchange rates would increase their exports by making their goods cheaper abroad and simultaneously check imports by increasing the prices of imported goods. Between 1933 and 1934 the United States devalued the dollar by raising the price of gold from $20.67 to $35.00 per fine troy ounce, a reduction of 59.06 percent. However, the competitive devaluations did not have the anticipated results, because the devaluation of one currency was frequently countered by that of another.

In World War II, as in World War I, most of the belligerents and many of the neutrals adopted stringent exchange controls in an effort to husband declining international reserves. The declines in reserves resulted from a dire need for imports and an inability to export in sufficiently large amounts to balance imports. The exchange controls were continued in the years immediately following the war and remained in effect during the postwar years until the late 1950s and early 1960s. In addition, the governments of a large number of countries intervened frequently and often massively on the foreign exchange markets in an effort to protect their exchange rates. The vestiges of those exchange controls are still in effect, and exchange market intervention has become a permanent feature of the modern foreign exchange system. Those developments have constituted a sharp reduction in laissez faire.

During the war years and for a number of years afterward, some nations maintained parities that overvalued their currencies. Since they had little to export and were in urgent need of imports, the overvalued parities held exports in check by rendering them more expensive and facilitated imports by making them cheaper.

The financial requirements of the Allies and some neutrals during World War II were met by United States lend-lease, totaling almost $45 billion. After the war, the financial difficulties of many countries suffering from the "dollar shortage" were ameliorated by the Marshall Plan and its successor programs as well as by substantial American loan programs. That still left a large number of problems facing the industrial countries, particularly those of convertibility and international liquidity, without which trade cannot grow.

Advent of the Bretton Woods System

At the end of World War II it was clear that the international monetary system was more a series of expedient innovations than a rational structure. Much of the impetus for reform came from John Maynard (later Lord) Keynes, an official of the United Kingdom, and Harry Dexter White, an official of the United States government, who exchanged papers spelling out their reform proposals during the war. In the summer of 1944, an international conference was held at Bretton

Woods, New Hampshire, to develop an acceptable reform of the international monetary system.

The articles of agreement of the International Monetary Fund and those of a sister organization, the International Bank for Reconstruction and Development (IBRD), which provided for long-term international loans, were drawn up at the Bretton Woods conference. Both articles of agreement were subsequently ratified by the requisite number of governments and, at an inaugural meeting of the Governors of the IMF and IBRD held in Savannah, Georgia, during the spring of 1946, both the IMF and the IBRD were established and put in operation.

The IMF Articles of Agreement provided for a system of fixed parities and limits to the fluctuations of exchange rates somewhat similar to that in effect when gold was the standard. A system of fixed parities was preferred to freely floating or flexible rates of exchange by a majority of the nations in attendance at Bretton Woods, and the question of the one system versus the other was settled until 1971. The parities were defined both in units of gold and in dollars. The system based on the dollar continued to support international trade growth, although it had a number of limitations that are discussed in Chapter 5.

Some Definitions

Most nations then established parities that represented the official values of their currencies in dollars or units of gold. The parity was fixed, although it could be changed from time to time. When the parity, or par value, of a currency is reduced, the currency is said to be *devalued;* when it is increased, the currency is said to be *revalued.* A few countries have not established a single par value but instead use different pars for various groups of commodities or types of transactions.

The par value of a currency is not necessarily the price at which the currency may be purchased or sold on free foreign exchange markets. That price varies over time in response to the demand for and the supply of the currency, as well as other factors. The price of one foreign currency in terms of another is its *rate of exchange.*

There are several rates of exchange for each currency; in fact, there is one for each other currency into which the currency is convertible. Thus, there are pound-dollar, pound–French franc, pound-mark, pound-escudo, and many other British pound sterling rates of exchange. Foreign exchange for delivery within two days is known as *spot exchange;* that which is deliverable at some other time in the future is known as *forward exchange.*

Currencies that are readily or freely exchangeable for all others and for merchandise and services transactions are known as *convertible currencies.* Those that are not thus freely convertible are held to be either *inconvertible currencies* or *currencies of limited convertibility.*

External Economies, Internal Economies, and Foreign Exchange

There is a marked interrelation of the external and internal economies of all trading nations, and it is from this interrelation that foreign exchange developments often arise. In countries in which foreign commerce is an important part of the economy, as it is in the Netherlands, Belgium, and Denmark, the impact of the external economy upon the internal one is great. Usually the influence of the external economy on the domestic one, and vice versa, is manifested by changes in income, prices, and interest rates.

A large number of statistical studies have shown a close correlation between national income and imports. As income rises, imports tend to grow and a downward pressure on a nation's rate of exchange may develop. As income falls, imports tend to drop and there is a resulting fall in the demand for foreign currencies and a lessening of the downward pressures on the rates of exchange.

Changes in domestic prices have an important effect on a nation's foreign economic position and are a frequent cause of fluctuations in the nation's rates of exchange and the devaluation or revaluation of its currency. Inflation is usually followed by declining exports and rising imports and brings downward pressure on the rates of exchange. Deflation is likely to have the opposite effect.

The movement of internal interest rates affects a nation's external business. Rising rates stimulate the inflow of capital from abroad and bring upward pressure on rates of exchange; falling rates stimulate the outflow of capital and exert downward pressure on rates of exchange. However, the effects of changes in domestic interest rates on the external economy are not always as clear-cut as are those of income and price changes.

The exports (imports) of one country are the imports (exports) of another; the investment and unilateral transfers inflows (outflows) of one nation are the investment and unilateral transfers outflows (inflows) of another. Thus the impact of the internal economy upon a nation's external economy finds its counterpart in the impact of the external economy upon the internal economy of another country or countries. From a global point of view, the internal and external economies are but two sides of the same coin, and declines in the rates of exchange of any one country find their counterparts in the relative increases in the rates of others. The effect of changes in income, prices, and interest rates in one country may be countered or offset by similar changes on the part of that country's trading partners.

The impact of the external upon the internal economy may be felt in yet another way. The export of goods and services and the receipt of investments and unilateral transfers from abroad mean an inflow of money from overseas. Such an inflow tends to have an inflationary effect and serves to raise incomes and prices as well as lower interest rates, all of which has the effects upon exchange rates that have already been noted. Imports of goods and services and the outflows of unilateral transfers and investments have the opposite effects.

When a nation is running a persistent deficit or surplus on its balance of payments, there may be reason to believe that its parity is no longer realistic, that it over- or undervalues its currency or that its internal economy is out of adjustment with its external economy. The remedy for such a situation involves a choice between changes in the country's internal economy, the establishment of new and more realistic or equilibrium par values, the installation of barriers to trade and exchange controls, or some combination of all these measures. The problem of why parities may or should be changed is discussed in Chapter 4.

Balance of Payments and Foreign Exchange Flows

A country's economic relationships with other countries is measured by the tabulation called the *balance of payments,* which is also useful for examining flows of exchange between trading countries. The modern balance of payments presents in tabular form a summary of all the international economic transactions of a nation with another country, a group of countries, international organizations, or the rest of the world. The balance of payments does not show totals; it shows only the movement of the items included for the period covered. More than a hundred members of the IMF now prepare these statements, which are published in a uniform format by the IMF in its *Balance of Payments Yearbooks.* The balance of payments of the United States is published in these yearbooks, but the primary source of U.S. balances of payments, in a format that differs from the one used by the IMF, is the monthly periodical of the U.S. Department of Commerce, the *Survey of Current Business* and the supplements to the *Survey.*

The full and official United States balance of payments, as carried in the *Survey,* is a highly technical tabulation of 64 rows of figures. A condensed summary version of that statement for 1970, without cumbersome technical detail, is presented in Table 1. It is based on the accounting principle of credit and debit, respectively represented by either a positive sign (+) or no sign and the minus sign (−). The positive-sign items represent transactions that give rise to currency receipts from overseas, and the negative-sign items represent those that give rise to payments to overseas residents. The balance of payments thus indicates the sources and magnitudes of the supply (receipts) of foreign currencies and the demand (payments) for them during the period covered.

Since the balance of payments is based on the accounting principle of debit and credit, it can, technically speaking, show neither a surplus nor a deficit; the debits must equal the credits, and vice versa. If the debits and credits do not balance, as they practically never do for all countries, one or more errors or omissions have been made. The account on line 13 of Table 1 shows the errors and omissions on the United States balance of payments for 1970.

Nevertheless, the terms "balance of payments surplus" and "balance of payments deficit" continue to be employed. As used, they refer to the

Table 1. Summary balance of payments of the United States, 1970.
[in millions of dollars; Debits (−)]

Account	Amount
(1) Merchandise trade balance	2,110
(2) Services (net)	1,480
(3) **Balance on goods and services**	**3,592**
(4) Remittances, pensions, and other transfers	−1,410
(5) **Balance on goods, services, and remittances**	**2,182**
(6) U.S. government grants (excluding military)	−1,739
(7) **Balance on current account**	**444**
(8) U.S. government capital flows (net), and non-liquid liabilities to other than foreign official reserve agencies	−2,029
(9) Long-term private capital flows (net)	−1,453
(10) **Balance on current account and long-term capital**	**−3,038**
(11) Nonliquid short-term private capital flows (net)	−548
(12) Allocations of SDR's	867
(13) Errors and omissions (net)	−1,132
(14) **Net liquidity balance**	**−3,852**
(15) Liquid private capital flows (net)	−5,969
(16) **Official reserve transactions balance**	**−9,821**

Source: IMF, *International Financial News Survey*, Vol. XXIII, No. 29 (July 28, 1971), p. 229.

increase (surplus) or the decrease (deficit) of a country's gold stock and certain highly liquid foreign short-term assets that are readily convertible into other currencies plus certain drawing rights on the IMF. Those assets constitute a nation's international reserves, and thus the balance of payments serves to indicate the movements of a nation's international reserves and its ability to maintain its parity, limit the fluctuations in its rates of exchange, and also continue to import, provide unilateral transfers, and invest abroad at its customary levels. The international reserves are also the domestic reserves of the central bank or the banking system of some nations, and their movement serves to condition, in part, the monetary supply.

There is no standard definition or measure of international reserves that is utilized by all nations; each nation uses a definition that corresponds to its institutions and practices. Since intervention in the exchange markets and the determination of the size of banking reserves are functions of government, only the items that either belong to the government or can be utilized by it in case of need are counted as parts of its reserves and as measures of its surpluses and deficits.

Formerly the United States employed what is known as the "gross liquidity measure" to determine its surpluses and deficits. There was, however, criticism that the liquidity measure gave an exaggerated picture of deficits and was also asymmetric, in that it did not include private short-term assets as offsets to private short-term liabilities, and so a second and additional measure, the official reserve transactions, was adopted in 1967.

In 1971 certain changes were made in the format of the U.S. balance of payments and in the definition of liquidity balance, and a new, but unofficial, measure of surpluses and deficits was added. Table 1 presents these changes. The liquidity balance or measure was revised to include both private short-term assets as well as private short-term liabilities, the new Special Drawing Rights (SDR's) of the IMF (explained in Chapter 3) and errors and omissions. This new measure, termed the "net liquidity balance," is a symmetric measure and is shown on line 14 of Table 1. The official reserve transactions balance remains unchanged and is shown on line 16. The new and unofficial measure, preferred by some analysts, is the balance on the current account and long-term capital and is frequently called the "basic and overall balance." It is intended as a rough measure of long-term trends, rather than volatile short-term movements, of the balance of payments and is shown on line 10 of Table 1. The United States now has one unofficial and two official measures of balance of payments surpluses and deficits, which causes confusion.

On the liquidity basis, in general terms, surpluses and deficits are measured by the changes in U.S. official reserve assets and in U.S. liquid foreign assets and liabilities, in SDR's, and in errors and omissions. The official reserve transactions basis, likewise in general terms, measures surpluses and deficits by the changes in U.S. official reserve assets and in U.S. liquid and certain nonliquid liabilities to foreign *official agencies.* The difference between the two measures can be substantial. On the liquidity basis, in 1970, there was a deficit of $3.9 billion, whereas on the official reserve transaction basis there was a deficit of $9.8 billion.

Of the two official measures, the liquidity one seems to have greater acceptance and is generally believed to be the more realistic, but neither definition is entirely satisfactory. No completely adaquate measure of the U.S. balance of payments surpluses and deficits has as yet been devised, if, indeed, it is possible to devise a measure that will meet all requirements. A similar observation applies to the surplus and deficit measures employed by other nations.

Theories of Foreign Exchange

After decades of relative neglect, economic theory, especially in its mathematical form, has taken new life since the end of World War II. The renaissance has included many aspects of international economics, but theories that purport to explain the levels and movements of parities and spot and forward exchange have been somewhat neglected. The result is that parities and spot and forward exchange are still a subject of research and controversy. There are, however, five leading theories that attempt to explain exchange movements, and each has some validity; they are purchasing power, balance of payments, and supply and demand theories and the psychological theories of pars and spot rates, together with the interest parity theory of forward exchange.

Purchasing power parity theory. In its simplest form, the purchasing power theory affirms that the rate of exchange establishes itself at a point that will equalize the prices in any two countries. One of the functions of the rate of exchange, according to this theory, is to equalize the purchasing power of the several currencies.

A rate of exchange that does nothing more than equalize price levels will not necessarily prove to be an equilibrium rate. Foreign trade usually includes capital and unilateral transfer movements, and the purchasing power parity theory does not pretend to equalize them. In addition, nations produce many commodities that do not enter into international trade, and the prices of those domestic goods obviously cannot be equalized internationally. Furthermore, studies of European prices and rates of exchange during inflationary periods indicate that internal price levels are frequently determined by rates of exchange, and not the other way around.

The purchasing power parity rate of exchange does have the signal advantage, however, of being relatively determinable, whereas some theories do not provide a practical method of calculating an exchange rate or a par value. In addition, since the merchandise trade is the most important element of world commercial relations, the theory does have at least limited applicability. For such reasons as these, it continues to have considerable acceptance as a workable approach to the general movement of exchange rates.

The balance of payments theory. The balance of payments or the equilibrium theory of rates of exchange affirms that the rate of exchange tends to establish itself where it will maintain balance of payments equilibrium and eliminate surpluses and deficits. The theory might be valid if the rates of exchange were allowed to float freely and attain their market, or equilibrium, levels. Under the Bretton Woods system, however, limits are set to the fluctuations of rates of exchange and government intervention in the exchange markets impedes the free movement of rates. Hence, the theory is more a statement of a tendency than a complete explanation.

In addition, the theory does not at present provide a workable mechanism for calculating an equilibrium rate of exchange, except, perhaps, in the cases of relatively primitive and small countries with a limited range of international transactions. When mathematical economics has become more sophisticated and electronic computers have been sufficiently developed, it may be possible to calculate balance of payments rates for large and highly developed economies.

The supply and demand theory. According to another theory, the rate of exchange is held to be determined by the supply and demand for foreign currencies. Actually, the supply and demand theory is not a theory but is instead a descriptive mechanism. To say that a rate of exchange is established by supply and demand is to tell *how* a rate is established but to say little about the factors that determine it or *why* the rate is at a given level and not at some other level. All of the forces, substantive, technical, and psychological, that have impact on a rate of exchange must, by the very nature of the market itself, act by determining the demand for, and the supply of, foreign exchange.

The psychological theory. According to the psychological theory, the rate of exchange is largely conditioned by the attitudes of those who deal in it. If, in their opinion, a rate is below its correct level or will rise in the future, they are inclined to buy it; they thereby increase the demand for the currency and work to raise its rate. If, on the other hand, they feel that the rate overvalues the currency or is likely to decline, they are apt to sell their holdings and thereby increase the market supply of the currency and push its rate down.

The theory has considerable merit because attitudes do affect the demand and supply of a foreign currency. Many of the movements in the rates of exchange can be explained only by the attitudes of those who deal in exchange. In addition, the psychological theory realistically stresses qualitative factors in exchange rate determination; the theories that rely solely upon quantative factors are incomplete. On the other hand, the psychological theory is vague and lacks precision. It does not provide a means of calculating either par values or rates.

The unsatisfactory state of exchange rate theory has recently led several countries to abandon the calculation of new parities by the use of academic theories. Instead, they have allowed their rates of exchange to float within limits and to seek new and equilibrium levels through the free play of market forces. The rates thus established may possibly form the basis of the new and realistic parities.

Interest parity theory. The interest parity theory is the most widely accepted explanation of the magnitudes of forward exchange rates. It is based on the fact that short-term interest rates differ from country to country and also the fact that banks, which buy or sell foreign currencies forward, usually like to cover their positions by the purchase or sale of these currencies spot.

The interest parity theory holds that the difference between the spot and forward rates for the currency of a given country is due to the discrepancy in the short-term interest rates between that country and another. Theoretically, the forward rate tends to move to a discount or a premium over spot large enough to equalize the interest rates prevailing in the two countries.

Experience with forward exchange indicates that the interest parity theory is basically sound but that there are many other factors that act on forward rates and serve to set their levels. They are discussed in Chapter 7.

3

The International
Monetary System, 1946-1971

THE international monetary system that prevailed from 1946 to 1971 was often called the Bretton Woods system and was based upon a form of the gold exchange standard. It was heavily in debt to its immediate predecessor, the gold standard, for some of its principal features.

The International Gold Standard

Under the gold standard, the par value of a nation's currency was the amount of fine gold embodied in its monetary unit in comparison with the amount embodied in that of its trading partners. For example, in the heyday of the gold standard prior to World War I, the pound sterling contained 4.8665 times as much fine gold as the dollar. The par of pound-dollar exchange was therefore $4.8665 per pound.

The parities were, of course, firmly fixed and could be changed only by altering the gold content of a country's standard monetary unit. A nation's rate of exchange fluctuated around the par value, but it could not exceed or fall below the gold export and import points. Those points were determined by the cost of shipping gold. Assuming that the cost of shipping gold between the United Kingdom and the United States amounted to 2 cents per pound, the upper limit, the gold export point, stood at $4.86 plus 2 cents shipping charges for a total of about $4.88 and the lower limit, the gold import point, stood at $4.86 minus shipping charges of 2 cents for a total of about $4.84.

Above and below the export and import points, it was profitable to buy gold in one country and sell it in another, with direct effects on the money supply of both countries. That in turn had an effect on the domestic situation of a country receiving or losing large amounts of gold; it would inflate or deflate the economy and so change the relationship of international prices. The price adjustment left the internal economy of one country open to pervasive influence of other countries. If a real run on a country's gold supply took place, the country was forced to reduce the value of its currency, that is, to devalue in terms of gold. It was, in large part, that automatic, direct effect on the internal economy, which was difficult or impossible to counteract by monetary policy, that led to the adoption of a new system.

Gold points, determined by shipping costs, existed between the currencies of all countries on the gold standard. Unlike the par values, the gold points were not firmly fixed; they tended to vary with the cost of shipping and insuring gold. The system of generally fixed parities and limits to exchange rate fluctuations were the main legacy of the gold standard to the IMF system, which was begun after the famous Bretton Woods conference of 1944.

The IMF System, 1946–1971

The IMF system controlled the limits to exchange rate movements of its member countries in a predetermined way. The exchange rates were permitted, under the original IMF Agreement, to vary by 1 percent above or below par. [Signatories to the European Monetary Agreement (EMA) agreed to limit their exchange rate fluctuations to $3/4$ of 1 percent in either direction, and some other nations also followed that practice.] As a country's rate of exchange attained or approached either limit, usually termed arbitrage support points, the country's central bank intervened in the market to prevent the rate from passing the limits.

Market intervention can require a nation to accumulate international reserves composed of gold and foreign currencies above normal trading levels; the reserves can, of course, be used by the nation to support its own currency when necessary by purchasing it on the exchange markets. Continued intervention when a spot currency is under pressure and threatening to go below the lower intervention point can mean depletion of international reserves of the country.

In 1971, in view of the unsettled international monetary system, some IMF members preferred to adopt "central rates," rather than new pars, as a temporary measure until more stable conditions prevailed when new pars could be established realistically. A few other nations preferred to refrain temporarily from establishing new pars and elected to allow their rates to float or to be established by market forces. Many nations also agreed in 1971 to allow their market rates of exchange to fluctuate within a wider band—2¼ percent above and below par—than that permitted by the original Fund Agreement. All of these changes fall within the provisions of the Fund Agreement and the decisions of its management. These topics are discussed more fully in Chapter 4. Table 2

Table 2. Par and central values of the currencies of selected IMF member countries as of August 16, 1971.

Country	Currency	Units per U.S. Dollar	Type of Rate
Austria	Schilling	23.3	Central
Belgium	Franc	44.8159	Central
Canada	Dollar	1.8598	Floating
Denmark	Krone	6.98	Central
France *	Franc	5.1157	Par
Germany	Deutsche mark	3.2225	Central
Ghana	New Cedi	1.81818	Par
Guatemala	Quetzal	1.0	Par
India	Rupee	7.27927	Central
Iran	Rial	75.75	Par
Italy	Lira	581.5	Central
Japan	Yen	308.0	Central
Kenya	E. African shilling	7.14286	Par
Mexico	Peso	12.5	Central
Netherlands	Guilder	3.2447	Central
Portugal	Escudo	27.25	Central
Spain	Peseta	64.4737	Par
United Kingdom	Pound	0.383772	Par
United States	Dollar	1.0	Par

* Maintains dual rates.

Source: IMF, *International Financial News Survey*, Vol. XXIV, No. 4 (February 2, 1972).

presents the pars and central rates for a selected group of countries as they stood on February 2, 1972.

The IMF arbitrage support points provided a more narrow band for spot movements than the gold export and import points under the gold standard. It might appear that, under the original IMF Agreement, the acceptable band of spread in exchange rate fluctuations amounts to a total of 2 percent: 1 percent in either direction. However, the IMF rules stipulated that those support points applied only to exchange rate movements with respect to other currencies than the dollar. It might, for example, be possible for the French franc rate to have been at its lowest dollar support point while the German mark was at its highest. The spread between the franc and the mark would then be 2 percent. Under the original IMF rules, the mark could then drop to its lowest support point and the franc rise to its highest for an additional 2 percent variation from par. That would give a total possible exchange movement in a range of 4 percent.

Since with the passage of time a nation's fixed parity may cease to be realistic and either over- or undervalue the currency, the IMF Agreement provided for orderly and reasonable changes in a parity upon the initiative of the country concerned. Such a system of alterable pars is often termed the *adjustable-peg*.

The provisions relating to parities and limits to exchange rate fluctuations, as well as certain other features of the original IMF Agreement, were designed to prevent a recurrence of the competitive devaluations of currencies that took place during the 1930s. In addition, the agreement stipulated that the members were to avoid restrictions on current payments (trade in merchandise, services including income, and unilateral transfers), as well as discriminatory currency practices.

The British economist Keynes, in the pre-Bretton Woods debates, apparently favored the creation of an international central bank or a national central banks' bank. On the other hand, Harry White, the American Treasury official, in those same debates, did not favor such an institution, and it was not adopted at the Bretton Woods conference. An international central bank would have raised some important political questions, some of which revolved around the surrender of a country's control over its money to an institution responsible to such a large group of members that it would be effectively responsible to none.

However, the lack of an international central bank made it difficult for many nations to trade at customary levels during periods of temporary balance of payments deficits and to protect their rates of exchange. Such countries had no institution to which they could turn for temporary short-term loans to tide them over the difficult periods. As a result, there was frequent recourse to exchange controls and other barriers to trade and a consequent decrease in world commerce. Unfortunately, for political reasons, many countries have not taken the internal steps necessary—deflation, price controls, and income policies—to combat balance of payments deficits in a more constructive way.

To counter those problems, the IMF was endowed with the power to create certain drawing rights. Under the drawing rights provisions, a member could draw the currencies of other members that were held by the IMF under certain conditions. The regular (not special) drawing rights were divided into two groups: the gold and the credit tranche

Table 3. Quotas, subscriptions to IMF capital stock, and
SDR allocations of selected members, 1972
(in millions of dollars).*

| | | Subscriptions | | |
| | | | Member's | Total SDR |
Member	Quota	Gold	Currency	Allocations
Austria	270	67.5	202.5	76.7
Belgium	650	162.5	487.5	209.4
Canada	1,100	275.0	825.0	358.6
Denmark	260	65.0	195.0	82.8
France	1,500	375.0	1,125.0	485.6
Germany	1,600	400.0	1,200.0	542.4
Ghana	87	15.2	71.8	30.1
Guatemala	36	9.0	27.0	11.9
India	940	162.5	777.5	326.2
Iran	192	48.0	144.0	61.9
Italy	1,000	250.0	750.0	318.6
Japan	1,200	300.0	900.0	377.4
Kenya	48	11.9	36.1	15.6
Mexico	370	92.5	277.5	124.2
Netherlands	700	175.0	525.0	236.5
Portugal	117	29.3	87.8	NP †
Spain	395	98.7	296.3	126.2
United Kingdom	2,800	700.0	2,100.0	1,006.3
United States	6,700	1,675.0	5,025.0	2,294.0

* Quotas and subscriptions as of December 31, 1971. Total SDR allocations include those of January 1, 1970, January 1, 1971, and January 1, 1972.

† NP = nonparticipants in SDR's.

Source: IMF, *International Financial Statistics*, Vol. XXV, No. 2 (February 1972), pp. 7–9; IMF, *International Financial News Survey*, Vol. XXIV, No. 1 (January 12, 1972), pp. 1–2.

drawing rights. Each member was assigned a quota based on its relative importance in world economic activity, and the member's drawing rights depended upon the size of its quota.

The quota corresponded in amount to the member's subscription to the capital stock of the IMF, which the member was required to purchase. Either 25 percent of a member's quota or 10 percent of a member's holding of gold and dollars, whichever was less, was payable in gold and is termed the gold tranche; the remaining 75 percent, or credit tranche, was payable in its own currency. Table 3 lists the quotas, subscriptions, and Special Drawing Rights (explained in a later paragraph) of selected IMF members.

A member was entitled to draw the currencies of other members virtually unconditionally up to the amount of its gold tranche, and that privilege comprised the gold tranche drawing rights. Those rights were therefore included by many members as a part of their international reserves. On the other hand, drawings above the gold tranche, termed credit tranche drawing rights, were subject to the specific approval of the Fund. Because credit tranche drawing rights were conditional rather than automatic, some members did not report them as a part of their international reserves, although others did.

When it exercised its drawing rights, a member tendered its own currency to the Fund against the currencies that it wanted to draw. The drawing rights were hedged by a number of considerations and provisions specified by the IMF Articles of Agreement.

As the volume of world trade increased and prices rose, the quotas established by the Fund in 1946 became increasingly inadequate to meet the members' requirements. Accordingly, in 1959, quotas were increased by about 50 percent and in 1966 by slightly more than 25 percent. Also, in 1962, the IMF negotiated an arrangement with ten important industrial members (the Group of Ten) that gave it the power to borrow currencies from the members of the group and so increase its capacity to lend. Under that arrangement, known as the General Agreement to Borrow (GAB), the Fund was authorized to borrow about $6 billion that could be loaned to members on five-year terms.

Special Drawing Rights

Despite the increase in the Fund's capacity to make short-term loans, it became increasingly evident that additional resources were needed if the Fund was to solve some of the problems of the international monetary system. After much debate and long deliberations on the part of the Fund itself, the Group of Ten, the finance ministers, and the governors of the central banks of the Fund members, new drawing rights, called Special Drawing Rights (SDR's), were created.

The SDR's, or paper gold, as they are sometimes called, were designed to remedy at least one important defect of the international monetary system: its lack of liquidity, its inability to supply adequate international reserve media to a world with rapidly growing foreign commerce. The SDR's are a form of special account entries on the books of the IMF that are separate and distinct from other drawing rights. Those accounts are distributed among the members who elect to participate in the plan —no member is required to participate—in conformity with their quotas.

At its annual meeting in 1969 the Fund authorized the creation over the ensuing three years of SDR's to a value of 9.5 billion units, or, since each unit has the value of $1, the equivalent of $9.5 billion. An initial allocation of SDR's amounting to about the equivalent of $3.4 billion was made on January 1, 1970, an additional allocation of about $2.9 billion was made on January 1, 1971, and another of almost $3 billion on January 1, 1972. The individual allocations to selected countries are presented on Table 3. The SDR's are a form of fiat money not convertible into gold. However, their gold value is guaranteed, and that helped to assure their acceptability.

Participants in the program are able to use their SDR's to meet balance of payments deficits in a way similar to that in which they use their holdings of gold and foreign exchange reserves. A participant with balance of payments problems instructs the IMF to draw down the balance of its SDR account in exchange for an equivalent amount of convertible currency to be used to reconstitute its reserves or finance its international transactions. When so instructed, the IMF designates one or more of the other participants, usually with a strong balance of payments position, to transfer convertible currencies to the participant making the request. The SDR accounts of the participants furnishing the convertible currency are increased by the equivalent of the amount of the currency involved.

Although the SDR's are designed primarily to finance countries that are in a difficult balance of payments position, and not to improve the composition of a participant's international reserves, they can be used under certain circumstances for some other purposes. Thus a participant could use them to purchase its own currency that was held by another participant, provided the latter consented. That provision was of importance to the United States in its past efforts to protect its monetary gold stock. A reduction in foreign holdings of dollars would have reduced the potential demand for the reimbursement of those holdings in gold.

The SDR's can be used only among the participants in the program, and they were not originally designed to replace gold or convertible currencies as reserves assets. Participants who hold SDR's receive interest on them at a nominal rate, and those who are allocated SDR's must pay interest on those allocations at the same rate. Consequently there is a small incentive for participants with surpluses to cooperate by acquiring SDR balances and for those with deficits to rebuild their balances.

This discussion has dealt with the original role of the SDR's. Chapter 5 explores the possible changes that may lie ahead.

The IMF System and International Reserves

If a country had freely floating exchange rates—rates that were allowed to seek their own levels without interference, it would not need a high level of international reserves. The rates of exchange would fall as foreign payments exceeded receipts and rise as receipts exceeded payments. They would tend to reach equilibrium levels that would automatically balance the country's international accounts.

However, if a country wanted to prevent its rates of exchange from falling below certain levels, it would require some international reserves. It would use those reserves to buy its own currency on the market and thereby decrease its supply and work to enhance its value. If it wanted to counter a rise in its rates of exchange, it would use its own currency to purchase currencies of other countries and thereby increase the supply and work to lower the price of its own currency.

When the exchange rates are pegged, a country has three reasons for needing international reserves: First, it must intervene in the market to prevent its rates from falling below the permitted limit. Second, if its balance of payments is in a deficit, it must have a reserve of foreign exchange to help pay for its imports if it is to continue to trade at customary levels. Third, it needs reserves to maintain confidence in its currency and acceptance of its currency by the international community. The narrower the range of support points, the larger the supply of reserves that will be required. The Bretton Woods system forced all members to maintain substantial international reserves.

Table 4 presents an estimate of the free-world (members of the IMF) holdings of the more important categories of reserves as they stood in 1958 and in 1970. As the table indicates, there has been a substantial change in both the amount and composition of those reserves in the 13 years covered. The total reserves grew from $57.5 to $92.4 billion during that time to accommodate the rapidly increasing world commerce.

Table 4. Free-world holdings of international reserves,*
December 31, 1958 and December 31, 1970 (in millions
of dollars and percents of totals).

	1958		1970 †	
	Amount	Percent	Amount	Percent
Gold	38,040	66.1	37,190	40.3
SDR's			3,124	3.3
IMF reserve position	2,557	4.4	7,697	8.3
Dollars	9,648	16.8	23,921	25.9
Sterling	5,998	10.4	6,636	7.2
Other currencies	1,304	2.3	13,863	15.0
Total	57,547	100.0	92,431	100.0

* Holdings of IMF members only.
† As of December 31, 1970.
Note: The division among dollars, sterling, and other currencies given for 1970 may not be exact because of the operation of the Euro-dollar multiplier, and the amount allocated to other currencies may be exaggerated. Data are not available to permit a more exact distribution.

Source: Computed from data in IMF, *International Financial Statistics,* Vol. XXI, No. 10 (October 1968), pp. 16–17, and Vol. XXIV, No. 9 (September 1971), pp. 18–23.

The role of gold in free-world reserves declined from 66 percent of the total in 1958 to about 40 percent in 1970. Its place was largely taken by dollars, which increased from 16.8 percent in 1958 to 25.9 percent in 1970. Sterling declined in importance as a reserve currency; it dropped from 10.4 to 7.2 percent. The part played by other currencies, however, rose from 2.3 to 15.0 percent. The role of IMF reserve position grew substantially more important in the period 1958 to 1970; the percent of total increased from 4.4 to 8.3 percent. SDR's constituted 3.3 percent of the total reserves in 1970. Because of the operation of the Euro-dollar multiplier (explained later), the allocation of reserves among dollars, sterling, and other currencies is at best a rough approximation.

The International Role of the Dollar

The dollar has occupied a unique position and played a key role in the IMF system. Together with gold, it was the reference point and the standard by which the par values of all other IMF members currencies were measured. As Table 4 shows, dollars have been, after gold, the most important component of the world's international reserves;

they amounted to 25.9 percent of the total in 1970. Using the foreign currency reserve holdings of all the IMF members as a base of 100 percent, in 1970 the dollar represented almost 54 percent of the total, followed by sterling at about 14.9 percent and all other currencies at 31.9 percent.

In addition to its role as a reserve currency, the dollar has been an important vehicle or transactions currency. Many transactions, including some between non-dollar countries, are negotiated and liquidated in dollars. When some residents of non-dollar countries desired to purchase the currency of another non-dollar country, they sometimes first exchanged their own currency for dollars and then used those dollars to purchase the other currency desired. Thus, for example, if a Liberian resident desired to buy French francs, he might first have exchanged his Liberian dollars for United States dollars and then those dollars for francs.

Although IMF members must have maintained their rates of exchange within 1 percent of parity in either direction against the dollar under the system that prevailed until 1971, the dollar itself, under the original IMF Agreement, need have been kept convertible into gold only when it was presented by member countries' official financial institutions. For example, if the escudo-dollar rate fell or rose by more than 1 percent of parity, it would have been up to Portugal to take corrective measures and not the United States. For those reasons, the United States was obliged to maintain certain gold reserves, but only smaller reserves of foreign currencies. The crux of that system was this undertaking to provide gold when requested; of course, other countries were expected not to turn in their dollar holdings capriciously.

The dollar's international position and its role as a reserve currency permitted the United States to run deficits on its balance of payments in every year since 1950, except 1957 and 1968, without undertaking severe policy steps to correct the situation. In the 20 years from 1950 to 1970, the U.S. balance of payments deficits measured on the liquidity basis totaled $48.4 billion, or an average of about $2.2 billion a year.

Those deficits have played an important international role. The need for international reserves is, in part, a function of the volume of world trade. As that trade has increased, the need for reserves has also increased. The amount of gold that is mined, and that is available for reserve purposes, has not kept pace with the rise in the volume of trade. Hence, trading nations have been obliged to augment their holdings of gold by increasing their foreign exchange assets. Because the dollar was the principal component of the foreign exchange reserves, more and more dollars have been demanded for reserve purposes.

Dollars usually became internationally available when the United States ran a deficit on its balance of payments, which gave the unfortunate illusion of a permanent necessity for such deficits. Other currencies, especially sterling, are also used as components of reserves, and conceivably their use could be substantially increased. But given the gold convertibility of the dollar until August 15, 1971, and the economic size of the United States, the dollar was heavily demanded in the past for reserve purposes. It might possibly be said, therefore, that until the advent of the SDR's, the United States was "obliged" or "condemned" to incur deficits if the international monetary mechanism was to avoid a crisis of liquidity. In addition, as will be seen later in this chapter, the dollars arising from the deficits served to support the Eurodollar market.

The deficits have placed a strain on both the dollar exchange rates and the U.S. monetary gold reserves. Although the United States is not necessarily obliged to defend the dollar exchange rates, it has done so from time to time when they have been under heavy speculative attack. It has taken that action with the cooperation of other central banks.

In addition to the downward pressure on dollar rates of exchange, some foreign countries have, from time to time, lost confidence in the stability of the dollar, the dollar exchange rates, and the continued ability of the United States to redeem foreign official dollar holdings in gold. That lack of confidence has been manifested, in part, by substantial requests for the redemption of foreign-held dollars in gold. As a result, the monetary gold holdings of the United States, which stood at almost $25 billion in 1947, have declined to about $10.2 billion (November 1971).

An international monetary system that relies on U.S. balance of payments deficits and weakens its principal reserve currency by reducing the U.S. gold reserve is not an indefinitely viable one. It was the hope of the IMF and the majority of its members that the SDR's would improve the international monetary system by reducing the responsibility and pressure that the system imposed on the dollar.

The Monetary Crisis of 1971

Before the SDR's had sufficient time to demonstrate their effectiveness, President Nixon on August 15, 1971, announced a series of measures designed to improve the American economy by reducing inflation and unemployment, stimulating production, and reducing or eliminating its balance of payments deficits. As far as the international monetary system was concerned, the most important measures he announced were the refusal of the United States to continue to redeem officially held dollars in gold and the imposition of a 10 percent surtax on the importation of a list of goods. Although the redemption of officially held dollars in gold had never been mandatory, it had been the policy of the United States ever since the Gold Reserve Act of 1934 became law.

Between 1950 and 1970, the net deficits of the United States totaled slightly more than $39 billion as measured by the gross liquidity concept. In 1969, the deficit amounted to $7 billion, that for 1970 was $3.8 billion, and that for 1971 gave promise of also being large. The dollar had finally become redundant on the world's foreign exchange markets. That is to say, the supply of dollars was in excess of the demand for them. However, the redundancy of the dollar cannot be blamed *exclusively* on balance of payments deficits. As explained subsequently in this chapter, some of the excess dollar supplies were the result of the multiplier effect of operations on the Euro-dollar market.

This redundancy became clearly manifest in 1971 when the dollar exchange rates came under heavy downward pressure, especially vis-à-vis the West German mark, the Swiss, Belgian, and French francs, the Dutch guilder, the Italian lira, and the Japanese yen.

To comply with the provisions of the IMF Articles of Agreement, those countries whose currencies rose in relation to the dollar bought dollars with their own currencies to prevent their currencies from rising above the support point in terms of dollars. This increased their stock of dollars and the amount of their own currency outstanding, thereby contributing to inflationary measures in their own countries. Some countries finally stopped supporting the dollar in this way by buying it against their own currency, and allowed their currency to float and to seek its natural market level against the dollar and other currencies.

The downward pressure on the dollar had its origin in the belief on the part of many of those who dealt in foreign exchange that the dollar would be devalued in terms of the stronger world currencies. Some of those who held dollars and had future payments to make in marks, French, Belgian, and Swiss francs, Dutch guilder, Italian lira, Japanese yen, and other currencies thought it wise to exchange their dollar holdings against those currencies before the dollar was devalued and the price of those currencies rose in terms of the dollar. In addition, speculators saw the possibility of making a quick profit by buying those currencies against dollars at the prevailing exchange rate and selling them later at a higher price in terms of dollars. As a result of these pressures, the dollar rates of exchange fell in terms of those and other currencies.

The impact of these events was especially great, because the dollar was not only the principal foreign exchange reserve asset and the leading vehicle and transactions currency—the currency in which many transactions were denominated—it was also the *numéraire* of the international monetary system. Together with gold, the dollar was the standard of value of all IMF members' parities as well as that of Fund subscriptions, quotas, and certain transactions among members and with the Fund.

According to the IMF Agreement, the United States was not obliged to maintain its spot rates of exchange within 1 percent of parity as were the other members. It was only obliged to buy and sell gold freely at the established rate of $35 per fine troy ounce. Thus, for example, if the pound rose close to its upper limit with reference to the dollar, it was up to the United Kingdom authorities to take appropriate action to prevent the pound from rising above its upper limit; the United States did not need to intervene on the foreign exchange markets to prevent the dollar from falling below its exchange rate limit. When the United States broke the dollar's link with gold, it may be said to have breached the IMF Agreement, at least technically.

Since the United States was not obliged to sustain the dollar exchange rates, and since the dollar was widely demanded by other nations as a reserve medium and the Euro-dollar market utilized increasingly large amounts of dollars, the United States was able to run balance of payments deficits for a long period of time and in substantial amounts. This "privilege" was denied all other currencies, and some nations, notably France, resented the fact that the United States could continue to invest abroad and buy foreign enterprises while running balance of payments deficits.

Several reasons underlay the decision to break the link with gold. By allowing the dollar to "float" without any attachment to gold, the United States hoped to force its trading partners to revalue their currencies. The United States monetary authorities had come to believe that many strong foreign currencies were undervalued, which gave these partners substantial trading advantages. Revaluation would have the effect of making the exports of the revaluing countries more expensive and their imports less expensive, thus working to reduce the U.S. balance of payments deficits.

In addition, the United States wanted to retain its slender gold, foreign exchange, IMF drawing rights, and SDR reserves—in July 1971 they amounted to slightly more than $13.8 billion—in the event that, under a revised IMF Agreement, it would have to limit dollar exchange rate declines by using these reserves to intervene on the foreign exchange markets. Finally, the U.S. monetary authorities desired to diminish or destroy the role of gold in the international monetary system, believing that it introduced an undesirable element of rigidity and that it had outlived its usefulness.

The addition of the 10 percent surcharge on import tariff duties was designed as a negotiating advantage for use in forcing certain U.S. trading partners to revalue their currencies realistically and to eliminate some of their barriers to imports and of favors to their export industries. This surcharge has since been eliminated.

The reaction of other countries to the U.S. measures was prompt. Some of the leading trading nations closed their foreign exchange markets for a few days. When the markets reopened, the rates of exchange of several of them were allowed to float within limits and not entirely freely. The governments of most of those countries wanted to prevent their rates from rising too high, which would endanger their balance of payments positions.

France adopted a "two-tier" exchange rate system, which was really a form of multiple exchange rates. Under this system, controlled rates, maintained within the prescribed limits, were adopted for current transactions and another rate was allowed to seek its uncontrolled supply and demand level for use in investment and speculative transactions.

After August 15, 1971, it also became evident that the international monetary system would have to be substantially altered or possibly restructured if it was to operate satisfactorily in the years ahead. Possible changes in the Bretton Woods system were discussed at meetings of the Group of Ten ministers (Belgium, Canada, France, Germany, Italy, Japan, the Netherlands, Sweden, the United Kingdom, and the United States); the finance ministers of the members of the European Economic Community (EEC); the Council of the General Agreement on Tariffs and Trade (GATT); and the Board of Governors and Executive Directors of the IMF.

Chapters 4 and 5 discuss those changes that were agreed upon in November–December 1971.

The European Monetary Agreement

The European countries participating in the Marshall Plan formed several organizations, one of which, the European Payments Union (EPU), was designed to facilitate payments between members, provide members with a source of short-term credit, and reduce barriers to foreign trade. At the end of the Marshall Plan, the EPU was replaced by the European Monetary Agreement (EMA), which is still in force. It consists of two principal parts or programs: a multilateral system of settlements to accommodate multilateral exchange clearance and a

European fund to provide temporary assistance to member countries in balance of payments difficulties.

The clearing facilities of the EMA were designed to be an alternative clearing mechanism and not to replace the free exchange markets. Since the EMA clears transactions at less favorable rates than those available on the foreign exchange markets, it provides an incentive for the members to use those markets. It does, however, require that balances arising from certain bilateral payment agreements be cleared through its mechanism. To date, few countries have taken advantage of the credits offered by the EMA, and so that aspect of the program has not proved to be very attractive.

The creation of the IMF, EPU, and EMA and the swap arrangements among government central banks are evidence of the cooperation that today characterizes the international payments system and is in agreeable contrast to the negative and competitive attitude that prevailed before World War II, especially during the depression-ridden 1930s. The new spirit is perhaps the most important characteristic of the modern world payments system.

The Euro-dollar Market

The term "Euro-dollar market" is really a misnomer, because the market deals in currencies other than dollars. However, dollars do account for about 85 to 90 percent of all the transactions carried out on it, and so it is customarily called the Euro-dollar market. Moreover, to simplify the following discussion, the market is assumed to deal exclusively in dollars. What is said about Euro-dollar transactions applies generally to transactions in other Euro-currencies.

The Euro-dollar market is informally organized; it consists of transactions between banks, mostly in London but also in other financial centers, that accept demand and time deposits in dollars and stand ready to extend credit in dollars.

Foreigners who receive payment in dollars in the form of drafts, checks, and bills of exchange and who want to retain the dollars and enjoy the higher rates of interest offered by their banks (in comparison with U.S. banks), deposit the proceeds of the instruments in the commercial banks of their own or other countries outside the United States in dollar-denominated accounts. The Euro-dollar market originated from that willingness to keep deposits in dollars and from the willingness of banks to accept and relend such deposits.

Euro-dollars may be said to originate in two ways: from primary sources and from dollar loans. The primary sources include the transfer of deposits in U.S. banks from U.S. residents to nonresidents. They also include dollars received in exchange for foreign currencies and the proceeds of dollar-denominated money and credit instruments that are deposited in dollar-denominated accounts in foreign banks. Other, or nonprimary, Euro-dollars originate when foreign banks and residents make dollar loans against their dollar deposits.

Since the Euro-dollar market deals most often in short-term funds up to one year, Euro-dollars have somewhat restricted uses. They are widely employed to finance foreign trade transactions, and that market has added a new dimension to the more conventional foreign trade financing facilities. They are also used by business firms abroad, including the subsidiaries of American firms, as a source of working capital.

Foreign central banks have used the Euro-dollar market as a source of additional dollar reserves and as an outlet for excess reserves. In recent years, American commercial banks have had recourse to the market on a large scale to adjust their U.S. liquidity and reserve positions, as well as to secure supplementary funds to meet customer credit demands. Recent (1968–1969) pressures on U.S. bank reserves, the declines in the large negotiable certificates of deposit (CD's), and exceptionally heavy demands for credit induced American banks to borrow heavily on the Euro-dollar market at that time.

More stringent controls on U.S. direct investments abroad have increased the number of bond flotations in foreign markets by American corporations. The proceeds of those loans are often placed temporarily in Euro-dollar deposits. Apparently, substantial amounts of foreign funds that were formerly used to purchase U.S. securities have been diverted to the Euro-dollar market.

The market owes its increasing usage and flexibility to several circumstances. Federal Reserve Regulation Q, which fixes the interest rates on time deposits, together with the rule that prevents American banks from paying interest on demand deposits, have made dollar deposits abroad more attractive. Foreign banks often offer higher time deposit interest rates than their American counterparts, and some of them may pay interest on demand deposits. The strict regulations applied on many European capital markets have created a demand for less highly regulated markets, and, until recently, the Euro-dollar market was relatively free from regulation. Present trends, however, seem to indicate that this market will be more and more strictly regulated in the future and that it may lose some of its attraction as an unregulated market in the years ahead.

In addition, there has been a shortage of attractive money market instruments in Europe. The relatively high interest rates and convenient maturities that frequently characterize Euro-dollar loans have interested many investors. Moreover, the growth of economies all over the world, especially the increase in world trade, has created a need for additional sources of short-term funds. Finally, until August 1971 the exchange rate stability of the dollar has constituted another attraction of the market.

The Euro-dollar market has been increased in part by U.S. balance of payments deficits. According to data prepared by the U.S. Department of Commerce, foreign-owned demand and time deposits in U.S. banks, together with foreign-owned liquid dollar assets such as U.S. Treasury bills and commercial paper, totaled more than $43 billion (December 1970). The foreign central banks and other official foreign financial institutions held approximately $20 billion of those funds and private parties $23 billion at that time.

The amount of Euro-currencies outstanding at the end of 1970 is estimated by the Bank for International Settlements (BIS) to total the equivalent of about $57 billion, including $46 billion in Euro-dollars. Evidence of the rapid growth of the market is that the total currencies outstanding on it were estimated at only $1.5 to $2 billion in 1961 and at $7 billion in 1964.

Although much foreign trade is financed on it, the Euro-dollar market is largely a private bank credit market supplying business working capital and conducted by foreign commercial banks in dollars and certain other currencies. It carries out internationally the basic functions that a domestic money market performs within a given country. It provides an international mechanism and the institutions for moving funds from corporations, banks, and others with temporary surpluses to those with temporary shortages. In that way it links together the domestic money markets of many countries.

A certain discrepancy is apparent in the figures showing Euro-dollar holdings and U.S. short-term liabilities cited in the preceding paragraphs: the total liquid U.S. liabilities to private foreign parties are estimated at $23 billion and the dollar component of the Euro-dollar market at $46 billion. In other words, the Euro-dollar holdings were estimated at approximately twice the U.S. dollar liabilities to private foreign parties. A similar discrepancy is found in the IMF international liquidity statistics showing the difference between the foreign exchange holdings of the various national monetary authorities, on the one hand, and the sum of the liquid liabilities of the U.S. and the U.K. to official foreign creditors on the other. This discrepancy has grown from less than $1 billion prior to 1966 to almost $14 billion at the end of 1970.

In view of all the available facts, it is too large to be explained solely by the increase in the holdings of other currencies.

These discrepancies are believed to be due to the fact that the dollar assets of the Euro-dollar market have what economists term a "multiplier effect." This effect results from the overseas commercial banks' use of their dollar deposits in the United States as "reserves" and the recycling by foreign central banks of their dollar deposits in the United States.

Assume, for example, that a private British resident, John Doe, draws a million dollar draft on his account in a New York bank and deposits it to his dollar account in Bank *A* in London (a Euro-dollar deposit). Bank *A* now deposits the draft to the credit of its account in another New York bank and also has a dollar deposit liability of like amount to John Doe. Realizing that all its dollar depositors are not likely to demand full payment of their dollar deposits at the same time, and that withdrawals are often accompanied by additional dollar deposits, Bank *A* regards its New York dollar deposit as a "reserve asset" in much the same way that an American national bank regards its deposits in a Federal Reserve bank as its reserve.

Bank *A* then lends another British resident, Richard Roe, $800,000 and opens a dollar deposit of this amount in Roe's name. The bank now has dollar deposit liabilities amounting to $1,800,000 supported by its New York bank deposit (reserve) of $1 million. Bank *A* might even make additional Euro-dollar loans, thus creating additional dollar deposit liabilities, if it felt that its New York dollar deposit would be large enough to support them. Thus by the use of New York dollar deposits as reserves, the overseas Euro-banks multiply the number of dollars available on the Euro-dollar market.

Now assume, for example, that the Bank of France lends $10 million to the BIS to take advantage of the attractive rate of interest this bank offers. It does so by drawing a draft on one of its New York bank accounts and handing it to the BIS, receiving a $10 million credit to its account with the BIS. The BIS now deposits this draft to one of its accounts with a New York bank.

To take advantage of still higher rates of interest, the BIS then lends $10 million to Bank *B* in London by handing it a draft on its New York account. Bank *B* deposits this draft to its New York bank account. Company *X*, in Paris, needing additional working capital, borrows $10 million from Bank *B*. Bank *B* draws on its New York account and turns the draft over to Company *X*, which in turn deposits it to its bank account in New York. Then Company *X*, needing francs, sells its newly acquired New York dollars to Bank *C* in Paris receiving an equivalent amount of francs in return. Bank *C*, desiring to increase its reserves, draws a draft for $10 million on its recently increased New York account in favor of the Bank of France, which then deposits it to one of its accounts in New York. In return, Bank *C* obtains a credit of an equivalent amount in francs at the current rate of exchange posted to its reserve account with this central bank.

The Bank of France now has an additional $10 million in its New York accounts, and still retains its $10 million deposit credit with the BIS. It now possesses $20 million in Euro-dollars whereas it started the round of transactions with but $10 million in its New York account. The Euro-dollars have been doubled by the recycling operations. The Bank of France could repeat such transactions several times more if the circumstances were propitious and several other central banks have carried out a number of transactions of similar type.

Although these hypothetical examples of the Euro-dollar multiplier are greatly oversimplified, they serve to indicate the manner in which it operates. Because of these multiplier effects, the large and perhaps redundant supply of dollars abroad, which overseas commercial and central bankers are sometimes wont to decry, cannot be attributed solely to U.S. balance of payments deficits. Perhaps as much as half of the Euro-dollar market's supply of dollars has been the creation of the overseas commercial and central banks themselves.

Data for the computation of the multiplier effect are not readily available. Several analysts have placed its value at approximately 2, meaning that for each U.S. short-term and liquid dollar liability held abroad, another Euro-dollar has been created by the overseas commercial and central banks. Some of the downward pressure on the dollar exchange rates has been due, in part at least, to these multiplier effects.

The basic funds of the Euro-dollar market on which the multiplier operates are supplied largely by U.S. balance of payments deficits. Should the measures taken by the United States since August 15, 1971, together with the possible revaluation of the currencies of its trading partners and the devaluation of the dollar, succeed in eliminating this deficit, the Euro-dollar market would be deprived of some new funds and might cease to grow at least as rapidly as it has in the past.

If the United States were to run a balance of payments surplus that was not compensated by an equivalent increase in SDR's, the dollar assets of this market might decline as traders draw on it for dollars needed to finance their transactions with the United States. The impact of such surpluses in reducing the Euro-dollar market's dollar assets could be exacerbated if the dollar were to continue to be used as a reserve currency.

Thus, the future size, growth, and effectiveness of the Euro-dollar market cannot easily be predicted at present (1972). It is likely to depend heavily upon the success or failure of United States efforts to improve its balance of payments position and on the impending changes in the international monetary system.

4

Parity Changes

PARITY, or the par value of a nation's currency, is today described as the official rate of exchange or the international value in terms of other currencies that a government is either obliged by agreement to maintain or tries to maintain for its own money. It is, with the exception of freely floating or multiple rates of exchange employed by some countries, a single fixed rate of exchange around which the market rate is permitted to fluctuate to some degree.

In the case of the 118 members of the IMF and as stated in the IMF original (1944) Articles of Agreement "the par value of the currency of each member shall be expressed in terms of gold as a common denominator or in terms of the United States dollar of the weight and fineness in effect on July 1, 1944." This definition is likely to be modified in the future. In the case of nonmembers that have par values, the parity may be similarly expressed.

The antecedents of the present system of parities are found in the gold standard that prevailed before the Great Depression of the 1930s. Under the gold standard the mint parities were automatically established and defined as the ratio of fine gold in the monetary unit of one country to that of another.

Alternative Exchange Rate Systems

In 1944, the participants in the Bretton Woods conference, where the IMF Articles of Agreement were worked out, were faced with a choice between several possible exchange rate systems:

- Freely floating rates of exchange.
- Flexible exchange rate systems.
- Fixed parities, subject to adjustment, with a wide or narrow band of permitted exchange rate fluctuations around them.
- Absolutely fixed parities, not subject to adjustment with no permitted exchange rate fluctuation around them, usually enforced by exchange controls.
- A system of multiple exchange rates.

With the exception of multiple exchange rate systems, the alternative systems shade into one another. They range from complete laissez faire, as in the case of freely floating rates of exchange, to totally directed systems, as in the case of fixed parities with no permitted exchange rate variations. However, all fixed parities are actually subject to change from time to time. Rigid, unadjustable parities may exist in theory, but they are seldom found in peacetime practice. That is why the Bretton Woods system of fixed parities was often called the adjustable-peg system.

Under a *freely floating system,* the rate of exchange is established on the foreign exchange markets without government intervention. There is usually no fixed parity under the system; the only prevailing rate is usually that established by supply and demand forces on free markets. Such a rate of exchange is often termed the "natural" or market rate. Theoretically, the freely floating system does not require holdings of international reserves, since no attempt is made to control the movement of exchange rates and government intervention on the exchange market is not involved.

When a *system of flexible exchange rates* prevails, a parity is usually not established and the rates are determined by the market. However, the government reserves the right to intervene from time to time in an effort to raise or lower the rate. It may also establish maximum and minimum rates that it attempts to enforce. Flexible rates require some holdings of international reserves; for the government's central bank or exchange stabilization institution could not intervene on the exchange markets without them.

Under a *system of adjustable fixed pars* a parity is established, as it was under the 1944 IMF Agreement, and is subject to adjustment from time to time. The market rates of exchange are permitted to fluctuate above and below par in either a wide or a narrower band. The fixed par system, which is still in general use, requires substantial holdings of international reserves; their actual amount is partially determined by the size of the permitted band of flutuations around par and the individual country's requirements.

A *system of rigidly fixed parities*, not subject to adjustment, and no permitted exchange rate fluctuations around them implies all-embracing exchange controls. The relatively free exchange market is abolished, and a monopoly of foreign exchange dealings is conferred on the central bank or an exchange stabilization institution. All buyers of exchange must purchase it from that institution, and all those who receive foreign exchange must turn it over to that institution in exchange for domestic currency. Under such a system, no international reserves are required theoretically, although most nations that use complete exchange control do hold some. Such systems may be used in wartime.

Multiple exchange rate systems lie somewhat outside the spectrum already sketched. Under such systems, and there are many types of them, no single rate or parity, either in fact or in effect, is applicable to all transactions; instead, two or more are applicable to a given group of transactions. Thus a country might have two official parities, a lower one in terms of the domestic currency that is applicable to exports and a higher one that is applicable to imports. Such a system would encourage exports and discourage imports. Also, the government would earn revenue by buying foreign currencies cheaply and selling them dearly.

Multiple exchange rate systems are usually designed to encourage some transactions and discourage other; in February 1972, multiple rates were employed by 35 of the 118 members of the Fund and by a number of nonmember countries, both Communist and non-Communist. The structures and mechanisms of such systems vary widely, and a full discussion of them lies beyond the scope of this book.

Determination of Parity Levels

As was seen earlier in this chapter, the determination of parities under the gold standard presented no problem, but under paper money standards, which prevail universally today, it presents a number of difficulties. Paper money, whether government currency or commercial bank demand deposit, has no intrinsic value and is a form of debt.

The value of paper money on the domestic market is generally held to be determined by what the money will purchase there; hence, it rises when prices decline and declines when prices rise. On the international or foreign exchange markets, the value of a national money may be said to be determined by the amount of foreign currency that can be obtained in exchange for the currency; it rises when more foreign currency can be obtained and falls when less can be.

However, that does not tell very much about how exchange value is determined. The two leading theories of how the determination is made are the *purchasing power parity theory* and the *balance of payments equilibrium theory*. The second is only an extension and development of the first.

The purchasing power parity theory was first fully described during the first decade of the 1800s. The most recent version compares exchange rates and price levels of two or more countries during a base period and a subsequent period. According to this version of the theory, the rate of exchange shifts to reflect changes in the price levels.

The following formula is often used to compute the purchasing power parity rate:

$$\frac{\text{Index number of prices in one country}}{\text{Index number of prices in another country}} \times \begin{matrix}\text{rate of exchange} \\ \text{in base period} \\ \text{between the two} \\ \text{countries}\end{matrix} = \begin{matrix}\text{purchasing power} \\ \text{parity rate}\end{matrix}$$

To illustrate, assume that prices in countries X and Y are both 100 in the base period and that two units of currency X are then required to purchase one unit of currency Y, both expressed in dollars. If, in a subsequent period, prices in X increase by 50 percent while those in country Y remain the same, the rate of exchange will be

$$\frac{150}{100} \times \$2 = \$3$$

Under those circumstances, the new rate would be $3 instead of $2.

The purchasing power parity theory has frequently been used to calculate new pars of exchange after the older pars ceased to maintain a balance of payments equilibrium. However, the theory has many shortcomings. In the first place, it is difficult to determine just what index of prices should be employed. Usually, in practice, many indices are used in an effort to provide a reliable basis for the calculation.

Another criticism of the theory is that such a rate of exchange can serve to equalize the prices of only those goods that are traded internationally. Also, the theory does not provide a basis for the equalization of exchange rate movements due to movements in investment funds and rates of interest.

Furthermore, the purchasing power parity theory does not explain shifts in rates of exchange that are due, not to price movements, but to structural changes in the economies, technological developments, changes in the source of supply, and so on. Finally, transportation costs may contribute to disparities in the rates.

The deficiencies in the purchasing power parity theory led to the elaboration of a more modern theory that has wide acceptance today: the balance of payments equilibrium theory. According to that theory, the rates of exchange of any country with other countries, on free markets, will tend to establish themselves at a point that will result in a balance of payments equilibrium. Actually, that is less a theory than a truism. On free exchange markets, the rate of exchange could scarcely establish itself at any other point.

The most important dffiiculty with the newer theory has been the impossibility of computing such a rate for countries with a wide variety of international transactions. With the advent of more sophisticated computers, however, it may be possible in the future to estimate such rates.

The practical advantage of the purchasing power parity theory over the equilibrium theory is, therefore, the possibility of computing a rate, and consequently a par, that has at least approximate accuracy. It is also possible to adjust a purchasing power parity par in an attempt to counter the shortcomings sketched in earlier paragraphs. However, even the most carefully estimated rates, whatever the method employed—and this will apply to computer-determined equilibrium rates also—are subject to a wide margin of error because of the inaccuracy of many economic data.

Even the most precise economic statistics, such as those for foreign trade, are inaccurate. The known inadequacies of the two theories described here have recently led several countries to experiment with another method of determining an appropriate par. The rate of exchange was allowed to fluctuate more freely until the data accumulated were sufficient to enable the exchange authorities to determine what the correct par should be.* In theory, the modal rate, or that which occurred most frequently, should be selected as the proper one to use as the new parity.

---

* In several cases there was some degree of manipulation by the authorities to limit the exchange rate fluctuations.

The experimental method violated at least the spirit, if not the letter, of the IMF Agreement, but the IMF has not taken any important action against the countries that employed it. In view of its utility, some think it advisable for the Fund to modify its Articles of Agreement to permit its use with, of course, appropriate safeguards against abuse. In a decision of the Fund Executive Directors on December 18, 1971, steps were taken in this direction.

Parities and the IMF

In December 1945 the IMF accepted the stated pars of 32 of its then 39 members. At that time the Fund realized that many of the pars were not realistic and that most of them overvalued the currency. They were accepted with the expectation that they would be reevaluated in the near future. In 1949 there were many devaluations, and a number of countries, including some of those that devalued in 1949, have devalued since. Of the present 118 Fund members, only a few more than 40 have not changed the value of their parties since joining the Fund. Almost all of the changes in parities have been devaluations; only a few have been revaluations. The rationale of the IMF parity system is presented in Chapter 3.

Supply, Demand, and Parities

A par is a theoretical or abstract rate and is, of course, not necessarily the rate at which a currency can be bought and sold. The actual, or market, rates of exchange tend to fluctuate around the official par only when the par approximates an equilibrium rate. If the par overvalues the currency, the market rates tend to fluctuate below it; if it undervalues the currency, they tend to fluctuate above it.

Foreign exchange, or the currency of another country, is usually wanted, not for itself, but for what it will buy in its country of issue. (An obvious exception is foreign exchange wanted for speculative purposes.) Thus, the demand and supply of foreign currencies may be said to be derived from that of the items bought and sold with it. In addition, the supply of foreign currencies comes from many different sources and may be said to represent a composite supply.

Under these circumstances, the demand for and supply of foreign exchange takes on the characteristics of the goods, services, and capital that it is desired to acquire or that gave rise to the supply. As far as the establishment and maintenance of a parity is concerned, the price elasticities of the goods, services, and capital from which the demand and supply of foreign exchange are derived are matters of prime importance.

The price elasticity of the demand for foreign exchange refers to the response of buyers to a change in the rate of exchange. When buyers are very responsive to alterations in the rate of exchange, demand is considered elastic. If, on the other hand, buyers react only slightly to changes in exchange rates, demand is held to be inelastic.

The demand for necessities, or goods for which there is no adequate substitute, is usually inelastic, and so inelastic demand is characteristic of many types of foodstuffs and raw materials. The elasticity of demand for foreign exchange desired for merchandise imports depends in part on the willingness or ability of domestic firms to produce substitutes or competing items.

The supply of foreign exchange of a given country stems from the sale of foreign merchandise, services, and capital to that country. When foreigners desire to buy a country's exports, they must purchase its currency with their own. Thus the supply of one country's currency available to a second country is closely related to the demand for the second country's currency. When the demand schedule of a given country for a foreign currency is known, the supply schedule of the foreign country's exchange can be frequently derived from it.

Similarly to the price elasticity described earlier, the supply elasticity of foreign exchange refers to the responsiveness of sellers to movements in the rates or pars of exchange. When the sellers are highly responsive to those changes, the supply is said to be elastic; when they are not, the supply is said to be inelastic.

For purposes of determining its elasticity, the supply is generally divided into two groups: an existing or market and a long-run supply. The market supply cannot be increased immediately and is therefore likely to prove inelastic. A long-run supply must be produced, and its price elasticity may depend on the nature of the costs involved in creating additional supplies of it. From that point of view, supply elasticity is related to the cost of production of exports, since, for most countries, the largest share of foreign exchange is that gained by the export of merchandise and services. When the supply of foreign exchange is derived from constant-costs industries (labor-intensive ones), the supply price is not likely to change much as the quantity demanded rises and falls. On the other hand, the supply price of increasing-costs industries (land-intensive ones) tends to rise when demand increases and to fall as demand decreases. When the supply is derived from decreasing-cost industries (capital-intensive ones), the supply price tends to decrease when the quantity demanded increases, and vice versa.

When a country has only a few exports and imports, it is relatively easy to establish the demand and supply elasticities for foreign exchange, but when it has a wide variety of exports and imports, elasticities have been difficult to estimate. In the future, thanks to the advent of computers and the development of statistical technology, estimation may prove easier.

Elasticities in the demand for and supply of foreign exchange are important in establishing and maintaining equilibrium parities. When both demand and supply are relatively elastic, small changes in the parity are likely to prove adequate in reestablishing equilibrium. When they are relatively inelastic, larger changes in parity would probably be required.

The supply and demand elasticities of foreign exchange are important in determining the effectiveness of changes in parities in correcting balance of payments disequilibriums. Assume that a nation with a persistent balance of payments deficit desires to restore equilibrium through devaluation. The first effect of devaluation would be to lower the *prices* of exports in terms of a foreign currency and to raise those of imports in terms of the domestic currency. If the devaluation is to prove effective, the *total value* of imports must be less than that of exports. If in certain special cases the foreign exchange supply and demand elasticities are unfavorable, devaluation could conceivably widen the deficit by increasing the payments for imports over the receipts from exports.

Parity Stability

The par value of a currency, once correctly established, will continue to reflect the correct international value of the currency, or its value in terms of other currencies, as long as the country's balance of payments remains in or near equilibrium over time. But since even the best balances of payments are not very accurate and many others are highly inaccurate, another and probably better measure of the accuracy of parity is the movement of international reserves.

When a country loses international reserves over time, its par is no longer an equilibrium rate and may be said to overvalue its currency. When it gains reserves, its par is likewise no longer valid and may be said to undervalue the currency. In the first situation, if the drop in reserves cannot be eliminated by other means, the currency should probably be devalued. In the second, unless the reserve gain can be reduced, the currency should be revalued. Some pars, of course, were not correctly established in the first place and sooner or later had to be, or should have been, rectified.

For many decades prior to the establishment of the Bretton Woods system, devaluation and, to a lesser extent, revaluation were in bad repute and nations usually had recourse to those measures only when all others had failed. Even today, and after so many nations have devalued, some of them several times, a certain stigma is still attached to devaluation.

Devaluation and, to a lesser extent, revaluation are difficult politically because they cast doubt, both internally and externally, on the capacity and integrity of the government and the value of the currency. For that reason, either change is usually postponed as long as possible and is made only after all other measures have failed. In this context it should be noted that the pre-1971 IMF did not have the power to force any individual member to change its parity, although it could, and often has, put considerable pressure on a member to do so. Other countries can, of course, exert similar pressure. Also, the Fund can, under certain conditions, change the par value of all its members.

Devaluation or revaluation can frequently be postponed by taking steps to combat speculation against the currency, by borrowing funds to replenish international reserves, by swaps and other cooperative measures between central banks designed to replenish a deficit country's reduced reserves, by drawing on the Fund under any of the rights that the member may have, by employing exchange, import, and export controls, and by preempting the foreign currency holdings or securities of residents.

Inflation. There are many reasons why parities, once correctly stated, lost their validity over time. Probably the most common cause of the difficulty is inflation. Usually inflation has an important impact on the value of a currency when some prices rise more rapidly than others and when some, fixed by contract, do not rise at all. In periods of inflation different costs increase at various rates; incomes, expenditures, and savings are higher; there is loss of international confidence in the stability of the currency, and the terms of trade of the inflating country and those of nations that trade with it are changed.

Inflation serves to raise the prices of the exports of the inflating country and thus reduce them in volume. In addition, because of rising prices, it tends to attract imports. Since there is a close and direct relation between income and imports, inflation, by raising incomes, serves to reinforce the increase of the volume of imports.

Decrease in exports and stimulation of imports together create a greater volume of holders of currency who wish to sell it (to acquire foreign currencies to pay for the increased imports) and a smaller volume of persons who wish to buy (foreigners who require it to pay for the inflating country's exports), which fosters downward pressures on the rates of exchange of inflating countries. If those pressures persist, they could cause parity to represent an overvaluation of the currency. If the measures designed to counteract those pressures are not successful, the ultimate alternative is devaluation. The rare case of deflation, would, of course, have the opposite effects on parities and rates of exchange.

When so many nations are inflating at the same time, it is not analytically correct to consider the inflation of any one country without regard to that of others. If, for example, county A inflates by 5 percent, country B by 5 percent, country C by 10 percent, and country D by 2 percent, country A has not inflated at all with reference to country B; it has deflated with reference to country C, and it has inflated with reference to country D.

The net effect of inflation on a country's rates of exchange and parity could possibly be determined by taking a weighted average (by relative volume of exchange transactions) of its impact on the several rates of its trading partners. However, in view of the role played by the dollar and other leading currencies in the Bretton Woods system and in world trading patterns, the rates of exchange with these currencies could well be the critical ones in determining the net impact of inflation on a national currency, as was demonstrated by the exchange rate movements in 1971.

Cyclical movements. A second important cause of upward and downward pressures on parities and rates of exchange is the cyclical movement of economies that occurs from time to time in industrial countries. During the cyclical upswing, production, employment, incomes, and general economic activity rise; during the downswing, they decline. In an upswing, since incomes are on the rise, imports are likely to grow. Exports may possibly increase as well, and the net effect on the rate of exchange will depend on the relative sizes of the increases in imports and exports.

If imports rise more rapidly than exports, as they are likely to, there will be downward pressures on exchange rates and devaluation will perhaps be the ultimate result. If exports rise more rapidly than imports, the pressure on rates of exchange will be upward and revaluation may eventually become necessary.

The downswings of the cycle are usually accompanied by falling imports and exports. The net effects of those movements on rates of exchange and parities will again depend upon the relative extent of the declines in both exports and imports.

Again it should be noted that no nation is an island unto itself, and cyclical movements are characteristic of all capital-intensive economies. Thus a cyclical upswing in one country might be met by a concurrent downswing or an upswing in another. As is true of inflation and deflation, the net effect of cyclical up- and downswings in various nations would be the weighted average of the several national pressures on a given rate of exchange or parity. Again, the necessity for devaluation or revaluation would probably be determined by the resulting relationship of the currency in question to the dollar and other leading currencies.

Terms of trade. Movements in a nation's terms of trade have frequently brought about devaluation or, far less frequently, revaluation. The expression "terms of trade" refers to the movement of the prices of a nation's exports with reference to those of its imports. If a country's export prices are declining while the prices of its imports remain the same or increase, the terms of trade are said to be turning against the country in question. When the prices of exports rise faster than those of imports, the terms of trade are becoming favorable.

Variations in the terms of trade arise from many sources; changes in taste, changes in the cost structure of goods, and shifts in demand are examples. If, for example, the people of the United States began to drink less coffee and more tea, the terms of trade would turn against Brazil and turn in favor of India and Ceylon, unless there were countervailing changes in the prices of U.S. exports to those countries.

When the terms of trade move unfavorably, downward pressures on the rates of exchange and parities become manifest; when they move favorably, upward pressures are to be expected. Again, any one nation trades with several others, and an unfavorable movement in its terms of trade with one trading partner may be either offset by favorable movements or reinforced by similar movements in those of another. It is the weighted average of all the changes in a nation's terms of trade that will determine the net effect. The impact of terms of trade on the rate of exchange with the dollar and other leading currencies is apt to prove crucial in determining if devaluation or revaluation will ultimately be necessary.

Interest rates. Shifts in a country's rates of interest can also have an important impact on the country's exchange and parity. When the rates rise with reference to those in other countries, investments are likely to be attracted from abroad; when they decline, domestic investment funds may flow outward. As funds flow out, they exert downward pressure on both rates of exchange and parities; as funds flow in, they exert upward pressure. These movements may have the effect that the parity of the country will over- or undervalue the currency.

A nation's rates of interest cannot be judged alone; those of other countries must be taken into account. It is not the interest rates of any one country that are crucial; it is those of any one country compared with those of the others that determine the direction of the flow of investment funds and the resulting impact on parities and rates of exchange.

Structural changes. Structural changes in an economy are likewise apt to bring about changes in exchange rates and parities. The term "structural change" refers to the creation of new industries or the growth and decline of existing ones. Such changes alter the composition of a nation's exports, imports, and investment and are followed by changes in the demand for and supply of its currency. When structural changes result in more efficient operations, lower costs and prices, they stimulate a nation's exports and curtail its imports. The result is upward pressure on its rates of exchange and parity. When they result in less efficient operations, they have the opposite effects.

Structural changes are likely to occur in several nations at approximately the same time, and the improvement or deterioration in the cost and price structure in any one country may be countered by the improvements or deterioration that take place in one or more of that country's trading partners. The net global impact of such changes on a nation's exchange and parity will thus also be due in part to structural changes in other countries.

Technological changes. Technological changes have effects similar to those of structural changes on costs and prices. As the name implies, technological changes involve the use of new methods and techniques in production and distribution. They often result in improved labor and industrial productivity and lower costs. When lower costs are followed by lower prices, a country's export position is improved and its imports tend to be reduced. The result is upward pressure on its parity and rates of exchange.

It is not probable that technological changes will occur in one country alone. Consequently, improved technology in any one nation may be offset by similar improvements in others. The global impact of technological change involves the "netting out" of the improvements of any one country against those of all of the others with which that country trades. If any nation makes net technological improvements with reference to the rest of the world, upward pressures on its rates and parity will doubtless be manifest; if it lags in that respect, downward pressures are likely to follow.

Speculation, market psychology, and leads and lags. The preceding basic causes of changes in parities are only the more important ones. Because of the close interrelationship of all economic forces, almost any major change in an economy will have either a direct or an indirect effect on rates of exchange and parity.

When people who deal in foreign exchange—both speculators and others—believe that a currency is soon to be revalued, they are apt to buy it forward, with the inevitable effect that the spot rates will tend to rise. They will also buy the exchange spot in the hope of selling it later at a profit and again tend to drive the rates up. When traders and speculators feel that a currency will be devalued in the near future, they will take the opposite steps and tend to drive both spot and forward rates downward.

Leads and lags arise when people who have overseas payments to make or who expect to receive foreign currencies feel that a rate of exchange will either decline or rise or that the currency in question will be devalued or revalued before the terms of their financial arrangements arrive.

If those who have debts to liquidate feel that a currency will fall or be devalued, they will endeavor to lag or delay their payments; when they feel that it will rise or be revalued, they will try to lead or advance their payments. When those who expect to receive payments feel that the currency involved will fall on the exchanges or be devalued, they will attempt to lead or advance their receipt of the funds; and when they expect the rate to rise or the currency to be revalued, they are inclined to lag or delay their receipts.

Speculation, market psychology, and leads and lags are, of course, very closely related. They are essentially short-term phenomena and, taken alone, usually do not have a long-run effect on either rates of exchange or parities. Combined with the basic economic factors, however, they may often exert a leverage effect upon rates and parities.

The foreign economic policies of nations have a most important effect upon pars and rates of exchange and, as a matter of fact, are often designed to protect international reserves, rates, and par as one group of considerations. There are a number of such foreign economic policies; they include tariff, tariff administration, import quotas, and import, export, and exchange controls. Of course, these economic policies often have other objectives, such as the protection of domestic industry and labor against foreign competition. However, they tend to reduce the demand for foreign currencies and the supply of the domestic currency and thus reduce the downward pressures on a country's rates of exchange and parity.

Central Rates of Exchange

The system of parities, and other measures, established in 1944 at Bretton Woods served the international trading world very well for about

25 years. Toward the end of the 1960s, however, it became increasingly manifest that certain changes in the system might prove desirable and that a realignment of the par values of the currencies of the IMF members was urgently required if the system was to continue to facilitate international commerce.

These manifestations came to a head in 1971 with, among other things, the flight from dollars into marks, French and Swiss francs, guilders, and other relatively strong currencies, which was effected by international traders, investors, international and multinational companies as well as speculators. A number of meetings were held during 1971, attended by central bank and government financial officials, to consider the problems of the international monetary system. Finally, between December 16 and 18, 1971, the deputies, ministers, and central bank governors of the Group of Ten (those countries participating in the General Agreement to Borrow and comprising Belgium, Canada, France, Germany, Italy, Japan, the Netherlands, Sweden, the United Kingdom, and the United States) as well as the Executive Directors of the IMF met to consider immediate measures to stabilize—temporarily at least—the international payments system. The IMF Executive Directors announced on December 19, 1972, its approval of the measures taken at these meetings.

As a temporary measure, the decision of the IMF Executive Directors permitted Fund members to allow their market exchange rates to vary by a total of $4\frac{1}{2}$ percent—$2\frac{1}{4}$ percent above and $2\frac{1}{4}$ percent below—from parity. By February 2, 1972, some 43 members had indicated that they desired to take advantage of this provision.

In addition, members were allowed to refrain from establishing new parities, but were permitted instead to indicate to the Fund new stable "central rates" which they desired to maintain in their place. For the time being, and until members can establish definite new pars, the temporary central rate will perform all the functions of a par value. Indeed, these central rates have been termed "professional" or "unofficial par values." By February 2, 1972, 31 members had established central rates instead of new pars.

The decisions of the Fund Executive Directors permitted members to establish neither new parities nor central rates but instead allowed their rates to float and be established by market forces. Eleven members had availed themselves of this privilege by February 2, 1972. Twenty-four members had decided to maintain their parities unchanged and ten had changed their pars by the same date. Members were also permitted, under certain conditions, to maintain multiple exchange rates or different rates applying to different transactions. Thirty-five members had opted for multiple exchange rates by this date.

The new pars and central rates were generally those which the Group of Ten had agreed upon during its December 1971 meetings and those established later by Fund members outside the Group of Ten. Perhaps the most important change in parity was the decision of the United States to devalue the dollar by about 8.57 percent through an increase in the dollar price of gold from $35 to $38 per fine troy ounce. In addition, and in view of the proposed changes in the pars and central rates of its principal trading partners, together with the agreement of these partners to reduce certain barriers to American exports, the United States agreed to eliminate the 10 percent surcharge on certain imports that it had announced on August 15, 1971. All of these measures are tentative and they may, or may not, accomplish the purposes for which they were designed. They are, of course, subject to change in the future.

5

International Monetary Problems and Proposed Solutions

AS was indicated in Chapter 2, the present international monetary system is the product of a long period of development that extends back almost as far as international trade itself. In addition to the system's natural development, improvements, or at least changes, have intentionally been made in it, partly through international conferences. System development has also been affected by the changes fostered by central banks, commercial banks, and business firms engaged in international trade and investment. This section deals with both the accomplishments and the apparent weaknesses of the system and the major suggestions for its reform.

Accomplishments of the International Monetary System, 1946–1971

The principal accomplishments of the international monetary system between 1946 and 1971 are:

1. It has sustained a rapidly increasing volume of trade and investment.
2. It has displayed flexibility in adapting itself to changes in international commerce.
3. It has proved to be efficient; it has performed its tasks with a decreasing percentage of reserves to trade.
4. It has proved to be hardy; it survived a number of pre-1971 crises, speculative and otherwise, and the down- and upswings of several business cycles.
5. It has allowed a growing degree of international cooperation.
6. It has already established a capacity to accommodate reforms and improvements.

The ability of the system to sustain an increasing volume of international commerce can be proved by a few figures. In 1946, for example, U.S. exports of merchandise (excluding military) amounted to about $11.7 billion; in 1970 they stood at $42.0 billion. During the same period, the merchandise imports (excluding military) of this country rose from $5.0 to $39.9 billion. In 1948, the IMF estimated the total world merchandise exports of its members at $52.3 billion and in 1970 at $278 billion. Also according to IMF estimate, the world merchandise imports of IMF members during the same period rose from $59.1 to $288 billion.

A major expansion in international investment has also been financed. In 1950, for example, U.S. investment assets of all kinds abroad amounted to $54.4 billion; in 1970 they totaled $166.1 billion. During the same period, foreign investment assets in the United States rose from $17.6 to $96.4 billion.

The international monetary system has displayed considerable flexibility and adaptability to change. It accommodated itself to the shift from the relatively free pre-World War II foreign exchange markets to the controlled markets of that conflict and also to a gradual return to the free foreign exchange markets in the years following the end of the war. Since its establishment, the Bretton Woods system has also permitted changes in the methods of financing foreign commerce of all types, such as through the Euro-currency markets.

If the efficiency of an international monetary system can be gauged by the size of the reserves that it requires to meet growing trade, the efficiency of the system may be said to have been high. The total international reserves of the IMF members stood at about $45 billion in 1948 and at $80.6 billion in 1970. The increase, though substantial, was smaller than the increase in international trade or international investment during the same period. Thus, the foreign commerce of the free world has been able to expand without the necessity for a proportional increase in free world international reserves. The international monetary system may be said to operate on the principle of fractional reserves in a fashion somewhat, but not entirely, similar to the fractional reserves of a banking system.

The international monetary system proved to be hardy, for it survived a number of crises. Some of those crises involved the devaluation or revaluation of the pound sterling, the French franc, the deutsche mark, and the Dutch guilder, among many others. The devaluations or revaluations were usually accompanied by heavy speculative activities in the currencies concerned, and often they were ultimately forced by outside pressures. Other pre-1971 crises had involved the drain on the U.S. holdings of monetary gold and some speculative attacks on the dollar and the free gold price. In addition, the system survived several up- and downswings of the international economy and has been able to accommodate itself to those movements. The system did not, however, survive the crises of 1971.

Another important accomplishment of the system appears to be a fostering of international cooperation in monetary matters, which is in striking contrast to the dog-eat-dog policies of the depression-ridden years that preceded World War II. The present monetary arrangements have permitted nations whose rates of exchange were under heavy downward pressures to obtain temporary relief in the form of loans and swaps. The swaps consisted of the actual or potential exchange of currencies under pressure for other currencies to be used in supporting the attacked currency. That cooperation has also included the organization of international monetary conferences on improving the system and increasing international liquidity.

The present international monetary system has been receptive to a large number of minor improvements and one major one, the installation of the Fund SDR's described in Chapter 3. The changes have been made without serious disturbance to Fund operations. Most of the changes have been designed to promote liquidity, and the Fund has responded constructively to the changes.

Criticisms of the International Monetary System, 1946–1971

The accomplishments of the international monetary system have not, however, blinded observers to some evident shortcomings. The principal criticisms are that the system:

1. Lacks a continued source of new liquidity as international commerce grows and has relied too heavily on U.S. balance of payments deficits.
2. Has not fostered the reduction or the elimination of national balance of payments surpluses and deficits.
3. Is not designed to promote confidence in reserve assets in the form of foreign currency holdings.
4. Does not provide adequate or proportionate reserves for all nations.
5. Lacks flexibility.

Liquidity. The one criticism that has been most frequently heard may no longer be valid. It is that the system lacked liquidity in that it failed to expand sufficiently as trade grew or that it could expand only at the price of continued U.S. balance of payments deficits, an obviously impossible long-run condition. If international reserves do not expand sufficiently to sustain an increasing international commerce, the growth of that trade may well be curtailed. Nations that are running short of reserves may be obliged to impose import and exchange controls in an effort to curtail the outflow of funds in payment for imports and investments. Alternatively, they may be forced to devalue their currencies. A crisis of liquidity could occur, and the level of international economic transactions could be reduced.

Until the advent of the SDR's, neither the mining of gold nor the IMF drawing rights increased sufficiently to meet completely the growth in international trade. Convertible currencies other than the dollar were not sufficiently attractive to central bank authorities to be used in amounts sufficient for international reserve needs. Therefore the burden of augmenting those reserves fell upon the dollar and U.S. balance of payments deficits. It was to avoid the potential crises of liquidity that the SDR's were created.

Balance of payments disequilibrium. A second criticism of the international payments system has been that it did not tend to correct, or to promote the correction of, balance of payments disequilibriums. Nations running balance of payments surpluses could continue to do so indefinitely, and there is little about the international payments system that induced them to reduce or eliminate them.

Countries that run deficits may, however, be impelled to reduce them as their international reserves are drawn down. They are likely to have recourse first to loans and other devices to supplement their dwindling reserves. When those resources are exhausted, deficit nations must take steps to reduce the outflow of funds, increase the inflow, or both. All too often, deficit countries have had recourse to the negative measures of curtailing outflows already discussed: import and exchange controls or devaluation. Unfortunately, the positive domestic and foreign measures required to restore balance of payments equilibrium are usually politically unpalatable, and many nations are inclined to take them only as a last resort. Deficit nations must reduce their prices and/or incomes, and then there is the strong possibility they will create or increase unemployment, reduce output, and lower standards of living.

Surplus countries might be obliged to attempt to inflate their money, raise prices and incomes, and increase employment and output. When a surplus nation has a domestic economy that is in a relatively stable position, it may hesitate to take those possibly disturbing steps. As a last alternative, a surplus nation might revalue its currency. But few surplus nations have been willing to take that step, and it has been taken only when it was evident that a currency was undervalued and under the pressure of trading partners.

Confidence in assets. There is ample evidence to sustain the third criticism that has been leveled against the international payments system: that it failed to promote confidence in some of the assets that compose international reserves. The gold and IMF drawing right components of those reserves (before conversion into national currencies) are not debt, but the convertible currency parts are the debt of the nations that issue those currencies. As such, their value, both market and psychological, depends in part upon confidence in their reliability and stability.

The principal foreign currency components of reserves have been the pound sterling and the dollar. Since the end of World War II, sterling has been subjected to several attacks on its rates of exchange that resulted in large measure from decline in confidence in its stability. Two of those attacks resulted in the devaluation of the pound; in 1949 the pound was devalued from $4.03 to $2.80, and in 1967 it was further devalued to $2.40.

The devaluations were especially serious for the members of the sterling area and some other countries that are heavy users of sterling as a reserve asset. Devaluation meant that the reserve holdings of those nations shrank by about 30 percent in 1949 and 15 percent in 1967.

The dollar was subjected to several crises of confidence during the same period; the first occurred in 1961. Declining confidence in the dollar led to a renewed demand on the part of the world's central banks for the redemption of their dollar holdings in gold. Such demands occurred on a large scale; the gold reserves of the United States, which stood at almost $25 billion in 1947, declined, as a result of redemptions, to less than $11 billion in 1971. Finally, on August 15, 1971, the pressures on the dollar had become so great that this country decided to cease to redeem officially held dollars in gold as had been its practice since 1934. The important results of this decision are discussed later in this chapter.

Underdeveloped nations and the IMF. Another criticism of the international monetary system has been that it was designed primarily for developed, industrial countries rather than for underdeveloped ones that rely largely on agricultural exports for their exchange earnings. If it has proved reasonably satisfactory to the former countries, the criticism goes, it has not to the latter; it has failed to provide the reserve-short underdeveloped nations with access to needed foreign exchange.

Since 1963, attempts have been made by the IMF to improve that situation through its program of compensatory financing of the export fluctuations of primary exporting countries. That program places additional drawing rights at the disposition of some countries that have "export shortfalls"—that is, countries that have insufficient exports to pay for their imports—and softens some of the Fund's rules insofar as they are applied to such countries.

In addition, some underdeveloped nations have endeavored to attach special conditions to the Fund's newly created SDR's to put more of those drawing rights at their disposal. Many of the more industrialized nations, as well as the United Nations, have provided grants and unilateral aid of various kinds to the less-developed countries, and that aid has supplemented the reserve earnings of those countries.

On the other hand, it is not clear that the lack of reserves of certain nations is primarily a problem of the international payments system and that one of the functions of the system is to supply, more or less automatically, additional reserves to nations that either need or want them. When a country cannot earn sufficient reserves, it is not likely to be able to service loans extended by a bank or other institution attached to the international payments system. The adequacy of reserves is a problem of the international economy as a whole and the domestic economies of particular countries. The problem is far too complex to be solved by international monetary measures, which, perforce, must attack only the symptoms of low reserves rather than the causes.

Flexibility. The final criticism levied against the present system— and which may cease to be valid if certain reforms, under discussion beginning in 1971, are put into effect—has been that it lacks flexibility; in part, this criticism stressed the rigidity of the Fund's system of par values. Those who leveled the criticism recognized that the Fund pars were not absolutely fixed, but they claimed that its adjustable-peg system moved too slowly and then by excessively large jumps. Changes in the pars could be made only by the member concerned in consultation with the Fund.

In spite of the apparently cumbersome procedure that surrounded them, changes in the members' parities have been made in large number since the inauguration of the institution in 1946. However, a relatively long period often elapsed between the time when a change in par became necessary and the date on which the change was made. In addition, the infrequency of changes in parities required a large change to be made each time. Some critics of the system feel that more frequent and smaller alterations of parities would prove desirable and realistic.

Critics of the Fund's par value rules maintained that the rules were adopted to prevent the type of competitive devaluations that character- ized the depression-ridden 1930s. The critics felt that, because the IMF has succeeded in preventing them, such unwarranted devaluations no longer constitute a problem. The Bretton Woods adjustable-peg system of parities is thus no longer "relevant." The critics hold that a new par value system is needed to lend greater flexibility to the international payments mechanism.

Opponents of greater flexibility contend that in addition to the trad- ing problems that greater par value flexibility—more frequent devalua- tions and revaluations—would certainly create, such a system could have a destabilizing effect on the international payments system. That system not only would hold more risk for international businessmen but would function less smoothly than it did. It would inject another element of uncertainty into a system that already had its full share of pitfalls.

Floating rates. Not all the critics of the rigidity and inflexibility of the present payments system rest their case on par values alone. Many of them have felt that the present Fund limits to the fluctuations of rates of exchange to within plus or minus $2\frac{1}{4}$ percent of parity are too narrow. They maintain that broader bands of fluctuations or freely fluctuating rates with no pars or limits should be permitted.

Among other things, a broader band or a floating rate would mean that nations would not need as large holdings of international reserves as they now do. It would also mean less frequent official intervention on the foreign exchange markets by central banks and exchange stabiliza- tion institutions than now prevails. In addition, speculation against cur- rencies would decline and crises of confidence in the national currencies would not occur as often. Finally, a broader band or floating rate would result in less pressure against the parities and perhaps less fre- quent changes in the par values. Broader bands or floating rates could, of course, mean, their critics maintain, wider variations in the prices of exports, imports, and investments. The problems associated with forward exchange would be multiplied and covering and hedging would become more complex and doubtless more expensive.

Proposed Reforms of the International Monetary System

Some of those criticisms of the international monetary system were brought into sharp focus by the crisis of 1971, which was sketched in Chapter 3. This crisis was far more severe than any of the previous ones and, together with the measures announced by President Nixon on August 15, 1971, shook the international monetary system to its very foundations. The defects that were revealed have probably made a revision or a restructuring of the system mandatory.

One important change, which does not involve a reform of the Bretton Woods system but which became manifest during the crisis of 1971, was the need to establish new parities for many of the more important members of the IMF.

Even before the crisis, it had become evident that either the dollar was overvalued in comparison with other leading currencies, or that those currencies were undervalued in relation to the dollar, which are but two views of the same phenomenon. The crisis also revealed that the amount of dollar overvaluation (or other currency undervaluation) varied from country to country. The changes in pars and the establishment of new central rates, sketched in Chapter 4, have provided a temporary, and probably a partial, solution to this problem. When the dollar was devalued, all those countries that held dollar—in preference to gold—reserves suffered a loss of about 8.57 percent on their dollar holdings.

The discussions that have taken place among the interested nations concerning new parities since President Nixon's announcement have apparently put greater stress on the relationships between the barriers to trade, the internal and external economies, and the national trading positions on the one hand, and the official parities on the other, than many previous conferences. Such recognition of the broad significance of parities bodes well for future negotiations and the future establishment of a system of realistic pars.

However, as long as some nations continue to intervene on the foreign exchange markets to regulate or to limit fluctuations of their rates of exchange, the rates will fail to reflect the market or natural rates of exchange established by the free play of demand and supply. Under these conditions, it will be impossible to determine equilibrium parities based *solely* upon these rates. If these rates are to form the basis for establishing new equilibrium parities, either they must be allowed to float freely without intervention or else some other means must be used.

Ever since the establishment of the Bretton Woods system, a large number of plans for its reform or improvement have been advanced. They follow the lines of criticism described in this chapter. All of the many plans fall into seven major groups:

1. A return to the semiautomatic international gold standard.
2. The centralization of international reserves in an international central bank or other institution.
3. Multiple currency reserves.
4. Crawling or sliding pegs.
5. Freely floating or flexible exchange rates.
6. A new *numéraire* in place of gold and the dollar.
7. A new role for the dollar.

Return to a gold standard. Some of the more conservative students of the international monetary system have advocated a return to the semiautomatic gold standard that prevailed prior to the 1930s. To counter the objection that not enough gold is being produced to meet the increasing demands for international reserves, they propose that the price of gold be increased. The increase, they say, should be sufficient to bring forth enough newly mined gold to meet the increasing reserve requirements.

The participating nations would agree to abide by the "rules of the gold standard game," whereby they would refrain from managing their money supply and its impact on prices, incomes, exchange rates, production, and employment. They would settle all international balances in gold. They would not, however, need to adopt a domestic gold standard currency.

Several advantages are claimed for the proposed system: it would lend stability to the international monetary system; the international reserves of participating countries would no longer be the debts of other countries; and a nation's reserves would have a permanent, intrinsic value independent of the will or the capacity of any other country. Also, the semiautomatic gold standard would eliminate the need for dollar reserves derived from U.S. balance of payments deficits.

It is extremely doubtful that any nation would be willing to relinquish the advantages of managed monetary systems and international reserves in favor of an automatic system over which they would have little or no control. The proposal for a new gold standard is generally rejected for the very reasons for the end of the historical gold standard.

Centralization of reserves. The second group of plans for reform, the centralization of international reserves, would involve the creation of an expanded IMF (XIMF) acting as a central banks' bank—a truly international bank or some similar institution. The reserves of the nations participating in such an arrangement would take the form of deposits in the international institution, where the world's reserves would then be centralized. The centralized reserves would replace national holdings of foreign exchange and perhaps even gold. The international bank would perform for the international economy functions similar to those that most central banks undertake for the domestic economy. It would grant loans and advances to the participating central banks (depositors) when needed and justified. It would be able to exercise considerable control over the world's payments system just as central banks exert control over the commercial banks and monetary systems of each country.

Another advantage of such an institution is that the international monetary system would no longer be forced to rely on U.S. balance of payments deficits for the required increases in international reserves. The proposed bank would thus eliminate one of the weaknesses of the Bretton Woods system. The required increases in national reserves would be met through the issue by the bank of claims on it, by its increased liabilities, or by deposits credited to the account of the participants. The central bank could also put strong pressure on deficit countries to reduce their balance of payments disequilibriums by tying the amount of credit it would be willing to extend to economic measures planned to reduce the deficits.

There are again political considerations that must be taken into account before an international bank plan could be adopted. A central bank or XIMF would doubtless be responsible to a number of "stockholders" or participants similar to that of the IMF (118 in number in 1972), and an institution that is responsible to so many is responsible to none. In addition, the participating members would be required to transfer some of their authority in monetary matters to the central institution. Under present concepts of sovereignty, it is doubtful that many nations would be willing to relinquish any control over their money to an international institution they could not hope to manage. However, it should be noted that the Common Market countries have plans for the creation of a Common Market currency, which would eventually replace national currencies. If this plan is finally adopted, the individual Common Market countries will have abandoned complete control of their currencies to a Common Market body.

Multiple currency reserves. The third group of international monetary system reforms, known as the system of multiple currency reserves, proposes that in the place of the dollar as the principal reserve asset, the assets be composed of a number of convertible foreign currencies. Instead of gold, dollars, and sterling as the main components of their international reserves, nations participating in the plan would agree to use gold plus a combination of several convertible currencies in addition to dollars, SDR's, and sterling and thus broaden their portfolios of foreign exchange reserves. The currencies to be so employed would be selected by mutual agreement.

The countries whose currencies were selected for use as reserves would agree to maintain the gold values of their currencies, to buy and sell gold freely at a determined price, to furnish foreign exchange to the user countries as required, and to maintain agreed-upon rates of increase in their currencies to permit the foreign exchange reserves of user countries to keep pace with the growth in world commerce.

To prevent some countries from switching in and out of the various component elements of the combined reserves and shifting the composition of their reserves, one form of the multiple currency reserve scheme envisages the creation of a composite reserve unit (CRU). The CRU's would consist of new type of international currency backed by a 100 percent "reserve" of the agreed foreign exchange components.

The foreign exchange instruments of the supplying countries would be held by a central authority, perhaps the IMF, as a 100 percent backing of the CRU's supplied to the user countries. In that way, it would be impossible for any country to switch in or out of a given national currency. Such a shift in the composition of the CRU's could be made only by mutual agreement.

The advantages of the scheme are that the arrangement would obviate the reliance that the Bretton Woods system placed upon U.S. deficits. It would bring some order into the reserve system, which has been haphazard and disorganized. In addition, the reserve plan would lend greater stability to the international payments mechanism.

This proposal has several obvious weaknesses. It fails to provide nations with either a mechanism for eliminating payments imbalances or an incentive to eliminate them. The system could expand its reserves only as the debt of the supplying nations increased. Thus, it would tend to substitute the deficits (debts) of a group of countries for the debt of the United States alone. Also, it fails to provide a source of additional reserves for nations that face temporary balance of payments difficulties. However, should the use of SDR's as reserves be extended, the resulting system might be held to constitute a form of multiple reserves. The SDR's are convertible into a group of designated currencies, which can be used as intervention, vehicle, or transaction currencies, and SDR's must be so converted to be used for these purposes.

Crawling-peg system. The fourth group of suggested remedies for the defects of the international payments system proposes to give the system greater flexibility by instituting a crawling peg. "Crawling peg," or "sliding peg," is a solecism (a peg neither crawls nor slides) used to designate a flexible system of par values whereby the par is allowed to move by very small increments over short periods of time. Thus, for example, a participating country might allow its par to decrease or increase by $\frac{1}{26}$ of 1 percent a week for a maximum change of 2 percent a year.

Proponents of the crawling-peg system hold that small, short-period changes are preferable to larger ones that devaluing or revaluing nations have customarily used. Only nations with convertible currencies would be permitted to utilize the crawling peg; if others were to use it, confidence in the international payments system might be compromised. In addition, the system would be employed only by countries whose currencies were either under- or overvalued.

To prevent other nations from transferring funds into or out of countries utilizing the crawling peg and thus either creating balance of payments problems or countering the effects of the changes, interest rates in crawling-peg nations would be shifted each week by an amount sufficient to prevent in- or outflows. Thus, a devaluing nation would gradually raise its interest rates and a revaluing one would gradually lower them.

A number of advantages are claimed for the crawling-peg system. For one thing, the system would avoid the necessity for a nation to take unappealing domestic measures to bring its external accounts into balance. Because very small changes in the parities would be made at frequent intervals, confidence in the currencies in question might be bolstered.

The crawling-peg system would be more equitable than the adjustable peg because under it devaluations and revaluations that primarily affected the current account might be offset by shifts in the rates of interest and consequently the capital value of investments. The present system of large devaluations and revaluations has no such compensatory feature. Also, it is claimed that the system of crawling pegs would reduce the rigidity of the Bretton Woods system of adjustable pegs.

The success or failure of the crawling-peg system would no doubt depend on the power of changes in interest rates to compensate for adjustments of the par. Otherwise, there might be a flight away from a currency that was being devalued into one that was being revalued. If the rates of interest should not prove to be compensatory, speculative attacks on currencies being devalued and speculative flows into those that were being revalued might well occur. In addition, if the compensatory rates of interest functioned perfectly, the movements of capital in and out of a given currency might counterbalance completely the effects of the shifts in the parities. The system is, of course, a highly contrived one and would necessitate the amendment of the IMF Articles of Agreement.

Freely floating rates. The proposal for greater permitted flexibility in the latitude of movement of rates of exchange and freely floating rates has already been explored in this chapter. That reform involves a broader band of permitted exchange rate fluctuations around the par and has already been authorized in some cases by the Fund. In some plans for reform, the broader-band exchange rate fluctuations plan is combined with crawling-peg arrangements.

A new numéraire. Under the IMF Agreement that was in effect from 1946 to 1971, the *numéraire,* or the international standard of value of member currencies, was expressed "in terms of gold as a common denominator or in terms of the United States dollar of the weight and fineness in effect on July 1, 1944." When the dollar's link with gold was broken on August 15, 1971, the dollar was no longer the full equivalent of gold and the official price of gold in dollars (which prevailed on July 1, 1944) no longer had any realistic significance. Consequently, the continuing validity of the gold and dollar standard of value of 1944 has been called into question.

In approaching the question of the *numéraire,* it is important to realize that it is merely a measure or a standard of value and has no other practical significance. A standard of value should possess stability, however; otherwise the parities it measures will, in turn, lack stability. This consideration is likely to be uppermost should a new standard of value be selected.

There are a number of possible *numéraires.* Under the present dollar devaluation, the dual standard could be allowed to stand but wth a new stipulation concerning the fineness and weight of the dollar to reflect the devaluation. Such a solution would have the advantage of requiring a minimum change in the present arrangements and a minimum disturbance to international payments systems. It would also continue the convenience of measuring the value of national currencies in terms of another currency.

On the other hand, the dollar may be said to lack the required stability for a standard of value, although it has displayed more stability than most other currencies. In addition, the dollar has become redundant —the supply of dollars has finally outrun the demand for them, and as a result its international value has declined. The dollar represents debt, and its value depends in no small measure on the domestic economic policies followed by the United States, which do not always have universal approval. Finally, a growing number of IMF members are becoming convinced that the standard of value of the international payments system should not be based on the currency of any single country, no matter how sound that currency might be. Since most other currencies show the same defects as the dollar—many of them to a greater degree—similar reasoning applies to the use of any other currency, together with gold, as the official *numéraire*. In addition, no other currency is as important internationally as the dollar.

If the present gold-dollar standard of value is to be replaced, the alternatives would appear to lie between gold and the SDR's. If gold were to be adopted, the pars of each country would be expressed in units of fine gold. Thus if the par of the dollar were set at 0.888671 gram of fine gold and that of the Belgian franc at 0.0177734 gram (their 1944–1971 values), the par of the Belgian franc would be 1 Belgian franc = 2 U.S. cents, or $1.00 = 50 Belgian francs.

Such a gold standard of value would most likely be a purely abstract one, since no currency is now redeemable in gold and gold is not widely used either in settling international accounts nor as an intervention medium to support exchange rates. The great advantage of gold as a standard of value is found in its relative stability. On the other hand, some international traders, bankers, and government officials feel that the international monetary system should no longer be linked to gold, because such a standard smacks too much of the now discredited international gold standard. This objection does not appear to be too serious, and a gold *numéraire* would doubtless constitute a workable standard provided that no currency or the SDR's were required to be redeemable in gold.

The use of the newly created SDR's as an international standard of value is receiving increasing attention. The value of the SDR's is expressed in terms of gold with each SDR (1971) the equivalent of 0.888671 gram of fine gold, the same as that of the dollar of 1944–1971. If the SDR's are selected as the new standard, their value in terms of gold would probably be guaranteed. Like gold, the SDR's are not a form of debt. They would constitute an abstract standard of value, for they are but a bookkeeping entry on the Fund's special account.

The SDR's are not *themselves* used to settle international accounts and are thus not a vehicle or transactions currency. Technically speaking, SDR's are not a currency at all. For the purpose of transactions, the SDR's must first be exchanged against the currencies of Fund members who participate in the SDR program. They are, however, a reserve medium and form a part of the international reserves of the IMF members who participate in the SDR program.

Defined and guaranteed in terms of a fixed amount of gold, the SDR's probably would have the same stability as gold. Since the SDR's are exchangeable for certain other member currencies, whose values are subject to fluctuation, their link with gold assumes importance. From the point of view of conversion into other currencies, they constitute an adaptation of the multiple currency reserve asset principle discussed in an earlier paragraph. Apparently the SDR's appeal to those who seek a stable standard of value but who prefer an abstract standard to gold. If the SDR's are selected as the international standard of value, the Fund agreement will require substantial modification to accommodate the increased role they would play.

The future role of the dollar. Since the dollar is not likely to form a part of the *numéraire* of the future international monetary system, and since it is no longer redeemable in gold, its future role calls for examination. The dollar's future involves the part it will play in international reserves, as an intervention currency, and its continued use as a vehicle and transactions currency. These issues *apparently* lie beyond the scope of the IMF, as constituted at present, to determine completely. The decision as to what reserves are to be used still rests with the world's central banks acting under the pressures exerted by commercial banks and the trading community. The IMF may be able to create new reserves of its own making and to alter the characteristics of its existing drawing rights reserves, but it does not now have the right to dictate what reserves central banks can hold, and it is not likely to be given this right.

An intervention currency is one that is used by central banks and exchange stabilization agencies to maintain national currencies within the band, or limits, set by the Fund, by other monetary agreements, or by the government itself. Thus if the exchange rate of the currency of country *A,* the unitas, for example, were to fall to its lower arbitrage support point (as set by the Fund, another monetary agreement, or the government), the central bank of country *A* would use its intervention currency to buy the unitas on the market in an attempt to drive its rate up. If, on the other hand, the unitas were to rise to its upper support point, the unitas would be sold against its intervention currency in an effort to bring its rate of exchange down. If SDR's are given a more important reserve role, the money used as an intervention currency would assume greater importance, for the SDR's are not currency and must be exchanged against designated currencies before they can be used for intervention on the exchange markets.

The dollar may or may not continue to form an important part of the international reserves of the world's trading nations. In spite of its recent vicissitudes, there is little reason to believe that it will be completely abandoned as a reserve or intervention currency in the immediate future. Since dollars continue to form a large part of the existing international reserves and are widely used as an intervention currency, it seems reasonable to assume that they will continue to do so at least until the dollar reserves are exhausted and other reserve or intervention currencies are used.

The future reserve role of the dollar may well depend on two sets of circumstances: (1) the future availability of dollars arising from U.S. balance of payments deficits, and (2) central bank preferences for SDR's, for dollars, or for other reserve and intervention assets.

If the United States does not continue to run balance of payments deficits, the dollar is apt to lose ground as a reserve currency because it might not be available in sufficient amounts. United States balance of payments equilibriums or surpluses would thus operate to reduce the reserve role of the dollar. The future balance of payments deficit possibilities for the United States depend, in a certain measure, on the demand for dollars as a reserve medium and on the Euro-dollar market's potential for absorbing additional dollar funds. If the dollar is not demanded as a reserve currency, and if the Euro-dollar market does not continue to absorb increasing amounts of dollars, the United States will no longer be able to run balance of payments deficits with impunity as it has in the past.

There is little doubt that the dollar will continue to play its customary role as a vehicle and transactions and intervention currency. Even if it no longer forms part of the international *numéraire* and if the SDR's replace it as an important part of international reserves, there is apparently no reason to believe that the dollar will no longer be used as the currency in which much international business is handled. The size of the United States, the large volume of trade it carries on, and the attractive financing opportunities offered by its money and exchange markets should continue to make the dollar a desirable vehicle and transactions and intervention currency.

Prospects for a New International Monetary System

It is, of course, impossible to predict the nature of the changes in the international monetary system or the form that any new system may take, and it is not the intention of the authors of this book to make such predictions. However, there seems to be a growing desire to make the new international monetary system less rigid than it was from 1946 to 1971. Chapters 4 and 5 sketched the changes already made in this direction in the form of a wider band of permitted exchange rate variations above and below par.

There is also a growing body of opinion among the IMF members that changes in parities should be more frequent and easier to obtain than at present. Whether such a system would involve a form of crawling peg or easier adjustments under the present system is less clear. Considerable attention is also being given to the establishment of a new *numéraire*, but no general agreement on what it is likely to be has yet emerged. The use of SDR's for this purpose apparently has a great deal of support. The days of the dollar as an international standard of value are probably numbered, and its continued use in this capacity does not appear likely.

There seems to be a growing body of opinion in favor of broadening the spectrum of reserves that the IMF is empowered to create, especially an enlargement of the reserve role of the SDR's. This opinion is based in part upon the possibility that additions to the supply of dollars for reserve and working balance purposes are likely to shrink if the United States eliminates its balance of payments deficits and starts to run surpluses.

The discussions for the reform of the international monetary system have considered the possibility of making other changes in the IMF but have not spelled them out precisely. Such changes might involve, among other things, an increase in subscriptions and quotas and a consequent enlargement of the gold and credit tranche drawing rights as well as new definitions of the rights and obligations of the members. In general, the discussions seem to favor an enlargement rather than a diminution of the role of the Fund, and it may well emerge as a stronger institution than it now is.

If a new *numéraire* is created involving either gold, the SDR's, or both, and if the role of the SDR's and their amount is increased, the Fund would come closer to constituting a government central banks' central bank or an international central bank than it now does. In this event, it would move in the direction of the British Lord Keynes' pre-Bretton Woods plans and away from those of the American, Harry D. White.

The changes in and the reforms of the international monetary system under discussion (1971), although important, are not as radical or as far reaching as some people thought they might be. The discussions have been projected against a background of opinion favoring increased international monetary cooperation and a reduction of barriers to trade including currency convertibility, lower tariffs and quotas, and improved tax policies.

The new international monetary system that emerges from these efforts is not likely to constitute the final system. It may well be subject to the alterations made by commercial banks, international traders, and speculators as they use its facilities and institutions in their practical day-to-day operations. Therefore many of the proposed reforms of the international monetary system discussed earlier in this chapter continue to be of interest and significance.

PART THREE

Foreign Exchange Markets, Rates, and Transactions

6

Foreign Exchange Markets
and Institutions

STRICTLY speaking, a foreign exchange market provides a mechanism
for transferring the money of one country into that of another. However,
because of the close connections between such a market and the money,
capital, and other financial markets, that characterization may appear
to be too narrow. In cooperation with the other markets, a foreign exchange market may also be held to provide a means of supplying credit
for and arranging the financing of international economic transactions
of many kinds.

Foreign exchange markets tend to locate in national financial centers near the related financial markets. The more important exchange
markets are therefore found in New York, London, Paris, Frankfurt,
Amsterdam, Milan, Zurich, Toronto, and the financial centers of most
other developed and industrialized nations.

The exchange markets are closely related to one another and are so well integrated that together they constitute a single world market, despite the distances and time differentials involved. In addition to the various national foreign exchange markets, the Euro-dollar market, discussed in Chapter 3, is heavily involved in foreign exchange transactions and may be said, in addition to its other functions, to complement the international foreign exchange markets.

Instead of by a written body of rules and regulations, the foreign exchange markets are usually governed by an unwritten code of conduct that all participants must follow on pain of ostracism. Most market transactions are handled in an informal manner by telephone or by other service and are not often written out in legal form. The apparently casual nature of the market transactions belies the strictness of the unwritten code and the swift punishment of anyone who reneges.

Foreign Exchange Intermediation

Generally speaking, there are two types of foreign exchange markets: the British–United States and the European types. Markets of the British–United States type are not markets in the *concrete* sense of the term; for they are not places where the participants actually meet face to face. The term "market" is applied in its *abstract* sense as a communications system whereby buyers and sellers contact one another for the purpose of transacting business. The communications system consists of a network of telephones, telegraph, cable, radio, Telex, and teleprinters that connects exchange markets all over the world and makes it possible to conduct business in an instantaneous and well-informed manner. That type of market is found in the United States, the United Kingdom, Canada, Switzerland, and some other countries.

The Continental or European foreign exchange market has been an actual place or locale in which buyers and sellers can meet to purchase and sell foreign currencies. Such markets are found principally in France, West Germany, the Netherlands, and Italy. The meeting places are sometimes located in a special and secluded part of the stock exchange of a country. They are sharply declining in importance, and many more transactions are consummated by telephone or other wire service than by personal contact even in the centers where the European-type market is found. In view of the increasing importance of the British–United States type of foreign exchange market and the decline of the European one, the rest of this chapter deals with the former type exclusively.

When parties interested in buying or selling foreign exchange do not meet face to face, they usually rely upon the services of intermediaries to consummate their deals. Thus instead of a company with, say, 1 million French francs for sale seeking out a buyer that wishes to purchase francs, the would-be seller disposes of its francs to a financial intermediary. The intermediary is willing to buy the francs; for it is certain of its ability to sell them at a profit to parties that require francs to meet their international obligations.

The financial intermediaries engaged in the foreign exchange business in the United States are now almost exclusively the larger commercial banks. Some foreign exchange dealers who specialize in the purchase and sale of foreign bank notes remain, and some firms, like the American Express Company, that deal heavily in traveler's checks and international credit cards continue, however, to do a large business.

The commercial banks commonly maintain balances abroad with their branches or correspondents, and the balances are usually denominated in the currency of the country in which the branch or correspondent is located. Conversely, they hold deposits, in their own domestic currency, of their branches and correspondents overseas. That system is the underlying constraint of foreign exchange dealings and, as will be seen later, of international money transfer and of acceleration programs for that transfer.

Although there is usually only one principal foreign exchange market in each country, there may be several secondary markets. Thus the principal U.S. market is in New York and secondary markets are located in Chicago, Philadelphia, Boston, Detroit, and San Francisco. Foreign traders located in cities outside those centers can find foreign exchange accommodation through the networks of correspondents that the New York and other financial center banks maintain.

Each foreign exchange market is a sort of clearing house in which a bank's sales of foreign exchange are set off against its purchases. The transactions may be said to take place between (1) a bank and its customers, (2) banks in the same market, (3) banks in different markets, (4) commercial banks and central banks, and (5) the central banks of different countries.

A bank's customers—the retail side of the market—buy foreign exchange from the bank to meet their obligations for payments in foreign currencies. They have foreign currencies for sale when they export goods and services, receive unilateral transfers, and sell investments overseas against payments in another currency.

Transactions between banks in the same market may be said to represent the wholesale side of the market. Since foreign currency holdings in the form of deposits in foreign banks or highly liquid foreign notes and investments usually carry only low interest, banks do not under normal conditions maintain any more foreign currency spot positions than are necessary for minimum working balances.

Banks in the United States and the United Kingdom, for reasons of tradition, efficiency, and competition, do not like to deal directly with one another for their foreign exchange requirements. Instead they use the services of brokers, as shown in Chapter 8. On the other hand, banks that operate on the foreign exchange market of one country do deal directly with banks abroad that are doing business on their own markets. Even when a bank does not have either a branch or a correspondent in a given country, it can buy and sell the currency of that country by using the services of one of its foreign correspondents that does have either a branch or a correspondent in that country.

Under modern managed monetary and banking systems there is in each country a close relationship between the central bank (the Federal Reserve System in the United States) and the commercial and other banks. Finally, the central banks of several nations deal constantly with one another and render considerable assistance to each other at times.

Orderly or Unbroken Cross Rates

An important function of bank trading activity is to maintain what are termed *orderly cross exchange rates* or *unbroken cross rates* between currencies. Non-bank dealers may also participate in the process. Orderly foreign exchange rates are maintained by means of what is termed *foreign exchange arbitrage.*

If the dollar-pound rate, for example, should stand at 2.60\frac{1}{16}$ in New York and the equivalent of $2.60 in London, a bank trader could quickly make some money for his bank—$\frac{1}{16}$ cent for each pound bought or sold—by buying sterling in London and selling it in New York. Such rates are "disorderly" or "broken" because they are different for the same two currencies in two different financial centers.

The purchase of the pounds in London would make the pound more valuable in that center, and the sale of them in New York would lower their value in that center. That would tend to bring the rates of exchange for those currencies to the same level in both London and New York, and the rates would then be orderly again. The sale and purchase of pounds in two different financial centers to take advantage of disorderly or broken rates is termed *two-point exchange arbitrage.*

A more complicated case of disorderly or broken exchange rates involving three-point exchange arbitrage can be illustrated by the following example. Assume that the par of the Belgian franc is 2 U.S. cents and that of the Mexican peso is 8 U.S. cents; the Belgian franc is thus worth ¼ Mexican peso. Assuming that the rates of exchange exactly equal the pars, an American who buys Belgian francs with $1,000 obtains 50,000 francs; and if he uses the francs to buy Mexican pesos, he receives 12,500 of them. If he now buys dollars with the 12,500 pesos, he obtains exactly $1,000, the amount with which he started (neglecting the costs of the transactions). Here the cross rates are orderly and there is no profit in buying the currency of any one country with the currency of another in any one of the three markets and selling it in one of the other markets.

Now assume that the Belgian franc–Mexican peso rate shifts and that the peso is worth 4.5 Belgian francs while the other rates remain the same. The American dealer now purchases 12,500 Mexican pesos with $1,000. With those pesos, and at the new rate of exchange, he immediately buys Belgian francs, obtaining 56,250 of them. With the francs he buys dollars in a simultaneous transaction and now receives $1,125. Since he started with $1,000 and has $1,125 when he finishes, he makes a profit, neglecting expenses, of $125, or 12.5 percent for a series of transactions involving minutes or even seconds.

The hypothetical dealer's profit was made possible by disorderly cross rates. Such rates would lead traders to buy Mexican pesos and use them to purchase Belgian francs. The increase in the demand for Belgian francs in terms of Mexican pesos would tend to force the rates of exchange for those two currencies back into line so that 4 Belgian francs, instead of 4.5, would equal one Mexican peso. The rates would again be orderly.

The examples given are exaggerated and are based on exchange rates that no longer prevail. Such large differentials are not likely to occur, and they would not last very long—a few minutes at most—if they did occur. Bank traders and other arbitrageurs rapidly bring disorderly or broken exchange rates back into line. There is thus a uniformity in the relations between the exchange rates of different countries on the foreign exchange markets of the world.

The terms "uniform cross rates" and "orderly or unbroken cross rates," are used chiefly for spot exchange and not for forward transactions, in which the same concepts do not apply. Forward rates depend on the rates of interest that prevail in different countries, and since there are usually rate differences in various countries at the same time, the forward rates are set by a different combination of factors. In addition, forward rates depend in some part upon the reputations or standings of the parties to a forward contract—the willingness and the ability of each party to honor his commitment to buy or sell exchange for future delivery. Since the reputations of participants vary substantially, the forward rates are likely to differ even on the same market.

As Chapter 7 explains, spot and forward exchange are intimately related by interest arbitrage and speculation, which involve both spot and forward exchange in a single transaction. In interest arbitrage, forward exchange is used as a cover against future movements in spot rates. Also, speculators anticipate future changes in spot rates and buy or sell exchange forward to take advantage of the anticipated shifts. Although spot and forward exchange are not the same kind of foreign exchange, they are traded in the same market, because the foreign exchange markets of all financial centers accommodate both types.

Financial Market Relationships

The foreign exchange market and the other financial markets in the same center are closely related. The other financial markets are usually a stock exchange, a money market (including the banking system), a long-term capital market, the mortgage market, other specialized financial markets, and, independent of those and having a locus of its own, the Euro-dollar market. One could also list the commodity markets, in which combined foreign exchange and commodity arbitrage transactions assume importance. Those relationships are so interwoven that it is often difficult to ascertain where one market stops and another begins. There are also relationships, although less close ones, between the financial markets in different centers around the world.

A portion of the foreign exchange market may be regarded as an extension of, or even a part of, the domestic money market because it deals in money for a somewhat specialized purpose: the financing of foreign economic transactions. A substantial part of the funds so used is borrowed from or finds its source on the money market.

Like the foreign exchange market, the money market in the United States is an informal organization without a fixed locale, rules and regulations, or established memberships. It deals in a wide variety of short-term credit instruments. If there were no easy access to such a market, foreign exchange would have a far less important position in the internal economy than it has. In addition, it is through the money market that foreign exchange links the external and domestic economies financially.

Movements of the volume of money in circulation in any country affect foreign exchange via the money market; conversely, it is through the money market that foreign economic transactions have an impact on the volume of money in circulation. The parties who trade on the money market include banks, business firms, and governments and their official institutions as well as individuals. When any of these parties are in need of funds, the market provides cash; and when they hold excessive short-term assets, the market provides an outlet. It is the arena in which demanders and suppliers, lenders and borrowers of short-term funds transact business.

Almost all financial centers include a stock exchange, in which the securities of the larger and better known corporations are bought and sold. Most stock exchanges are organized institutions with a locale, charter, bylaws, official membership, and a body of rules and regulations. The principal functions of stock exchanges are to provide a ready market for the securities of the listed corporations and render investment in those securities as liquid as possible. Stock exchanges are related to the foreign exchange markets in several ways; for there is considerable international business in the purchase and sale of the stocks and bonds of the leading corporations of other countries.

Stock exchange transactions are usually limited to older securities that have been on the market for some time; long-term, newly issued securities are usually handled otherwise. The investment banker in the United States or his counterpart in foreign countries handles most such transactions, although some are carried out by stock and bond brokerage houses.

There are often a number of specialized markets in the financial centers; the mortgage market is one of the more important of them. The specialized markets ordinarily do not have a direct connection with the foreign exchange market, but they have an indirect impact on it through their effect on the total demand and supply for money available for conversion into foreign exchange.

Ordinarily, the commodity markets have a similar indirect effect on the foreign exchange markets, but under certain circumstances they may have a direct effect. That happens when commodity–foreign exchange arbitrage transactions are undertaken, as when commodity price–foreign exchange rate differentials make it profitable to buy a given commodity in a market where the price, translated through an exchange rate, is lower and sell it in a market where the price, similarly translated, is higher. Commodity–foreign exchange transactions are sometimes undertaken in an effort to avoid (by legal means) or to evade (by illegal means) foreign exchange controls.

In addition to foreign exchange transactions, a number of related operations are carried out on the foreign exchange markets; they increased substantially during the late 1950s and early 1960s. The borrowing and lending of deposits denominated in foreign currencies has also increased; the development was fostered by the growth of the Euro-dollar market. Finally, interbank sterling transactions—or money lent in large round amounts in London between banks without security—grew in importance in the 1960s.

Today, the international departments of banks undertake foreign currency lending and borrowing operations more frequently than they did a few years ago, and they do so more systematically. In that way, foreign exchange departments of banks may be said to overlap partially with the lending departments.

Foreign Exchange Controls

Like some other markets, foreign exchange markets have freedom from government intervention that depends on the country in which the market is located. Government interference with the free market in foreign exchange may be said to take at least two forms: *intervention* on the market to maintain a rate of exchange within certain determined limits and the *elimination* of all or some freedom by the use of ex-change controls.

As was noted in Chapter 3, members of the IMF were formerly bound to maintain their spot rates of exchange within 1 percent of parity, either above or below, and members of the European Monetary Agreement and certain other countries have decided to maintain their spot rates within ¾ of 1 percent of parity. Therefore, the nations that respect such bands must sometimes intervene in the foreign exchange markets to maintain their rates within the agreed-upon limits. Under those circumstances, the prevailing rates of exchange no longer always reflect true market rates, or the rates determined solely by the play of the demand for and supply of a currency. The IMF band of permitted exchange rate fluctuations has since been widened to 2¼ percent above and below par.

In addition, central banks intervene on the domestic money market in order to apply managed money policies. The growing volume of in-ternational trade, investment, and unilateral transfers has increased the demand for and supply of foreign currencies, and the result has been an impact on the volume of money available for domestic circulation. Efforts to control the domestic money supply have an inevitable impact on the amount of funds on the foreign exchange market, and they may be said to constitute indirect intervention on that market. These ob-servations do not apply with the same force to forward rates, which may vary from par by substantial margins. Forward rates of exchange may be said to reflect the interaction of supply and demand more accurately than the spot rates. However, and especially since the early 1960s, governments have from time to time attempted to influence forward rates through intervention.

At times when the dollar has been under heavy speculative pressure, the Federal Reserve Bank of New York has intervened on the forward market to support it. Other central banks also have conducted operations in the forward sector. Nevertheless, intervention on the forward markets is less frequent and extensive than on the spot markets.

Exchange controls imply, to a greater or lesser degree, the end of free markets in foreign exchange. Although they were then not exactly a novelty, they were greatly extended and widely adopted during World War II. Exchange controls were utilized not only by the belligerents but by many neutrals as well. In addition, many of the overseas members of the sterling, French franc, and escudo areas were obliged to adopt exchange controls patterned after those of the metropolis.

Under the exchange controls of this period, the government central bank or some other official financial institution was granted a monopoly of dealing on foreign exchange. Those who needed foreign exchange were obliged to buy it from the central bank at the official selling rate, and those who had somehow acquired foreign exchange were obliged to sell it to the central bank at the official buying rate. In that way, the government was able to control its rates of exchange and protect its parity without having to engage in foreign exchange transactions and sacrifice its reserves. Exchange controls thus provided a cheaper method of enforcing pars and rates than that afforded by intervention on free exchange markets.

The financial institution charged with the administration of exchange controls generally appointed a number of commercial banks throughout the country to act as its agents and thus take administration of the controls closer to the residents who wanted to sell or buy foreign exchange.

In countries where import and export controls existed alongside exchange controls, as they frequently did, prospective importers had to apply for licenses to import items not on the free list. If the license was granted, the requisite foreign exchange was usually available automatically under most exchange control systems. For all other transactions requiring an allocation of foreign exchange, an application had to be filed and might be either granted or denied.

National exchange control systems differed in many important respects, and the system of any one nation usually changed substantially over time. The granting of foreign exchange under all control systems usually depended upon the nature of the transaction and its importance to the national economy, as well as its impact upon the currencies concerned by the transaction.

Exchange control, like all institutions calling for a bureaucratic adminstration, was either well or poorly administered and offered an almost ideal opportunity for corruption. It was easier to administer an exchange control system when the official par, and with it the rates of exchange, was at or near the equilibrium level. During the war, however, the official pars of almost all nations became less and less realistic and more and more overvalued the currencies. Consequently, black markets in foreign exchange developed in those nations that had exchange controls. Generally speaking, the rates that prevailed on the black markets were usually closer to the true market values of currencies than the official rates were. It became harder and harder to eliminate the black markets as the official rates became more and more overvalued, and in some nations the black markets became the gray or tolerated markets. Finally, in some countries, the black or gray markets were given official sanction when some traders were allowed, and even encouraged, to buy or sell a part of their foreign exchange on them.

Relatively complete exchange control systems persisted for a few years after the end of World War II. Beginning in the 1950s, they were relaxed, first insofar as they applied to current account transactions (transactions in merchandise, services and unilateral transfers), and then as they applied to capital movements.

However, exchange controls have not as yet been abolished, and today many nations apply them on a reduced and partial basis, especially for certain capital movements and investments. The United States maintains (1972) a form of exchange control against certain capital movements in the Office of Foreign Direct Investments program, although that has not been termed an exchange control. The IMF publishes annually a *Report on Exchange Restrictions,* which describes in some detail the controls still in effect in the member countries. Commercial banks that do a large foreign exchange business keep abreast of controls and are in a position to provide their customers with accurate information on the subject.

In addition to the direct controls, the free exchange markets are subject to the indirect influence of various other controls over international commerce. Foreign funds controls, for instance, are utilized as both hot- and cold-war measures to block the funds of certain foreign countries held to be actual or potential enemies and to eliminate or reduce financial transactions with those countries. Other regulations, such as bilateral trade agreements and international barter arrangements, also impinge on the free market for foreign currencies through their impact on potential total demand and supply for foreign currencies.

In summary, the modern foreign exchange market may be said to provide a framework for the play of supply and demand forces on foreign exchange within the limits provided by government intervention, as well as within the limits of the various systems of exchange and other controls that prevail at any given time.

7

Rates of Exchange
and Their Determination

THE *spot rate* of any currency is the price at a given time that holders
of that currency agree to accept in terms of a second currency and that
the holders of the second currency agree to pay in terms of their own
for "immediate" delivery. Under market conventions and with few ex-
ceptions, spot foreign exchange transactions are settled two business days
after the actual trade. Thus, there is no immediate exchange transaction except in specially negotiated instances or the limited case of
foreign currency notes.

In a sense, foreign currency is a commodity both held and sought
after by various parties for a number of reasons, but since it can earn
interest while held in the form of bank deposits, and since its primary

function is as a means of payment, the commodity analysis should not be overdrawn. Nevertheless, spot foreign exchange rates do follow the basic principles of supply and demand interaction, just as the price of a commodity does. When the price of foreign exchange in a given market is not affected by government or speculative action, it will be determined by the agreement of holders and seekers of that currency—that is, by supply and demand. Also, since the advent of instantaneous Telex and telephone communications, the exchange market is a roughly homogenous one that binds together major industrial countries throughout the world.

The interactions of supply and demand for foreign exchange should not be thought to result in a firm, lasting price or an equilibrium rate. Foreign exchange transactions take place chiefly through bank traders, who combine the demands of their customers on both sides of the market with bank policy, in a sensitive market with competing banks, brokers, and central banks as integral parts. Not only the bare mathematical input of supply and demand but also the traders' intuitive or studied considerations as to future developments in their markets will affect the spot price. A spot trade at 10:00 A.M. may thus warrant a different price than one at 10:15 A.M., although with the same bank. Other than traders' feelings and transactions, new information about political or economic events or even the 10:00 A.M. deal itself may have changed the price. A good deal is now being written about the psychological factors in the foreign exchange markets and the human element of the trader, particularly in light of the nervous and often chaotic markets of the late 1960s.[1]

There is no equilibrium or lasting price for spot foreign exchange that can be identified; instead there is a price that shifts from day to day and within a single day. Over the long run, the spot price will revolve around the par value of the currency, although it may remain consistently under or over its stated par value if suppliers of and bidders for the foreign currency have disproportionate needs, particularly if balance of payments conditions foster a preponderance of buyers or sellers. Of course, any price actually consummated in a spot transaction represents a transitory equality of the supply and demand functions at that particular point in time.

Not only will personal deliberations affect the supply and demand functions, but artificial barriers also can limit price movements.

Under the type of fixed parity system with upper and lower intervention points, a definite and agreed limit to spot rate prices exists.

---

[1] See, for example, Paul Einzig, *A Textbook on Foreign Exchange*, particularly chapter 3.

Unless the spot rate of a currency is actually floating and the central bank of the country issuing that currency has announced it will not support the spot price, any transitory equilibrium price will lie within the band. Diagramatically, that is shown in Exhibit 1, in which the actual demand for (DD) and supply of pounds (SS) coincide within the actual trading limits.

If demand should fall to D'D', however, the price of pounds cannot under the support system fall below the lower intervention point (excluding devaluation at that stage). By dipping into its international reserves, the U.K. treasury is obligated to buy, at its stated lower intervention point, all pounds offered. (That support operation can be very costly; the 1967 defense of the pound sterling before its ultimate devaluation was estimated to have cost the United Kingdom several billion dollars.)

In practice, the limits of spot rate movements become horizontal at the lower intervention point, reflecting the obligatory support (via purchase of pounds) of the British government, and at the upper intervention point. The latter reflects a similiar obligation, when the spot rate is rising under speculative or other pressures, to offer that currency to all purchasers at the upper limit of its band. Pound spot rates, no matter what the market demand or supply functions may be, will thus remain within the price range, as shown in Exhibit 1.

Exhibit 1. Supply and demand for pounds.

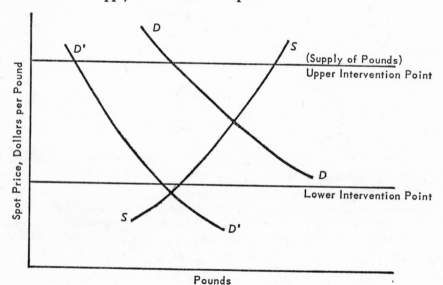

Elasticity

The simple diagram of Exhibit 1 does not attempt to reflect the elasticity of either supply or demand of spot foreign exchange. Like other commodities that respond to price change, response in the supply of or demand for a foreign currency may approximately equal or be greater or less than the change in price. Behind the supply of and demand for a currency lie the fundamental trade patterns and structure of the country. Upward changes in the price of a currency tend to depress its export and increase its import; depreciation of the currency has an opposite effect. Clearly, the underlying price elasticity of the country's internationally traded or purchased products will ultimately be a determining factor in the elasticity of the demand for and supply of the country's currency. Fritz Machlup has summarized this fundamental relationship in four rules: [2]

1. The elasticity of demand for foreign exchange will be higher, the higher the elasticity of the domestic demand for the articles we import.

2. The elasticity of demand for foreign exchange will be higher, the higher the elasticity of supply of domestic products which compete in the domestic market with our imports.

3. The elasticity of demand for foreign exchange will be higher, the higher the elasticity of supply by foreign producers of the articles which we import.

4. The elasticity of demand for foreign exchange will be higher, the higher the elasticity of the foreign demand for their own products.

The significance of all this for an individual business is more specific than general; for it is the specific price elasticity of its own products that is most affected by and that in the aggregate affects the foreign exchange markets.

The lower and upper support limits of a currency are superseded when a country (1) changes its par value or (2) lets the price of its domestic currency find its own transitory levels without major intervention, called floating the currency. Reasons for unilaterally changing the par value of a currency are given in Chapter 4.

The change in par value method of adjusting a currency to inter-

---

[2] Fritz Machlup, *International Monetary Economics* (London: George Allen & Unwin, Ltd., 1966), pp. 17, 18. Published in the United States by Charles Scribner's Sons as *International Payments, Debts and Gold*.

national trade or capital movements and inflationary differentials generally follows a period of monetary speculation and wide forward rates; typically, it can be hedged against, although at a cost. A floating rate reflects a compromise attempt to find a new or more "realistic" rate for a currency, usually under strong speculative pressures; that attempt is often "guided" by central bank action behind the scenes.

The first experiment in floating a currency was made by Canada in several periods and West Germany in 1969, but there was admittedly some influence on the movement of the spot rate by the central banks concerned. In 1971, a number of countries followed that pattern and floating rates proved more difficult to hedge against. However, the key aspect for businessmen in a floating rate situation is the ability to cover exposed exchange positions in the forward markets at a reasonable cost. When this availability of cover exists, floating rates are not as disruptive to trade and commerce as many commentators have feared.

The in-band movement of spot rates may appear insignificant, but it is of prime concern in decisions about short-term borrowing or investment in a foreign currency. The movement of the currency from one intervention point to the other during the period of the loan or investment will have a very large effect on a percent per annum basis. If, for example, there is a one-month deposit, a rate change of 1.5 percent will mean a flat per annum effect of 18 percent (12 months $\times$ 1.5 percent = 18 percent per annum) for or against the investor.

The movement of spot rates, even within the bands, could be overlooked by companies that consider lower short-term interest rates abroad to be advantageous compared with their own. For example, a U.S. company needing U.S. dollar finance might borrow short-term deutsche marks for three months when there is an interest differential in its favor of 2 percent per annum. But if the mark appreciates by 1 percent by the end of the period of borrowing, the company will have to supply approximately 1 percent more dollars to repay its deutsche mark obligation. On an annual basis, that is an adverse factor of 4 percent which makes the borrowing uneconomic compared with using domestic sources, despite the explicit interest differential.

The chance of loss from spot rate changes is greater when the period of investing in or borrowing foreign currency is shorter and the range of movement of the currency to a breakeven point becomes much smaller. For that reason, many opportunities to invest in or borrow a second currency become too risky for the multinational corporation unless the corporation has offsetting transactions. (It is, of course, possible to borrow or invest in a second currency on a protected basis through swaps, discussed later in this chapter, but the swap cost will most often eliminate the interest differential.) For example, if the French franc moves down 1.5 percent and the deutsche mark moves up 1.5 percent, the actual movement of marks relative to francs is 3 percent in normal market conditions, twice the relative movement vis-à-vis a fixed dollar or gold price. That eventuality magnifies the risk of in-band movements of foreign currencies and puts a substantial limitation to multicurrency investment and borrowing schemes.

Under the former IMF system short-term uncovered movements between two currencies (or Euro-currencies) were generally limited to investment when the currency to be loaned was at or near its lower intervention point and the currency to be borrowed was at or near its upper intervention point. In that case, any in-band movement of the second currency could be beneficial to the investor or borrower. As the currencies moved away from their limits, the risk of further negative movements had to be carefully calculated in advance by corporations that wished to use interest differentials in other countries to their advantage. This situation becomes substantially more complex if one or both of the currencies are floating.

The risk of spot rate movements can be quantified statistically, and the entire range of investment or borrowing potentials can then be put into a simple computer program. The computer can compare the probability and effects of spot rate movements against the mix of investment possibilities and, following the company's own constraints, come up with an optimum investment or borrowing solution. That simple form of linear programming, however, is only as good as its input, which depends on the expert views of traders and others as to the short-term movement of various currencies.

Demand for spot exchange. Demand for spot foreign exchange exists for a variety of trade and capital reasons. The first and most fundamental one is to pay for imports of goods invoiced in a currency other than that of the importer. Practically all of the estimated $280 billion of world trade in 1970 involved a foreign exchange conversion for either sellers or buyers across country lines. Conversion and foreign exchange transactions are unnecessary only when the invoiced currency is that of both importer and exporter, and that can be so only when a multinational group uses a common currency for reciprocal sales.

The demand for foreign exchange also arises from so-called invisible trade such as shipping, insurance, and tourism and other service-related transactions. Royalties, management fees, and similar payments typically require foreign exchange purchases, as do salaries of managers and employees abroad. Monetary transactions that arise from foreign aid also affect the spot foreign exchange markets, particularly when aid is not tied to purchases of goods from the donor country.

The second major element of demand for spot foreign exchange is for capital transfers covering a variety of transactions. A borrower may have to repay outstanding loans in a foreign currency, or a company may wish to place short-term deposits in another country and currency for higher yields. Direct and portfolio investment abroad likewise require the purchase of large amounts of foreign exchange.

Government action, such as the internal restructuring of international reserves or the attempt to support currencies under pressure, is also an element of demand in the spot foreign exchange market, although it is due to technical rather than trade reasons.

Banks are not only the major conduit through which foreign exchange is traded but also major participants in the market for their own account. Banks maintain spot positions in a number of currencies in order to meet normal working requirements; they also maintain large spot holdings, largely offset by forward sales, as a concomitant of their international financing, or lending, operations. Their transactions for their own account and also those at reporting dates for balance sheet purposes can influence spot trading appreciably.

Finally, speculation and hedging influence the spot market, although perhaps to a lesser extent than the forward exchange market. When a currency is under pressure and a parity change is expected, there will normally be a rush to build up a net long position in a currency that is likely to revalue or appreciate. That will mean the purchase of the currency in order to hold sight or time deposits; it can also mean that obligors in that currency will try to prepay outstanding payables and obligations and thus accelerate or "lead" their purchases of exchange. That is part of the so-called lead-and-lag mechanism commonly utilized by companies to conform foreign exchange positions to expected developments in various currencies. As was explained in an earlier chapter, lagging payments—delaying payment for trade and other obligations indefinitely or within legal constraints—is practiced by companies with payables in a currency that is likely to devalue or whose own domestic currency is expected to be revalued. Leading, or accelerating payments, is found in the opposite situation. Lagging induces a lessening, leading an increase, of spot demand for the affected currency.

All of the elements discussed in the preceding pages make up the constantly shifting demand for foreign exchange. It is apparent that normal trade and capital movements are only one component of demand and that technical transactions of governments and banks, as well as speculative responses, are an equally important and often more volatile component. Seen as a medium of exchange, spot foreign currency holdings will be demanded by all those groups for that into which they can be converted, whether domestic purchasing power, adjustment of exposure, or possible economic gain.

Supply of foreign exchange. The elements of supply of spot foreign exchange are analogous to those of demand. Holders of foreign currency earned through exports or other international transactions will usually wish—or be required by law—to convert those receipts into domestic currency. Banks will supply foreign currency both to serve in their normal role as principal dealers and to adjust their own foreign exchange positions and strategies. Each government has been required to supply its own domestic currency to the market under IMF rules when the currency has reached its upper intervention point in order to keep the price from rising under conditions of heavy demand. Speculative holdings of foreign exchange will be supplied to the market after speculators' short- or long-term goals have been met.

There is also a chronological aspect to the supply and demand functions for spot foreign exchange. Most countries have seasonal patterns in their international trading. Agricultural producers tend to have large inflows at and just after the harvest; countries in which tourism plays a major role will increase foreign currency holdings during the tourism season; and large industrial countries may have independent seasonal fluctuations in which the holdings of foreign exchange in the private sector follow balance of payments flows. Those patterns are reflected directly in the foreign exchange markets. The supply of foreign exchange, although partly a function of its price, thus tends to be a constantly shifting and independent variable.

Forward Rates

The area of forward foreign exchange is more complex than that of spot exchange and presents more ramifications and opportunities for the business sector. A forward exchange transaction involves the purchase or sale of one currency against another and the delivery of the agreed amounts at some future time. In common practice, neither party puts up any funds until the actual settlement or maturity date. Forward exchange transactions can, theoretically, be negotiated for any period from two days up to several years, although not much business is done for future dates of over two years. The most common trading dates are round numbers of months, such as 1, 2, 3, 6, or 12. There is obviously more concern about the credit worthiness of each partner in a forward foreign exchange transaction than in a spot or cash transaction, and firms that do not have prime credit ratings may be asked to furnish some type of collateral until the time of settlement.

Some authors regard the forward foreign exchange market as distinctly separate from the spot market, but that conclusion seems tenuous. Just as spot rates primarily reflect the immediate requirements of seekers and holders of a currency, so forward rates reflect anticipated needs for a currency. In both spot and forward markets, there is also, from time to time, a certain demand or supply that is activated by judgment or expectation of immediate or future rate performance. Whereas spot foreign exchange market participants are chiefly concerned about getting the best applicable rate in a conversion, forward purchasers or suppliers take into account future economic and political developments, likelihood of parity changes, and so on.

Spot and forward currencies are traded in the same market and by the same participants. The most important difference is that there are no formal limitations on the price of forward exchange. Furthermore, governments typically assume a neutral position vis-à-vis their forward rates unless speculation or money market flows create enough pressure that they feel forced to intervene for domestic reasons. There have been many cases of government intervention in the forward markets to induce foreign monies to flow into or domestic funds to flow out of internal economies; they have not always been successful. A case can be made that defending forward rates can prove to be a costly and self-defeating operation because, without concurrent domestic measures, the action may inspire further lack of confidence and even greater speculation against a domestic currency. The result can be a major loss of international reserve holdings. There is still a good deal of controversy about this policy area.

There are, therefore, wider variations in the forward rates than in the spot rates of the various currencies; at times the forward discount or premium for a currency can widen sharply, even precipitously. This type of widening of forward exchange rates—to a greater premium or discount—in itself signals both greater activity and, if constant, one-sidedness of the market or heavy speculation. If it is carried on over a period of months and coincides with heavy additions to or losses of reserves, a foreign exchange crisis is at hand. The alert international company will have picked up the problem as the forwards begin to widen, and it will attempt to take whatever adjustments or hedging measures are necessary before the cost reaches a maximum or the possibility of taking them disappears.

Forward exchange rates are expressed as being at a premium, at par, or at a discount vis-à-vis the spot value of the currency. The British pound, for example, may be quoted for six months forward at $2.6010 when the spot rate is $2.5845. The differential amounts to a 1.276 percent premium on a per annum basis; it reflects in part the market's monetary evaluation of the strength of the pound over the coming three months. More importantly, it is a reflection of the difference between short-term money market rates in the United Kingdom and those in external markets, as well as expected interest rate developments.

Trade and capital transactions. Forward rates are a function of future demand for and supply of currencies. In the examples given earlier it was assumed that an exporter would wait until he obtained foreign currency receipts before converting or that an importer would wait until his contract date to purchase foreign exchange for imports. Actually, in order to have an absolutely fixed future obligation and precise costs, an importer—say a commodity dealer buying foreign grain for future delivery that perhaps has not yet even been harvested—may enter a forward contract for the foreign currency. A premium on that currency forward may add marginally to the price, but that is preferable to the possible loss from an appreciation or revaluation of the currency owed under the contract. Similarly, an exporter selling for payment at a given future date will sell those receipts forward to fix his proceeds precisely and beyond effect of exchange market vagaries. That is shown in quantitative terms in Chapter 13.

Capital transactions, like visible trade and service transactions, augment the supply of and demand for forward foreign currency. With the gradual liberalization of foreign exchange control since World War II and especially since the Euro-currency market has reached massive proportions, borrowing in a currency other than a company's own has become commonplace. The foreign borrower of short-term dollars or deutsche marks, for example, may wish to protect himself against appreciation of that currency vis-à-vis his own by purchasing an equivalent amount for delivery at the loan repayment date. An entity receiving deferred payment for a capital transaction, such as sale of a stock interest in a company, may likewise sell its expected receipts forward to eliminate the risk of exchange loss.

In both trade and capital transactions, the purchase or sale of forward exchange is a form of insurance, of protection against depreciation of an asset or increase of a liability through exchange fluctuations. In both transactions a loss probability is averted, usually at a modest cost relative to the underlying transaction.

Banks affect the forward market both as principals and as dealers.

Each major bank will have a net position limit in the major currencies other than its own, and the position will be defined as the arithmetic sum of its spot and forward assets and liabilities in each currency. Forward transactions are used to even out or consolidate a bank's position, especially because the bank usually will have long spot positions for normal working purposes or for interest arbitrage transactions. Forward commitments can be used to spread risk over a longer period of time or to prepare for a net long or short position in a currency at a future date. It is not uncommon for a bank to be heavily involved in both ends of the forward market in a currency for position and strategy reasons; perhaps it will be long in short forward dates and owe the currency in long forward dates.

Speculation. As it is broadly defined, speculation represents the body of liquid funds that can readily be transferred between countries in order to realize gain on exchange fluctuations. True speculators, or pure risk bearers, are not as large a factor as might be deduced from the prominent mention given them in the financial and popular press. (The "gnomes of Zurich," perhaps the most often cited group of supposed speculators, are actually the very experienced financial institutions and banks of Switzerland using foreign exchange market movements to their own legal advantage.)

By taking uncovered risks in the various foreign currencies, speculators add both positive and negative features to the exchange markets. It could be stated that speculation helps give the exchange market more depth and breadth by increasing the number and variety of transactions. More typically, though, speculation increases the disruptive forces present in any marketplace in which psychological and political factors play as large a role as economic ones play. By increasing transactions on one side of the market for a currency—accumulated sales of spot pounds sterling as a case in point—speculation increases the pressure on IMF member governments to maintain their currency within IMF limits, adds to their reserve losses, and creates distortion in the forward rates. A convincing argument could be made that pecuniary speculation, when added to economic factors, may have been a decisive factor in each of the parity changes of the late 1960s. A. P. Thirlwall aptly describes the culmination of market forces which led to the British devaluation as follows: [3]

> The decision to devalue was taken on the 18 November. It was taken
> against the background of a lack of confidence, not so much in

[3] A. P. Thirlwall, "Another Autopsy on Britain's Balance of Payments: 1958–1967," *Quarterly Review of the Banca Nazionale del Lavoro*, September 1970, pp. 324–5.

Britain's ability to pay her way through an underlying worsening in her trading position, but in her ability to cope with the sorts of emergencies and contingencies such as were suffered the bleak months of July to September. . . . As it was, Britain was "blown off-course" and, in the face of pressure in the foreign exchange market, had little choice but to alter the par value of the pound. The basic deficit against which Britain devalued, however, was considerably less than in 1964. It was the "market" balance, not the "accounting" balance of payments, which proved decisive.

However, the volume of pure speculation is not ordinarily of the same magnitude as that of international business transactions in hedging and speculative adjustment of foreign exchange positions. The leads and lags instituted by multinational companies reach enormous proportions at times of actual exchange crisis, as does the covering of exposed positions by forward purchases and sales. The role of the business community in legitimately trying to protect its own exposure and to profit by parity changes as well should not be overlooked.

Interest arbitrage. Interest arbitrage is a further significant factor in the forward exchange market. It represents the placing of a deposit or investment in another currency to obtain a higher yield than could be realized by placing a deposit or investment of the same tenor and risk in the original currency. A true arbitrage profit ensues if there remains a positive differential in the investor's favor after the exchange risk has been covered by hedging. Given the dynamic nature of the forward exchange market, the act of interest arbitrage and its concomitant forward purchases will by itself tend to eliminate the interest differential. For example, a U.S. investor may find that interest rates on short-term local authority obligations in England are 2 percent per annum above the yield on paper of similar risk and tenor in the United States. If he can hedge his pound sterling exchange risk at a cost of less than 2 percent per annum, it is profitable for him to invest in the British obligations. His act of selling forward sterling (together with the acts of short-term foreign investors in the aggregate) will tend to depress forward rates of sterling and make the ultimate hedging cost equal to the interest differential between the two countries, if only in a transitory stage.

Swaps

A swap combines a spot transaction with a forward one; it provides a fixed amount of foreign currency for a specified period of time and at a known cost. In the preceding example of interest arbitrage, the short-term investor will purchase the spot pounds and will sell them forward for a future date to coincide with the maturity of his intended obligation. In the case of a currency with forward rates at a discount, the simultaneous purchase and future sale of the currency results in a net cost that can be expressed in percent per annum terms. That percentage becomes the actual cost of the swap or hedge; it must be subtracted from the gross yield on the short-term foreign deposit or investment to arrive at a net (pretax) yield.

A swap with a forward sale that is at par with the spot rate involves no cost, and one with a premium on the forward portion results in a net percentage gain, which is added to the yield on the short-term investment in that currency. The latter situation will often occur, particularly when the foreign currency in question is under speculative upward pressure. There may, however, be government action that restricts the inflow of funds or the payment of interest on nonresident funds at such a time.

Interest arbitrage via swaps is particularly practiced by banks; as participants in the market, most commercial banks see relative investment yields and hedging costs on a constant and momentary basis, yet they do not typically take sizable open positions for speculative purposes. As stated earlier, swap rates have a tendency to approach the interest differentials between countries and to lessen the amount of net advantage on an arbitrage transaction. Conversely, swaps can be used by companies for short-term borrowing of a foreign currency. By borrowing a foreign currency, selling it spot, and buying it back at a fixed rate for the future maturity, a company can obtain working capital for itself at a known rate without exchange rate exposure. The swap cost must be added to or the premium subtracted from the gross interest on the borrowing.

Commercial banks provide swap opportunities by matching the spot supply of a foreign currency with a future demand as part of their normal trading activities. Swap transactions can have a short-term effect on the international reserves of the country whose currency is involved. For that reason, forward rates are carefully monitored by central banks, despite the absence of formal obligation to support forwards. Governments may induce artificial forward rates for international monetary purposes, because market forces will react in a predictable way to artificial interest differentials created in that manner. For example, a country with a large balance of payments surplus, relatively low rate of inflation, and low rates of interest may experience speculative inflows of money in anticipation of appreciation or revaluation of its currency. Its central bank may then offer unrealistically low forward exchange contracts to induce a short-term outflow of funds by resident entities and banks to offset temporarily the funds inflow and the effect on its international reserves.

The Present System and International Business

The basic framework of foreign exchange allows businessmen to concentrate on fundamental areas of finance, marketing, and other aspects of management in an international setting. The foreign exchange elements in international business are manageable and, to some extent, predictable. Exposure can be ascertained and generally hedged, if at a certain cost; the cost is minor in most cases when compared with the overall advantages of an international configuration.

The exchange structure need not automatically be more difficult under a system of flexible rates. The key element is in the relative stability of exchange parities and the availability of a range of forward transaction possibilities at rates corresponding to interest differentials between countries. Flexible exchange rate enthusiasts base their advocacy of exchange market freedom on the development of such an orderly and predictable market. If their thesis has value, the free determination of exchange rates and its impact upon international operations would not result in significantly changed operating constraints, because exchange rates, while flexible, will tend to stabilize around predictable poles determined by the economic conditions of the countries concerned. Of particular determinant effect will still be inflationary rates, productivity gains, terms of trade, and free flow of capital between international participants in a freer market.

The growth and interaction of multinational firms have had a number of effects on the foreign exchange markets. The markets have increased not only in volume but also in complexity, particularly if one considers the Euro-currency market as an extension of the foreign area as well as a link between it and the local money markets of participating countries. International business presents both endogenous (internal) and exogenous (external) elements—endogenous because its transactions in the foreign exchange market are the bulk and the determinant force behind the market, exogenous because demands for foreign exchange techniques, particularly in the forward area, have by themselves broadened and changed the functions of the international market. It is the growth, development, and responsiveness of the foreign exchange market, taken as a whole, that has greatly contributed to the expansion and diversity of international trade and that promises to respond to complement its future growth as well.

8

Buying and Selling
Foreign Exchange

IT is clear from the preceding chapter that the foreign exchange market primarily serves the framework of international trade. Behind the bulk of transactions in the exchange marketplace lie the supply and demand for foreign currency arising from trade and capital movements, and thus the individual corporate participants.

Corporate entities, however, do not themselves deal directly in the marketplace; instead, they use their banks for the purchase and sale of exchange. Governments, when they deal in currencies, may act through their central banks or, if secrecy is desired, through commercial banks. The first of the following sections describes the role of each market participant; the second depicts the ways in which a corporation can approach the market in order best to consummate its exchange dealings.

Role of Market Participants

Central Banks

The central bank of a country has as its primary obligation the maintenance of an efficient monetary system, one that encourages domestic growth without inflation. That internal objective is affected by external forces. Balance of payments surpluses, if no action is taken, may raise the liquidity of a country to undesirable levels and add to inflationary forces; deficits can create liquidity pressures and eventually affect the domestic economy or undermine the international reserves on which the money supply is theoretically based. In either situation, a central bank, particularly through its exchange control arm, may be forced to intervene actively in the external economic sphere to attain domestic goals. In that way central banks often have a pervasive influence on foreign exchange markets.

In simplest terms, central bank dealings in foreign exchange are undertaken to maintain orderly markets for the respective currencies and thereby foster international trade and investment. Actually, a central bank acts in response to the complex interplay of its own country's economic course, balance of payments—trade and capital—and reserve position, domestic and international interest rates, current market psychology, and other factors. Furthermore, each central bank acts in its own way. The methods, extent, and frequency of intervention of central banks vary sharply from one to another; some of them are described below.

In the event of a severe balance of payments disequilibrium, a central bank will attempt to neutralize the adverse effects of the disequilibrium on the internal economy. That may not involve the bank directly in the exchanges; instead, the bank may adopt structural measures designed to limit the flow of funds into or out of the country. The measures will have a major, if indirect, effect on the other exchange market participants, and if like the exchange controls of Britain, France, and other European countries the measures are institutionalized, there will be a permanent framework within which the exchange markets operate. That framework may continue even when there is no severe balance of payments disequilibrium.

International interest rate differentials may force a central bank to change domestic interest levels by adopting a different discount rate or by taking some other action to control the speculative flows of funds seeking a higher yield. Again that may not involve direct participation of the bank in the spot market; on the other hand, interest rate differentials may induce the bank to intervene in both the spot and the forward markets. A central bank can offer swap opportunities to its domestic banks at rates not applicable to market conditions. For example, the Euro-dollar rates for short-term deposits might be in the 8 percent per annum range and German rates at about 6 percent per annum. Under the interest parity theory and in normal markets, the forward premium on the mark vis-à-vis dollars would be approximately 2 percent per annum. A German investor, such as a commercial bank, would not tend to gain in that situation by buying dollars spot and selling them forward, while placing them on deposit meanwhile, because the swap cost would tend to eliminate the interest differential.

For policy reasons, a central bank such as the German Bundesbank might offer swaps at a net 1 percent per annum cost to its local banks. In that case, the banks would be induced to enter into a large volume of outward interest arbitrage via dollar swaps. The internal result in Germany would be to reduce bank liquidity and international reserve holdings, although both on a temporary basis. In effect, there would be an artificial reduction of the forward premium on the domestic currency, in this case the deutsche mark.

A central bank may also intervene in the forward market to keep the discount on its own currency to a lower level. That may be done in some cases to disguise indecision or inaction, in others to maintain confidence in a currency. From 1964 to 1967 the British government supported the forward pound continually, but it did not couple that tactic with adequate internal measures to protect Britain's trading position. The policy proved to be very expensive and finally ineffective.

Although by its nature a central bank might be categorized as a non-profit-seeking participant, an element of profit and loss can be inherent in both its spot and forward dealings. Protection of either a forward rate or a lower IMF spot limit may result in severe losses of reserves, which constitute part of the "real wealth" of a country. In that sense, foreign exchange market participation is not riskless, even for a central bank.

Central bank cooperation. To strengthen and defend the present international money system, the central banks of Western Europe and North America have recently begun to cooperate closely. They have contact through monthly meetings in Basle; at times they have taken action to minimize exchange market disturbances. Central banks have offered very large swap facilities to each other on a formal or ad hoc basis. In those transactions, one central bank purchases large amounts of another country's currency (on a covered basis) to assist in that country's own adjustment or currency protection measures. Lessening the drain on the second country's reserves gains time in which corrective actions can take effect.

A cardinal rule is that no central bank will deal in another country's exchange without prior consultation, because, in an indirect way, such dealing can constitute interference in the internal economic affairs of another country. The exception to the rule is when countries other than the United States deal in dollars, the availability of which still forms much of the basis of international monetary relations. The dollar is typically the currency through which intervention will take place.

With agreement, very large spot and forward transactions have taken place between central banks. They are most frequently undertaken to protect international reserve positions and the related currencies during times of speculative pressures. For instance, Great Britain might undertake large swap transactions directly with central banks abroad; it might sell them pounds spot against forward, which would give it larger, if temporary, holdings of foreign exchange. That addition to its reserves would be available to defend sterling's existing parity against speculative attack.

The focal point of central bank cooperation has been the Federal Reserve, which had bilateral swap facilities with 15 central banks and international institutions totaling more than $11 billion by early 1971. Central bank intervention and cooperation, however, have practical limits. Even a central bank has a borrowing limit beyond which other monetary authorities and international organizations such as the IMF are unwilling to lend it additional hard currencies on a short-term basis. Further aid may be conditional on a promise to take strict and often painful measures to correct external imbalances and the resultant erosion of confidence in that country's central bank and currency. Failure to take such measures will eventually curtail the amount of aid other central banks will give.

The effect of external economic forces on domestic monetary policy can be substantial, and that interaction and the response of central banks must be known and followed by participants in the exchange markets, which in a significant way link the internal economies of all major trading nations.

Brokers

Foreign exchange brokers are small, individual firms that go between and combine commercial bank dealers in local exchange markets, particularly in the United States. They supplement either the system of a physical meeting place, or bourse, for foreign exchange dealings or direct dealings between banks. The broker is both agent and middle-man. Unlike a stockbroker, he will not carry a position for his own account; instead, he acts solely on a commission basis.

A typical exchange broker will have a very small capital (another reason for his not taking open foreign exchange positions) and an office in the financial district of a city such as London, New York, or Frankfurt. A brokerage firm will consist of a small number of individuals whose role it is to seek out and bring together buyers and sellers of a currency. It operates wholly through telephone calls and has direct lines to the major bank participants in a market. The broker's day will be spent in calling, and being called by, banks wanting to offer one currency, buy another, or simply check the current market quotation on a specific exchange.

The broker's coordinating and communicating role facilitates the working of the foreign exchange markets. A large commercial bank, for reasons of competition and efficiency, cannot seek out partners by calling every other bank in its own market continuously. Much of that action is taken by the broker, who may make several hundred calls daily in the course of his intermediary functions.

A second major reason for using a broker is that absolute secrecy is required. A commercial bank that wishes to alter a substantial exchange position will not let its competitors know of its strategy, because they would undoubtedly react in a manner that would make the dissolution of the position more costly. Instead, the bank dealer will call a broker to indicate a desired purchase or sale of a certain currency and will indicate his rates. For example, the dealer may say that he wants to sell £2,000,000 when the range is $2.5980–85. The broker will then contact a number of banks in the same marketplace to determine potential buyers and their rate ideas. If the selling rate is attractive, another bank accepts the offer, at which point the sale is confirmed and the selling bank is identified. In this case, a broker is an active agent of his bank clients, although he does not, of course, know their underlying position or strategy.

The broker is thus an information point and a nerve center in his own marketplace. He may be called at any moment by several banks wanting to know of rate developments, and he thereby facilitates the ultimate transactions. Between countries, brokers are not ordinarily used, for international banks deal directly with each other by telephone or Telex. The broker's role is more important when a local market is isolated from others by reason of time differential, particularly New York after about 11 A.M.

Brokers act on a commission basis, which varies with the currency involved. They receive their commission from seller or buyer; in some markets the commission is shared by both buyer and seller. Commissions are small in percentage terms; for example, Canadian-U.S. spot transactions in the U.S. market bring the broker only 0.01 percent, or $100 per million Canadian. A broker's commission income is thus a direct function of his ability to stay in contact with and bring together the larger bank participants in his respective market. A corporation will not have any contact with brokers and may be unaware of their function, yet these non-risk-bearing market participants are vital to the smooth operation of national exchange markets.

Brokerage charges are usually passed on to the customer, but sometimes U.S. commercial banks themselves absorb the charges when they are dealing for prime customers. In Europe, brokerage commissions are routinely added to the cost of buying or selling foreign exchange.

Brokers are used more intensively in the United States than in Europe because the U.S. market is isolated from direct European dealings during much of its trading day by the time differential. European banks have less need of brokers as intermediaries and prefer to go directly to their foreign correspondents or branches for the bulk of their business.

Commercial Banks

The foreign exchange market is primarily a market of banks trading directly with each other on a worldwide and instantaneous basis. Banks act both as agents for their customers and as active participants for their own account. Both functions involve risk of a passive or active nature.

In the case of sizable purchases of spot exchange from customers or other trading banks, large holdings of exchange in the form of demand balances with correspondents abroad can be built up. In the case of substantial sales of spot exchange, a sufficiently large supply of the currency sold must be acquired in order to make the contractual delivery. All trades of currency between banks and between banks and corporations involve transfers of funds on the books of banks in the country whose currency is involved. (There is no physical transfer of funds except in the marginal cases of individuals' own requirements.)

To accommodate trading requirements, banks maintain *working balances* in accounts with correspondent banks abroad. Purchases or sales immediately involve the bank in an exchange exposure in each currency that must be weighed against its overall exchange strategy. The level of foreign balances is also affected by the bank's other dealings in the exchange market, such as swap transactions. Equally important is the fact that spot holdings represent a charge on the bank's own sources and uses of funds. Foreign balances are only marginally interest bearing or return nothing at all, and the funds could be used for other bank purposes such as short-term investment or lending. Typically, therefore, the internal accounting system of a bank will charge the foreign exchange department, at the average cost of funds or *treasurer's rate*, for the amount of bank funds tied up in the department's spot position. The charge becomes an element of the exchange department's own profit and loss account and puts a substantial limit on the holding of long spot positions.

The transactions that customers bring to their banks are varied and not entirely predictable. On the average, spot purchases and sales of the various currencies tend toward a relative balance for the international banking system as a whole (a basic requirement of normal market equilibrium), but they may not for any individual bank. A single bank may experience demand that is asymmetric to the market, owing to the needs of particular customers or industries it serves. Its spot holdings in any case will not cover, and are not intended to cover, all of the spot requirements over time or even a single day. Thus it will be constantly entering the market as an active buyer or seller as much to balance its cash position as to even out its exchange position.

Although supplying customers' needs is a major extension of normal banking services, banks often assume an active principal role on their own behalf. As the volume of international trade and capital transactions has grown in recent years, the exchange markets have also grown in depth and scope. In keeping with those developments, the larger banks are now more likely to take a net exposed position for their own account, whereas formerly banks tended to even out their positions to neutralize the effects of their customers' transactions. This is still a disputed area of banking philosophy. Banks are profit-seeking and risk-bearing institutions; they accept risks in the process of maximizing returns to their shareholders. Profits can be made by participating in the foreign exchange area, and losses can be sustained as well. Recent banking history has recorded a number of prominent, even spectacular, losses in bank foreign exchange dealings. In contrast, profits derived from the acceptance of exchange risks have received almost no publicity.

Two types of risk can be identified: the in-band movement of spot exchange rates over time, which can involve only relatively small profits or losses, and the larger risk involved when the official parity of a currency may be changed. The first area is typically a matter of daily concern only to the head of exchange operations; experienced traders will identify that risk as one of their normal constraints and an area in which certain profits can be made. A bank will usually be more heavily involved in the forward markets, both for its own account and as a result of customer demand, when the second element of risk arises.

A bank's exposure in a foreign currency is the net of the bank's spot holdings and forward commitments. A typical position sheet, which is prepared each day for control purposes, will include the same items for each currency as those given here for the determination of a bank's position in Italian lire.

Spot balances with Italian correspondent banks	1,385 billion
Future purchases of lire	2,100
Subtotal	3,485
Less future sales of lire	2,400
Net position	1,085 billion

The 1,085 billion lire represent a net exposure of over $1.8 million, a risk of substantial losses if the lira should be devalued against the dollar, and a minor risk if the lira should merely move down but remain within its bands. The exposure will vary daily or even hourly, but the main thrust of the bank's position will take a certain direction until the bank's view of the currency concerned changes.

The usual method for controlling and limiting the exposure incurred in foreign exchange trading consists of the following:

1. *Limits.* A net position limit will be set by a bank's management for each major currency. It may range from very modest amounts for the less-traded or inconvertible currencies to sizable figures for the principal European ones. The internal limits may be reinforced by the banking regulations of a specific country, particularly as to forward commitments for or against the currency of that country. Most major banks also impose, in addition to limits on net positions the traders are permitted to carry, quantitative limiits on the degree to which forward commitments may remain unmatched as to date and amount.

2. *Position determination.* A position clerk will prepare the bank's precise net position by currency each morning to reflect the preceding day's changes. The trader keeps a running log throughout the trading day to keep track of his net position and to make sure that he stays within the position limit set by management. The position clerk, or more often the bank's computer, gives the trader a complete runoff accounting of his net forward positions so that he can keep track of his forward exposures also through the trading day.

3. *Policy setting.* Banks vary widely in their policies with respect to

positions vis-à-vis exchange risk and exposure, and it is precisely that difference that makes a heterogeneous market more interesting and profitable for the corporate officer. A bank with wider limits and larger forward dealings and commitments is, on the whole, more likely to give a more flexible service to any major customer. An advantage is the ability to consummate a single deal with one bank rather than divide it among several traders.

Moreover, banks have widely different attitudes about the role of foreign exchange as a profitable activity. In some countries, foreign exchange dealings and their resultant commissions and float are a major source of revenue. Particularly in continental Europe, where demand deposits and their inherent profitability do not play a dominant role, exchange trading is used more as a profit operation than as a customer service. That is reflected, in very general terms, in larger exchange spreads (and thus higher costs to customers) and in the acceptance of larger exchange risks. In the United Kingdom and the United States the servicing of customers, with whom there may be very extensive and profitable existing relationships, plays a larger role.

The extent to which a bank divides its exchange activity and emphasis between trading for its own account and serving its customers depends on the policies of its management, on the makeup of and the role played by its shareholders, and to some extent on legal and banking restrictions. Banks evaluate risk in different fashions; one bank may put a high contingent risk assessment on forward commitments, and another may take a much more liberal view. The risk inherent in forward dealings is not the full amount of the trade unless one partner to the deal, *after* receiving its foreign exchange, defaults or otherwise fails to provide the agreed counterpart. The chances of that are slight. A more pragmatic estimate would be the cost in obtaining cover for an obligation when a forward partner defaults, which could involve expensive borrowing costs, loss of time, and availability of funds if for a limited period or, in the case of a change in parity of the currency originally sold to a defaulting trading partner, the loss in selling the depreciated currency at the new parity rate. One rule of thumb that is commonly used is that forward contracts are carried on a 10 percent risk factor; a $1,000,000–FF 5,500,000 forward transaction has a nominal $100,000 risk. Internally, banks may calculate their risk at above or below 10 percent.

In addition to net position limits, banks will set different forward and overall exposure limits for outstandings vis-à-vis customer names, which constrain their trading. The opportunity cost (that is, the alternative yield if used elsewhere in the bank) of funds used in the foreign exchange department also varies greatly among banks of different sizes, geographical locations, and nationalities. All these divergent factors influence both the way in which a bank deals directly in the exchange market and the way in which it approaches its customers.

Corporations

As indicated in the preceding paragraphs, corporate transactions provide the background for an important part, perhaps the bulk, of the exchange market turnover. The way in which companies deal with their banks in the foreign exchange sector is described in detail in the balance of this chapter. To describe the role of the companies as participants requires a division into those that are non-risk-bearers and those that deliberately assume an uncovered exchange position.

Normal, or non-risk-bearing, transactions are purchases or sales of foreign exchange for working purposes. They include hedging or covering operations undertaken to protect an exposed exchange position, whether in the liability or asset category, according to the company's own definition and conceptual framework of exposure. Covered interest arbitrage, and also any other covered transaction, falls into this category.

Risk-bearing transactions consist of the assumption of risk for potential profit. Both the holding of spot balances or forward positions unrelated to trade obligations or underlying balance sheet items and the assumption of liabilities in a weak foreign currency fall into the risk-bearing category. In a number of countries there is nothing to prevent a corporation from speculating on the movement of currencies in a fashion unrelated to its actual sphere of business. It is an unresolved question whether management energies should be so directed or shareholders' equity so exposed. However, the number of corporations aggressively speculating in this manner is not large.

Normal leads and lags—accelerating or delaying certain foreign exchange transactions in anticipation of parity changes—usually fall into the non-risk-bearing category as a means of covering exposure or increasing potential gain without active engagement in a forward position.

Assumption of unnecessary debt in a currency likely to devalue and maintenance of idle balances in a revaluation-prone currency are typical examples of speculative activities that bear an actual or opportunity cost. Accomplishment of a net short or long forward position in either of the two cases may produce the same result without incurring the cost of idle funds or risking capital.

Consummation of Exchange Transactions

The best way to describe the mechanics of a foreign exchange is to detail the steps in a simple purchase of currency.

Company *A* in the United States wishes to buy 2 million French francs for capital equipment purchases from a French manufacturer. The company speaks with several of its banks to get a feel for the market, and on the day of actual dealing, it requests their specific quotes. One rate is accepted; without other arrangement, that particular bank debits the local dollar account of company *A* on the contractual settlement date, normally two days later for a typical spot deal.

Behind the bank's franc selling offer was either a prospective purchase of francs in order to satisfy company *A*'s needs or a prospective sale of its own holdings of spot francs. In either case, a French correspondent bank must enter into the transaction for the actual transfer of the francs. Assuming the U.S. bank purchases the francs in order to fulfill its sale, it gives, at the time of purchase, instructions to its source as to the disposition of the francs it has bought. The francs might flow into its franc account at the Crédit du Nord, Paris; the transfer in its favor will then take place two business days later. Similarly, following the instructions of company *A*, the U.S. bank instructs Crédit du Nord where to transfer its 2 million francs, which may be to another French bank in favor of the French payee. Note that, although both the customer's order and the market transaction take place on, say, Monday, the actual crediting of the U.S. bank's franc account and the immediate further movement to the ultimate payee of company *A* follow on day three, or Wednesday. The two-day lag is a market convention based on the time when communications were slower and banks could not be sure of getting their currency payments to an exchange partner on time.

A standard procedure can be deduced from even such a limited example as that given. A company with a large order to buy or sell exchange will approach several banks to get their rate quotations, because foreign exchange prices are not uniform but instead, as has been shown, vary from bank to bank. Assuming several banks are asked for their quotes at the same time, the variance will stem from a number of factors but will lie chiefly in the amount of spread, or the bank's margin. (The bank margin may not be obvious and will not normally be revealed to the customer, who is interested in the most advantageous rate and not the bank's own spread over its cost of buying the exchange.)

The spread charged to a particular customer will depend on the bank's overall relationship with the customer and the size of the transaction. A close bond with a customer will tend to reduce the spread charged (the service versus profit dichotomy). Non-customers can expect full spreads—up to perhaps $\frac{1}{8}$ percent on European currency transactions—unless, again, they are major solicitations of the bank. Simultaneous but varied quotations from different banks will reflect the relative ties of the banks to the buyer and relative emphasis on customer service. The size of a transaction also will determine the spread, which as a percentage tends to be in inverse proportion to the actual amount.

An alert treasurer will realize which banks tend to quote better rates on average, and he can limit his rate checking to a small number of house banks. It is, of course, feasible to concentrate all transactions with a single bank, but that can eventually lead to different rates than if a competitive element existed.

However, in certain cases when a bank is used as a direct agent of a corporation in coping with a large foreign exchange position, it is desirable and even necessary to use a single bank. For example, a U.S. corporation may expect to receive a very large amount of foreign currency in the form of dividends. The sale of that currency on the exchange markets could sharply reduce the spot price and thus the net amount of dollars received. In that case, only one bank should be entrusted with selling the exchange over several days and perhaps in several markets. Painful losses have occurred when different banks have been charged with consummating the same substantial transaction in a thin market. This particularly may be the case after an exchange crisis, such as that in late 1971, when both the spot and forward markets are unsettled and trading volume may be small. In such markets, transactions, which could readily be absorbed without affecting rates in "normal" markets, can have a disproportionate effect on the price of the currency dealt in.

There are variances between rates charged to corporate customers in different countries. Differences in traditional spreads and practice can lead to higher prices to the same customer in two or more markets. Yet it would be misleading to be dogmatic about the advantages of any geographical market. A large multinational company will be a valued customer or solicitation of major banks in any location, and it should command as good rates on the Continent as in New York except to the extent that transaction commissions may be applied on the Continent. Generally speaking, the lowest margins and most attractive rates tend to be found in the largest and most active markets, which amounts to a preference for London and New York. There is no essential reason, however, why a sharp Paris or Frankfurt trader cannot be as competitive on a case-by-case basis as his London or New York counterpart. After all, today's foreign exchange market, because of advanced communications, is truly international. Curiously, traders in less active locations may sometimes undercut those in world financial centers.

The way in which a bank determines its spot rate quotation at a given time depends on additional factors other than the bank's relationship with its customer. In straight bank-to-bank dealings for their own position, for example, the customer relationship plays no role. Before quoting, the bank trader must analyze many factors in the few seconds in which he is obliged to make up his mind. Some of them are described in the following paragraphs.

Present bank position. In this area the trader will have to review his overall position in the currency concerned and the effect of the pending trade on it. He may expect to move out of the changed position immediately or during the course of the day. Both the exposure aspect and the cost of spot holdings by country will influence his decision.

Direction of the market. The preceding trades of the day will have given an indication of the temporary direction of the market for each currency, particularly the in-band movement. The trader will react to concurrent brokers' and competitors' quotations and market comments; his determination of the present direction of the currency will also be based on trading of the past several days. His personal feeling as to rate direction will influence his rates significantly.

Time of day. Chronological factors, even within the trading day, affect rate quotations. Early trades, as the market in one country is opening, will be approached with caution, because the general movement and demand of the day's trading cannot yet be seen. Midday transactions can be more easily undone than those at the end of the day, for a net position taken near the end of the day may have to remain overnight.

Exogenous factors. Important to change in rates throughout a trading day are the exogenous, or external, factors—those not inherent in the foreign exchange fields. They can arise in political, financial, or economic spheres; their dissemination by Telex, news ticker, or radio during the day changes traders' forecasts, strategy, and analysis and thus their rates. Particularly critical, of course, are any changes in interest rate structures and bank reserve or lending regulations. Trade figures are eagerly awaited and often cause a sharp reaction in the relevant currency if they are other than those anticipated.

Since banks have different exposure positions and policies, different determinations of the movement of the market, and asymmetric reactions to exogenous events, they too go into the elusive process of rate setting. That complex, and often chaotic, function cannot be easily formulated, but the points discussed in the preceding pages show the necessity for dealing with several competing banks to develop the most profitable conversion rates.

The degree of involvement of individual banks in the foreign exchange markets adds to the distinction between the banks. The banks can be knowledgeable, competitive, and flexible only if they are active dealers in the markets for many customers and for their own account; their experience from being actively involved is actually the greatest advantage to the customer.

In the United States and in some other countries as well it is not normally necessary for the commercial customer to provide local funds for exchange transactions two days before receiving the counterpart in foreign currency. As noted earlier, many banks are willing to waive the two-day period on spot trades for good customers and debit a domestic account only on the actual day of receipt of the counterpart funds. That practice, designated as value compensation, reduces the cost of foreign exchange dealings.

Forward Dealings

Forward exchange transactions constitute part of the same markets as spot transactions and are made through the same channels. Forward rates, as shown in Chapter 7, reflect future supply of and demand for currencies, as well as market opinion as to the future course of the currencies and interest rate differentials between local money markets. Again there is a rate differential that can vary between banks for much the same reasons as outlined earlier: timing, position, size of transaction, and relationship with customer.

In forward transactions, the company's counterpart is not put up until the actual date of transfer of funds, provided the company's credit standing is acceptable. Most banks have internal limits on the total of forward exchange commitments they will book with any one company or any one correspondent bank. The bank trader must be constantly aware of how much leeway remains under those limits.

Forward rates reflect a net discount from or premium over the daily spot rate (except in the rare cases of being at par with spot), and that difference is often cited in terms of an annual interest rate. Forward quotes are made for regular periods at future dates, and they are given as so many points ($\frac{1}{10,000}$) above or below the spot price. For example, an interbank quote for dollar-sterling forward might be made as shown in Table 5. The rates given in the table reflect the narrow interbank trading band rather than the actual rates to customers; those will be

Table 5. Typical forward exchange quotations and annual percent equivalent.

Spot (middle rate)	Forward rates (buy and sell) for the following periods, in months				
Dollars per pound	1	2	3	6	12
$2.5845	2.5880–90	2.5915–25	2.5955–65	2.5975–85	2.5960–75
Difference, points	35–45	70–80	110–120	130–140	115–130
Per annum premium,* percent	1.86	1.74	1.77	1.04	0.48

* Based on middle forward rate.

at a larger margin from the interbank quote. For example, a bank may offer to purchase pounds six months forward from a customer at $2.6010, or 165 points off the current spot rate. A transaction of £100,000 for a six-months delivery date would thus involve a dollar counterpart of $260,100 to be received at that date. The amount of pounds and dollars to be received is precisely fixed and forms a legal contract protecting both partners.

The seller of pounds forward can ascertain the percent annual cost, or gain, on his forward transaction by the following formula:

$$\text{Percent difference from spot rate} = \frac{\text{difference in forward rate}}{\text{spot rate}} \times \frac{12}{\text{months to delivery date}}$$

$$= \frac{0.0165}{2.5845} \times \frac{12}{6}$$
$$= 0.638 \times 2$$
$$= 1.276\% \text{ per annum premium}$$

The position of the spot rate is clearly important. When the spot rate of a currency is under pressure, the forward rates often widen and put the ultimate price of the currency far below the lower intervention limit. The interaction of the spot and forward markets is appreciable, for the markets are neither independent nor static. (The recent discussions about the dynamic role of the forward markets have pointed out the obvious fact that marked changes in forward rates cause movement in currencies between countries and ultimate responses of the spot rate, interest rates, and government policy.)

As distinct from bank participants, corporate participants in the forward market may not wish or be able to pinpoint their forward dealings to exactly 1, 3, 6, or 12 months. For that reason, a system of optional-date forward contracts has arisen. Contracts can be made with a maximum and minimum time limit, within which the company can take down the counterpart funds purchased. For example, a six-month forward pound purchase may include an option to take down the funds any time after the beginning of the sixth month. An alternative is to make the option operative on any of certain fixed dates centering around the period of probable need of the currency.

Rates on optional contracts vary from those on standard forward contracts. The rule is that the bank, since it has uncertainty as to when the customer's option will be exercised, assumes the least favorable circumstance and quotes its rate accordingly. In the example given earlier, the option to buy pounds between the start and end of the six-month period would be quoted to include the full six-month discount. A purchase of dollars against pounds at three months with an option of taking the dollars before that period would cost the U.K. participant the full three months' premium.

Option contracts can take many forms, even one that allows exercise from day one to some fixed date in the future. In that case, the practice would be to charge the spot rate on a currency with forwards at a discount, because the bank cannot intelligently quote on a hypothetical discount for an unknown date. Quotes for purchase of a currency at a premium starting from day one would be based on the full premium for the final option date.

Once it is committed to a forward exchange contract, a company can, under certain circumstances, end its commitment prematurely, sometimes at a profit. Suppose, for example, that a foreign investor in Great Britain had covered his potential exposure vis-à-vis the devaluation of the pound by entering into a one-year forward sale of pounds at a discount of 2 percent per annum. Assuming that was done in August 1967 when the spot rate was at $2.78, the company would have an obligation to provide pounds at approximately $2.7244. During the period of the contract the pound would have been devalued in November, with a new parity of $2.40. In the period November 1967 to August 1968, the foreign investor would have an unrealized pretax profit of approximately $0.32 per pound, because the fulfilment of his obligation in pounds would ultimately cost considerably less than the contractual amount. Such a contract can be regarded as a salable asset, and its sale can be negotiated with a bank at a price profitable to both.*

---

* The gain on such a sale has tax consequences, and it may be treated as ordinary income in the country of origin. The problem is described in detail, with suggested tax-ameliorating techniques, in Marianne Burge, "Devaluation and Its Tax Consequences," *Price Waterhouse Review*, New York, October 1968.

In summary, the foreign exchange markets should not be viewed as unduly complicated or restrictive. They form one of the elements of the international framework in which the multinational corporation has its operations. Although exchange transactions add complexity, they also offer opportunities for profit and for rational international money management. To optimize a company's foreign exchange dealings is thus challenging and even intellectually stimulating; it adds to the depth and breadth of the finance function. Close ties with house banks, through which exchange dealings must be consummated, can lead to additional and mutually profitable cooperation in the international finance area. Among other things, knowledge of a company's foreign exchange position, needs, and problems will help a bank offer hand-tailored exchange and money management advice. That area is discussed in detail in the next four chapters.

PART FOUR

International
Money Management

9

Initial Stages of
International Money Management

THE next four chapters are concerned with delineating a specific area of international financial operations that encompasses foreign exchange management and the rationalization of the movement, collection, short-term investment, and borrowing of funds within and by the international company.

Definition of International Money Management

An intrinsic part of good management is optimization of the assets at company disposal. For the international company, that is both more difficult and more critical because the assets may be denominated in several currencies and physically dispersed. Company controls over liquid assets break down into two areas; the first is the rationalization of technical foreign exchange transfers, intercompany payments, collection of receipts from third parties, and netting of such payments where possible. Programs and systems that deal with such collections and disbursements of funds are commonly called international cash management. The second area, which is closely related to the technical management of cash movements, consists of short-term financing programs, investment schemes, and control over foreign exchange exposure, all of which is often designated as financial management.

The two areas overlap; a change in the cash management of a corporation, such as the acceleration of export receivables, has a direct effect on financial management. We have chosen to include both areas in the term *international money management*, which reflects both technical and discretionary aspects of the control over and the utilization of liquid assets of the international corporation.

International money management (IMM) is effective within the legal, banking, and regulatory constraints of individual countries. Much of the purpose of this book is to describe the foreign exchange and international monetary framework within which IMM systems operate, as well as the IMM systems themselves. Chapter 9 shows the beginnings of international money management in the rationalization of the international transfer of funds. It illustrates ways of accelerating payments between affiliated companies and reducing the time in which funds are unavailable because they are in transit in banking or postal systems. It gives the steps that an international financial manager would take in setting up IMM systems for the optimum movement of funds, and it justifies a central control point for such systems. Chapter 10 moves into a further area of IMM: aspects of which currency to use in export invoicing and the collection of export receivables. Chapter 11 develops a number of more sophisticated financial management systems, such as multicountry netting and pooling accounts, that can be studied after cash movement per se has been rationalized. Chapter 12 gives further considerations of money management, particularly the utilization of funds after automatic systems have been established, and comments about the relationship of foreign exchange trading to IMM.

The four chapters, taken together, attempt to show the general outlines of international money management, which, of course, has a unique application to each individual company.

The International Transfer of Funds

A variety of instruments exist for the international transfer of funds. Lodged in and flowing between banks, they can be simple payment in-

Exhibit 2.   Request for mail transfer.

MORGAN GUARANTY TRUST COMPANY
OF NEW YORK
33, LOMBARD STREET, LONDON, E.C.3

London

REQUEST FOR MAIL TRANSFER

Name of Payee...

Address...

Town..

Payment to be made
under advice
on application
by credit of account

in (Sterling
(or
(Currency

(Delete lines not applicable)

Amount ....

By whose order..

MORGAN GUARANTY TRUST COMPANY
OF NEW YORK
33, LOMBARD STREET, LONDON, E.C.3

Please advise the above credit by mail, it being understood that you are not to be held liable for the consequences of any delay, mistake, omission, misinterpretation or irregularity which may arise from conditions beyond your control.

Charge my/our account in payment   Cash/Cheque herewith.

N.B.—This form must be signed by the applicant, or in case the applicant is a firm or company, by a person duly authorised to sign on their behalf.

Signature...

Address...

....

Date..

Form No. 17A

structions in written form or they can evolve from documentary sales incorporating some form of credit.

The standard method of transferring funds internationally is by mail payment order. In it, the remitter of funds asks its bank to make a transfer in its own or another currency to the recipient. A standard form giving all pertinent details of the transfer, such as that shown in Exhibit 2, is used. The remitter's local currency account will be debited on the day the remitter presents the payment order to its bank (in some countries with one-day back value). If the transfer is made in the remitter's own currency, the debit will be for the amount on the order, except that in certain cases a payment commission will be added. If the transfer is made in a foreign currency, the local bank will make the conversion at the mail transfer rate, which reflects in part the time involved before the bank's nostro account (its own working current account) abroad is charged.

Mail transfer is a lengthy process despite the routine use of airmail. In our example the remitter's local bank may not maintain foreign currency accounts abroad; they are chiefly held by the head offices of the larger indigenous banks. It must then send the payment instructions through its main office, central savings bank organization, or domestic bank correspondent, which passes them on abroad. If the foreign bank named in the payment order is not a direct correspondent of the remitting bank, it must pass on the payment order to a fourth or final bank in the chain. Allowing for mailing time and processing at each bank, a mail transfer that involves several banks in two countries can take eight to ten business days or more.

Cable transfers reduce the remittance time appreciably. By instructing its local bank to pass on payment instructions by cable, the remitter insures that the recipient of funds is paid as soon as the foreign bank of account receives cable orders from its correspondent. That is the more desirable when the payee is an affiliate of the remitting company, because the funds are lost to the group during the transit time. Furthermore, cabling is the safest way to transfer funds. Cable orders, which by necessity have no signatures, are usually transmitted via a system of tested codes set up between banks to assure validity. Since only the larger international banks have test codes, the chance of mistake or fraud is negligible.

A cable transfer results in a debit to the paying bank's foreign account more quickly than mail transfer does, and so it can command a higher cost or less favorable rate of exchange when a conversion is involved. In addition, a nominal charge is made, usually $5 to $8 per cable, depending upon the length of the text.

Other international payment instruments include bank drafts, checks, and trade bills. A subsidiary may wish to bypass the normal bank mail transfer routing and instead purchase a bank draft from its house bank to send directly to the payee (Exhibit 3). A bank draft is payable to order

Exhibit 3. U.S. dollar bank draft used for international payments.

upon presentation and is drawn by a bank upon itself or another branch of the same bank. A check for export payment drawn on an account in a bank in the country receiving funds is also used, and it lends itself to interception and acceleration in the export lockbox scheme described in Chapter 10.

Certain international payment instruments, such as sight and time drafts, acceptances, and letters of credit, are connected with types of documentary credit. A sight draft is an international financial instrument in which the importer's (drawee's) obligation to pay a certain amount at sight to the drawer is formally confirmed in writing. Time drafts add an element of credit in that the payment is designated as due at a certain future date and the obligation is accepted by the drawee. During that period, there is a risk that the obligor will not pay at maturity. Acceptances—time drafts drawn on a foreign buyer whose obligation is accepted by its bank—and even letters of credit are only extensions of payment orders that take the credit risk of dealing with distant customers into account.* The instruments are well known and are generally processed by international banks in a structured manner that has proved over time to be efficient. Less improvement is to be expected when physical docu-

---

* See *Export and Import Procedures* (New York: Morgan Guaranty Trust Company, 1965) for a full description of export instruments.

ments with a legal status and strict handling requirements are involved, as opposed to cash movement without documents; the latter should be the point of departure for money management analysis.

The underlying principle of all international payment is that currencies are ultimately transferred on the books of banks in the country whose currency is involved. Dollars sent from Tokyo to Frankfurt will, at some point, become entries in the books of a U.S. bank in which the working accounts in dollars of international banks are held. That means that acceleration or interception of international dollar payments by necessity lies in the U.S. banking system. Even Euro-dollar transactions between two London-based banks, themselves British and sterling-oriented, are consummated via cable transfers across the Atlantic. (Some movement is underway to have a European dollar clearing for such transactions. The Euro-dollar market would be greatly facilitated by the innovation, particularly if it were located in London, but at the time of writing only tentative discussions, not including the predominant American banks, are being held.) Deutsche mark transactions are made over the books of German banks, pounds over those of British banks, and so on with other currencies.

Intercompany Transfers

Intercompany transfers arise from sales between affiliates and from such financial transactions as royalties and dividends. Since the time lost in transferring funds from one affiliate to another represents a loss of availability of funds to the group, it is important to rationalize intercompany transactions and reduce the transit time to a minimum.

It is apparent that intercompany transfers of sizable amounts should automatically be made by cable. Some concerns leave the decision to local subsidiaries; others use cable transfers only for six-figure amounts. Yet a simple comparison of cable cost and interest saved by reduction of overdrafts or gained by short-term investment of accelerated payments shows that even relatively small payments can profitably be made by cable. The breakeven amount, that is, the transferred amount above which it is more economical to incur a cable cost than use mail transfer, under various assumptions of interest rate, payment delay, and cable cost, is shown in Table 6.

Intercompany transfers above the breakeven amount (to be set by the international financial manager) should be sent by cable. If overseas subsidiaries are concerned about their income statements and so are reluctant to absorb recurring cable costs, they should be instructed to make payments net of the cable charge. From a global point of view, the company has greater availability of funds, and by using value compensation methods, the paying company gains as well.

The same principle should be applied to receipts from third parties. A foreign customer has no reason to accelerate payments abroad after its own account is debited. In most cases, the foreign bank has no incentive to expedite the transfer of funds to a foreign entity. Quite to the contrary: European banks traditionally are more dependent on float and commissions than on compensating balances, and that accounts for some of the slowness of mail transfers. The cost savings by earlier availability of funds that are given in Table 6 will accrue to the recipient even if it absorbs the cable charges of its customers. A minimum should be set and strict instructions should be given to customers to make all payments above that minimum by cable net of the cable cost. Acceleration of export proceeds in small amounts, that is, their most rapid and efficient collection, requires different techniques and is described in Chapter 10.

Table 6. Breakeven amounts for cable transfers under various assumptions of cable costs, interest rates, and time saving.

Saving, Calendar Days	Breakeven Amounts at Following Interest Rates		
	6%	8%	10%
Cable cost $5 or equivalent			
1	$30,000	$22,500	$18,100
2	15,000	11,250	9,050
3	10,000	7,500	6,030
4	7,500	5,625	4,525
5	6,000	4,500	3,620
7	4,280	3,210	2,585
10	3,000	2,250	1,810
14	2,140	1,610	1,290
Cable cost $8 or equivalent			
1	$48,040	$36,030	$28,880
2	24,020	18,015	14,440
3	16,020	12,010	9,630
4	12,000	9,010	7,220
5	9,600	7,210	5,780
7	6,860	5,150	4,125
10	4,800	3,600	2,880
14	3,430	2,570	2,060

To reduce further the transit time of intercompany transfers when a foreign exchange conversion is necessary, value compensation should be obtained. Under standard foreign exchange procedures, the remitter's account is often debited two days before the foreign currency counterpart is actually provided. Assuming two-day notice is given, the remitting bank should be amenable to debiting the local currency account on the actual day of transfer and thus saving two interest days for the remitter. The bank gives up its normal two-day float, but it maintains its spread on the conversion.

American bank branches that make payments between two subsidiaries, both of which are customers, offer value-compensated cable transfers as a matter of routine. They can look at their relationship with a multinational company globally and make concessions at one paying branch in light of activity or relationships at another. They may even waive cable charges for intercompany, intrabank payments. European banks, however, have not been in a comparable position, and they are often more reluctant to offer such cash management techniques to a single company in their country when they result in loss of income without an offsetting better relationship.

The IMM Role of the Financial Manager

A corporate financial manager will try to analyze all intercompany payments to make sure they are handled as effectively and quickly as possible. He will go through the calculations described earlier in this chapter to determine whether cable or airmail transfers are to be used. He will have local subsidiaries arrange value compensation with their local banks, and he will institute a series of cash balance and forecast reports to control the overall cash position as well as movements among members of the group. Acceleration of transfers not only increases availability of funds to the company but also enhances the credit control process. Accounts receivable are reduced and payments are more readily identified.

The rational transfer of funds is the initial step in international money management. Companies that grow to a certain size or are concerned about traditional methods when the Office of Foreign Direct Investment program, exchange controls, high borrowing rates, or credit limitations are affecting their liquidity position and financial arrangements abroad, typically begin their approach to IMM in the foreign transfer and payment acceleration area. Since the savings involved are a direct percentage of the aggregate flows, that first step can by itself be rewarding when the amounts are substantial.

Exhibit 4. Sample IMM questionnaire used to secure the data necessary for the development of initial and technical systems for the acceleration of transfers, collections, and other cash movement.

1. *Entity.* Name and location of entity; whether it is of the manufacturing, marketing, or financial type; and percent of ownership.
2. *Export sales volume.* Annual volume (projected if significantly different from actual) broken down by countries.
3. *Distribution by country.*
   a. Number and location of distributors and whether or not a distributor is controlled by the company.
   b. Average amount of remittances. (Example: 30 percent of sales are to a large number of distributors with average amount under $5,000 or local currency equivalent, and 70 percent are to three customers with average amount over $100,000.)
4. *Invoicing procedures.* Breakdown of volume by:
   a. Country and currency of billings.
   b. Categories—terms of sales and discount offered when applicable, open account, documentary collection, and so on.
5. *Collection.* Methods used for open-account export customers:
   a. Present payment instructions—printed on invoices, standing instructions, or other.
   b. Typical collection delays experienced in transfers from each country, that is, time that elapses between instructions of customer and receipt of funds by company.
   c. Breakdown of collection method by percent: bank mail transfer orders, bank cable transfer orders, bank drafts purchased by customer and mailed to company, customers' checks mailed to company, giro transfer, and other.
6. *Intercompany payments.*
   a. Currency of billing and terms of payment.
   b. Method of payments (mail, cable, and so on) and frequency of payments.
   c. Whether payments are netted or offset against other subsidiary payment.
   d. Breakdown of total annual intercompany trade by selling subsidiaries, such as subsidiary *A* sells $5 million to *B*, $10 million to *C*, and $7 million to *E*, including sales from parent company to subsidiaries and sales to and from trading companies.
   e. Any relevant special conditions, common settlement date, and so on.
7. *Disbursements.*
   a. Annual payments in local currency and foreign currencies.
   b. Breakdown of disbursements by means of payments: percentages for both domestic payment and imports by checks, drafts, bank transfers, cable, and other means.
   c. Whether accounts are maintained in currencies other than the currency of the subsidiary.

International money management requires a central decision point for analysis and instructions to group members. Centralization may be lodged in the corporate treasurer, the international treasurer or controller, or a new position created to carry out the function. The financial manager in charge of IMM, having a staff function, ideally represents an independent element that can best see the interactions, global position, and international problems of the group.

Such a money manager, when newly appointed, would first review the flow of funds within the group and from third parties. He might do so by devising a questionnaire that asks for data on the flow of funds; the bulk of the data required by such a questionnaire would be terms, currencies, methods of transfer, average amounts, and delays experienced. From the analysis of the answers would evolve not only systems for the accelerated receipts of large amounts via cables and value-compensated transfers but also programs for the interception of small-amount, large-volume export sale proceeds. Exhibit 4 is an example of the content of such a questionnaire. The data would be required of each manufacturing and/or billing entity.

Moving from the rationalization of cash movement, the money manager would analyze disbursements within the group, because funds paid out to affiliates but delayed in the banking pipeline are equally unavailable for corporate purposes. For example, sales representatives or offices abroad may operate on imprest drawing accounts, which have to be replenished periodically. Delay in providing funds to such accounts may interfere with the company's representative or sales functions. Techniques for the efficient payment of funds to affiliated companies, similar to those for collections, should be inaugurated.

The Beginning of Foreign Exchange Policy Formulation

Concurrently with the rationalization of cash movement will come analysis of and control over group exchange exposure. In fact, the accelerated movement of cash across international lines will itself affect the foreign exchange position of individual group members.

The management of foreign exchange is a substantial portion of the treasury function, and it can best be seen from a central point. Chapters 11 to 14 show the very real effect that foreign exchange developments can have on short-term borrowing or investment programs, as well as on consolidated balance sheet items. The following paragraphs describe the type of internal reporting and data gathering that the money manager should institute so his corporation can have a rational system for controlling its foreign exchange position and net exposure.

The corporate foreign exchange position is typically made up of the individual net position of each consolidated subsidiary and the parent company; unconsolidated subsidiaries have a different and less immediate effect on the parent balance sheet. The reporting system should give enough data to analyze the exchange position on a regular and recurring basis; monthly reports are perhaps the most appropriate. The monthly balance sheets and income statements from affiliates form a nucleus; to them can be added a more detailed description of working capital items as well as cash forecasts for an ensuing period. Each subsidiary should supply a detailed breakdown of its balance sheet to show all items denominated in its own currency and all assets carried or liabilities payable in foreign currency, specifying individually each currency. The reports from subsidiaries are integrated with similar reports of the parent company to formulate the net exchange exposure of the group.

Economic Exposure

Exposure determination in the accounting sense points out those items which will have a negative effect on consolidation if the currency in which they are denominated should change in value. (This is explained in detail in Chapter 14.) Whichever translation convention is used, the resultant consolidation merely indicates the reported position of a group at a given point in time, based on historical events. However, this does not necessarily show the operating impact of a parity change on any single member of the group or the effect on future flows of income in the group. Both of these are included in the term "economic exposure," which attempts to give management an additional means of analyzing effects of foreign exchange movements on operations, profits, and net worth. It can be important to identify economic exposure from the very beginning of foreign exchange policy determination.

The more immediate effects of economic exposure arise in the actual financial operations of a foreign subsidiary. For the local subsidiary, changes in any of its assets or liability items can result in a negative effect, which is not recorded in the consolidated exposure determination. Cash is a typical example; it is among those current assets always translated at current rates and affected by devaluation. The group position may show, due to hedging or offsetting, a neutral position in a particular currency. A subsidiary's ultimate liquidity position, however, can be significantly different depending upon the expected disposition of its cash balances when its own currency devalues. If liquid balances have been built up for imports or dividend payments, a local devaluation will have an impact on the subsidiary not always identified by the parent. Even if the group is covered against the currency in question, the liquidity of the subsidiary is impaired; the parent may not be able to augment it. A similar effect on liquidity can arise from parity changes involving accounts payable, accounts receivable, or short-term debt of the local subsidiary.

The realization of inventory presents a further example. Inventory to be sold in only one market may be considered an exposed asset if its price cannot be raised after a local devaluation. It is, however, important to identify the price elasticity of inventory and its ultimate destination (hard currency markets, for example) to determine which portion is exposed and which is not. This should be included in the identification of economic exposure; knowing the elasticity element can allow the group to raise prices before the event.

The importance of economic exposure is in identifying balance sheet items which are considered to be offset in terms of the consolidated balance sheet, but which could affect the operations of any subsidiary after a parity change. In this area, it can be as important to identify the "economic exposure" of *unconsolidated* subsidiaries as it is to determine that of consolidated ones.

Corporate Policy Regarding Exchange Exposure

After the initial data gathering and consolidation, the corporate policy vis-à-vis its foreign exchange position should be established, usually by a senior management committee with representatives of treasury, controller, and sales divisions. Foreign exchange policy must be consolidated with the general financial policy of the company. For example, short-term borrowing by a subsidiary for working capital purposes and anticipated future borrowing will affect both corporate liquidity and exchange exposure. Short-term investments in several currencies have both exchange and liquidity, as well as risk, aspects. At the senior management level, the company will determine whether its foreign exchange policy should be basically cautious or aggressive. If it is to be cautious, management essentially wishes to remain covered against foreseeable exchange risk and devote managerial attention to more basic areas such as product development and marketing. Under a cautious policy the attitude is that the firm's operations should basically be protected against risk of loss in foreign exchange, that is, insulated from the international environment in that regard.

It is possible to formulate a more aggressive policy and accept certain foreign exchange risks in either asset or liability categories as a potentially profitable method of doing business. Then exchange risk is deliberately assumed and yields on foreign currency deposits or profits from sales in foreign currencies are considered to outweigh the cost of a parity or spot rate change, depending on the probability of such a change. Now management will compare the cost of hedging its exposed assets or liabilities, when weighted by the probability factor that exchange markets will move against it, with the potential profit to be made by remaining uncovered. For example, the short forward rates for the pound sterling may result in a hedging cost of 2 percent per annum for periods up to a year when the pound is under moderate pressure. A cautious international company with net current exposure in pounds would usually cover by selling pounds forward (or by other means); a more aggressive group might well remain uncovered after weighing the cost of hedging against the probable change of parity of the pound in the period.

Under a system of constant and continuous review, the aggressive corporation should have the ability to hedge appropriately when the hedging cost or the probability of parity movements changes significantly. This review is even more critical under chaotic market conditions and when there is the possibility of frequent parity changes.

Inherent in the analytical control process is use of outside sources of information on factors that will affect the company's foreign exchange exposure. Tied in with short- and long-term policy judgments will be economic and political developments in the various countries that affect the possibility of parity change. Hedging costs and their probable movements will be obtained from sources close to the exchange markets, particularly from commercial banks; those elements of input complement the raw statistical data from subsidiaries. In certain cases a house bank will be willing to help the corporation determine exactly what its net exposure is and also the costs and various means of covering it. Such a service should be sought by companies that are becoming more involved in international operations and manufacturing abroad.

The justification for a central control point for foreign exchange analysis and policy is obvious and is analogous to that for rationalization of the transfer of funds: each subsidiary can see only a part of the aggregate exchange exposure of the group, and it may not have access to or awareness of a full range of hedging possibilities. The setting of a cautious versus aggressive policy can be done only by a high-level and central entity; what is more important, a central control point can best determine if different exposures of subsidiaries offset each other and thus reduce exposure, and hedging costs, on a global basis.

Once he has control over cash movement, under a framework of strict management of foreign exchange positions and purchases, the international financial manager can move into further areas of global money management. A parallel to rational transfers is acceleration of export receipts, described in the following chapter. Beyond that lie the more sophisticated areas of netting of intercompany payments, pooling, and short-term investment of international funds in several currencies.

10

Export Invoicing
and the Collection
of Export Receivables

AFTER intercompany transfers are rationalized, the next integral part of
international money management is the acceleration of the proceeds of
exports. Such proceeds are unavailable for corporate purposes while they
are delayed in the banking system abroad, and there are a number of ways
in which they can be brought back more rapidly. "Control over liquid
assets on an international scale" would relate here to accounts receivable
and the reduction of the amount of time receivables are outstanding by
reason of slow collection. This chapter also discusses the foreign exchange
problems connected with export invoicing and the implications of using
the exporter's or the importer's currency. Dollar invoicing is used as an

example of the position of U.S. exporters, but the implications of using the exporter's currency in invoicing from other countries are similar.

Dollar Invoicing and Its Implications

As part of the background for this section, some sixty major U.S. companies that primarily invoice in U.S. dollars were asked their reasons for doing so. Very few companies used currencies other than U.S. dollars when exporting from the United States, although two raw material producers, out of marketing considerations, did use a system of customer's option as to currency. The reasons for U.S. dollar invoicing were varied, but they fell in one or more of the following categories:

• Tradition
• Lack of knowledge of foreign exchange dealings
• Weakness of the importer's currency
• Unwillingness to bear hedging costs
• Fear of currency blockage by foreign governments

There are several advantages to dollar invoicing for a U.S. exporter. When the foreign exchange problem is eliminated, more attention can be given to marketing or financing. Dollars can be readily collected by the larger U.S. banks throughout the world, regardless of payor. Special IMM systems can be set up to accelerate the flow of export proceeds in dollars directly into the main working accounts of the exporter, as shown later in this chapter. There is no exchange exposure leading to a possible negative *translation effect,* or decrease in an asset denominated in foreign currency, on the firm's financial statements. Bookkeeping and accounting remain in a single common unit of account.

Marketing considerations, however, may point out the attraction of billing in currencies other than dollars. In a strong buyers' market, the importer may be able to extract concessions as to the currency used (its own or even a third currency under pressure). Jerome L. Stein, in his excellent study on *The Nature and Efficiency of the Foreign Exchange Market,* describes a period of international competition between British and German exporters to Imperial Russia. The German firms were willing to invoice in rubles, particularly because of the existence of a forward ruble-mark market, whereas the English exporters insisted on sterling payments. The result was the transfer of a substantial volume of trade from England to Germany; in the end, over one-third of Russia's imports in the last quarter of the nineteenth century were supplied by Germany.

The historical example cited has validity in the 1970s in light of the well-developed forward exchange markets presently existing. An importer in a country with a weak or soft currency can prove a more malleable prospect if it has the possibility of paying in local currency. The importer is then freed from the cost of hedging, and so the price in the equivalent of the exporter's currency can often be correspondingly raised. International competitors, as in the German-Russian example, may offer to receive payment in weaker currencies, and the exporter must respond in kind.

An important consideration for the exporter, of course, becomes the exchange exposure it formerly avoided. It must either have an offsetting liability in the foreign currency to counterbalance the receivable or be prepared to risk a financial impact—the translation effect—on its balance sheet. (The translation effect is discussed in detail in Chapter 14.) To bring foreign currency receivables to a neutral exposure position can involve the exporter in hedging costs it did not have before. Floating rates complicate the problem of delineating the foreign exchange risk of receivables in such currencies. All this implies an agreement between the export department and the financial staff that the costs and/or risks of moving into foreign currency invoicing are of net benefit to the company. The decision will no doubt be on a case-to-case basis, and primary considerations will be the relative market positions of buyer and seller, the strength of the foreign currency, and the cost of hedging, that is, insuring against the possibility of depreciation of an asset denominated in a foreign currency. Discussion of such matters may break down the traditional avoidance of billing in a currency other than the exporter's.

The other reasons for invoicing in the seller's currency can similarly be altered as a firm deepens its international involvement. Opportunity profits can be made by invoicing in appreciating currencies. Lack of knowledge of foreign exchange transactions can be reduced by frequent discussions with banks or by attendance at exchange and financial seminars, although nothing will substitute for actual dealings in the foreign exchange markets. Subsidiaries abroad will complement the educational process, particularly because they have assets and liabilities denominated in other currencies and see their foreign exchange positions in a different light. An excellent way to develop and clarify ideas on foreign exchange and IMM problems is to hold annual or semiannual conferences of local finance managers together with the parent financial staff.

It is not the relative vulnerability of a foreign currency to devaluation that is a deterrent factor; instead, it is the cost of avoiding forward risks in that currency, which will generally be inverse to the actual or believed strength of the currency. Analysis of the global exchange position of the group may point out areas in which liabilities in weak currencies offset exposed assets in the form of export receivables invoiced in such currencies.

Whether to bear the cost of hedging must be decided on both marketing and financial grounds. Hedging costs can be put on a per annum basis; marketing and production analysis will then show whether profit margins will allow the cost of hedging on a currency-by-currency basis. For example, the cost of taking out a forward exchange contract to protect export proceeds in a weak currency may approximate 1 percent per annum over a period of time. If the profit margin on export sales is large relative to that cost, the 1 percent additional cost may be readily accepted. Lowered unit costs or other economies of scale may also encourage increased production for export, even if incremental sales are invoiced in weak currencies; such effects increase the overall profitability of the concern. It is necessary to weigh each of the underlying production and financial considerations, rather than isolate the cost of the hedge alone, although the latter appears to be the practice of some companies.

Currency blockage is a recurring problem, not only in Latin American and other countries where funds have historically often been blocked, but also in a number of countries with new or unsteady governmments. This is a foreign exchange problem of a different nature, in that there are few means of protecting against it through banking or exchange market channels. One method is to obtain an all-risk guarantee from the Overseas Private Investment Corporation (OPIC), which is available to U.S. companies for certain priority foreign loans and investments that normally finance U.S. exports.

The credit and political risks attendant on remittances that result from U.S. export sales on terms of up to five years may be reduced substantially by obtaining either the guarantee of the Export-Import Bank of the United States (Eximbank) or the export credit insurance of the Foreign Credit Insurance Association (FCIA). Under FCIA policy, the U.S. exporter may obtain comprehensive coverage that relieves him of all credit and political risks, such as inconvertibility, expropriation, and confiscation, except for the usual 10 to 30 percent exporter's participation.

Under the medium-term guarantee program of Eximbank, the guarantee is issued to the bank that purchases the receivable without recourse to the exporter. On U.S. export sales that require terms in excess of five years with long lead times, Eximbank usually lends jointly with commercial banks to the buyers to finance 90 percent of the contract price. In addition, Eximbank may guarantee the repayment of the bank's portion of the loan.

FCIA also provides an insurance policy to cover U.S. export sales on terms of 180 days or less. In that case FCIA requires the exporter to insure a reasonable portion of its exports and provides an acceptable pre-negotiated spread of risks on the total volume of the export sales. Information on that and other programs offered by Eximbank and FCIA to U.S. exporters is available from major U.S. banks or directly from the Eximbank and the FCIA. Similar programs are offered in the major European industrial countries. With the exception of those aids, however, the risk of potential loss due to blockage of foreign assets has to be accepted—or avoided by eliminating certain countries—as part of the general risk of doing business abroad.

In some countries certain techniques, such as direct loans between unaffiliated foreign subsidiaries in the same country, permit the internal use of blocked currencies. One subsidiary may lend excess local currencies to a branch or subsidiary of another company and receive interest at a rate that is related to local market rates and takes into account the rate of inflation in the country. In some cases, part of the interest is paid in convertible currency outside the country. A bank guarantee of the loan can eliminate the credit risk.

Acceleration of Export Proceeds in Dollars

After the primary decision as to currency has been made, it is the money manager's concern to accelerate the proceeds of exports in order to increase the availability of funds to the company. His goal is to effect a reduction in time that export receivables are delayed in the banking or postal pipeline abroad, like the one sought in rationalizing intercompany transfers.

As was pointed out in Chapter 9, export proceeds can often be intercepted in the country whose currency is involved. For U.S. dollars, that involves directing dollar payments to a U.S. bank, typically in New York, rather than using the lengthy payment procedure that typifies most international transfers. When export receipts are in large numbers but in amounts that do not warrant cable transfers, the standard procedure is to use a *dollar lockbox* system. A typical cutoff point for mailing amounts might be payments below $10,000 (following the considerations of cable cost versus time saved discussed in the preceding chapter). Analogously to the U.S. domestic method, a lockbox system for U.S. dollar export proceeds incorporates a post-office box in a major U.S. money center. Since New York is dominant in international banking and the majority of foreign banks deal through New York correspondents for their U.S. business, the lockbox is typically processed by a New York bank.

The bank will have authority to open and empty a postal box held in the name of the exporter, which will instruct its customers to have dollar-denominated checks or drafts sent directly to the numbered postal box rather than to a bank for account of the exporter or to the exporter itself. The importer is indifferent to the means of payment in that its local currency account will debited at the same point in time whether a normal mail transfer is used or a dollar check is purchased. The check, drawn on a U.S. bank, will be airmailed to the New York postal box, whereupon the responsible bank will process and present it immediately to the Federal Reserve clearing system. The lag time is thus reduced to the time for mailing plus one day for clearance and credit to the exporter's U.S dollar account when a New York bank check is involved. Usually the standard time of receiving export mail payments is reduced by three to five days or more. For control purposes, a photocopy of each check can be sent on to the exporter, which otherwise does not receive a physical document. Written listings of amounts received will routinely be transmitted by the bank to the exporter as substantiation for aggregate daily credits.

Since the underlying principle is that U.S. dollars are transferred by banks in the United States, an identical procedure can be followed even if the exporter is not a U.S. company. For example, an international sales company located in Brussels may invoice in dollars for reason of market practice or the source of its products. It can also use a dollar lockbox in New York to accelerate dollar collections. Ideally, it will maintain one account in New York and another with the Belgian branch of the U.S. bank that processes the lockbox items. The U.S. head office will collate payments made and cable-advise its Belgian branch of the amounts received, and it will give details of each remittance to comply with Belgian exchange control regulations. Larger amounts can be received by cable and credited in much the same manner. Similarly, dollar amounts received in favor of a British exporter can be intercepted and credited to a retained dollar account in the United Kingdom by permission of the British Exchange Control.

Acceleration of Export Proceeds in Other Currencies

Interception of export proceeds in the local currency of the exporter is not limited to U.S. dollar payments. In most major European countries, IMM systems can be set up to allow interception of a currency in its home country, the purpose again being to avoid the lengthy pipeline of normal banking transfers. The principle remains to intercept the funds from abroad at a point physically and chronologically close to the account to which the funds are directed. Belgian franc payments, for example, can be requested from an importer or foreign dealer in the form of a Belgian franc check sent directly to the bank holding the exporter's model B documents (the formal documents that show pertinent details of the export and are necessary for the crediting of exports proceeds to a domestic account). The Belgian house bank will present the check directly to the clearing system after matching payments and documents and immediately credit the proceeds to the exporter's account after clearance. Both acceleration of receipts and compliance with exchange control are assimilated in such a system. Similar mechanisms can be inaugurated for British exporters invoicing in pounds sterling, Dutch exporters invoicing in guilders, and so forth.

Export proceeds that are in currencies other than the currency of the seller also can be accelerated, usually through an international bank and its correspondents. For example, a U.S. or European exporter may have marketing reasons to bill its Swedish customers in Swedish kroner. There are in Sweden no foreign bank branches that form part of an international group which can be used to rationalize payments. However, kroner can be collected within Sweden by one of the major commercial banks through the bank giro system.

The giro system is a domestic arrangement of money transfer found in many European countries. One type of giro is offered through the post-office system; it can be used by commercial banks and commercial firms as well as by individuals. In some countries, giro transfers, which are effected by a simple transfer form, have become the primary method of local payments where the use of bank checks is not widespread. Payments are made through the central network of post offices rather than through a bank. The payor sends a transfer notice to the giro office to transfer funds to the payee, whose account is credited under advice while that of the payor is debited. This type of bookkeeping transfer system is quite efficient, and amounts can be credited to other giro accounts within the country very rapidly. In some countries, there is an analogous system operated by the banks themselves.

By use of a bank giro arrangement for the Swedish transaction example given earlier, the kroner would be credited to an accumulation account in the exporter's name maintained by a bank in, say, Stockholm. The funds thus collected would be paid by cable in Swedish kroner, or converted to another currency upon direction of the exporter or his bank, when they reached a certain amount or according to a chronological system. That Swedish banks offer such a service reflects their increasing awareness of money management as well as their close ties to large international banking correspondents. The availability or applicability of giro systems for foreign currency receipts should be studied on a country-by-country basis, as amounts become substantial.

Retained Foreign Currency Accounts

The use of retained foreign currency or hold accounts complements the control over international cash flows. The specially authorized accounts allow exemption from normal exchange control practices in the major European countries. The object of foreign exchange control is to limit the effect of international economic transactions and fluctuations on the domestic economy, particularly by restricting the amount of outflow of domestic currency without prior approval. Another principal feature is that receipts of foreign currencies that arise from trade and capital transactions usually have to be converted into domestic funds within a limited period of time. In both cases, the intent is to protect the international reserve position of the country that institutes exchange control.

Countries that have an exchange control usually have a relatively high foreign trade ratio and are therefore dependent upon foreign trade for their standard of living. Their exchange control authorities will, then, necessarily be concerned that certain legitimate business reasons for holding foreign currencies are honored. For example, exchange control commonly recognizes that a trading or exporting company, which receives foreign currencies for its exports, may have foreign currency obligations against which such proceeds can be applied. In most European countries that have exchange controls, domestic exporting companies are permitted to hold foreign currency receipts in local accounts set up for that purpose. Upon presentation of the proper documents, foreign currency export proceeds can be credited to such accounts held at local banks, and in a few cases abroad, and held in suspense until they are needed for authorized or legitimate payments in that currency. There should be a reciprocal, although not necessarily identical, flow; funds usually may not be held in such accounts for an indefinite period.

There is a twofold advantage to the exporter in having foreign currency accounts. They avoid exchange conversion costs, which would normally be borne twice if proceeds were converted and reconverted, and they maintain a neutral exposure position in the currency for those transactions. In fact, such foreign currency holdings may constitute a short-term hedge against the exporter's local currency, although the exchange authorities will not view that as desirable. Conversion costs in transferring dividends in foreign currency to a parent company can also be avoided. In certain countries, currency accounts can earn interest at Euro-currency rates, which transforms them into a type of accumulation account.

If interest-bearing deposits are maintained continually, however, the exchange control authority may require that they be converted into local currency, because investment of foreign currencies is not their underlying justification. Of course, the same advantages of and rationale for foreign currency accounts exist for exporters in countries where there are no restrictions on international transfers or foreign exchange holdings.

A Note on Intracountry Collections

The principle of maximizing availability of funds to the company through accelerating sales receipts applies to purely local or domestic transactions. Delays in receiving funds that are due from various parts of a single country can also arise from postal and banking processing time. Although that area does not usually involve foreign exchange per se, it is typically the responsibility of the corporate money manager that intracountry movements of funds be handled as efficiently as possible. There are systems and techniques for the interception and concentration of sales receipts domestically, and they are comparable with those used for export transactions. Analysis and implementation of such techniques would complement other IMM efforts such as acceleration of export receipts and intercompany transfers. Use of domestic giro arrangements for intracountry movements of cash can also foster domestic accumulation and short-term investment programs.

Export collection forms the second leg in international money management, and it is essential to the institution of more refined systems. Although it is often neglected by even relatively large corporations, export collection is a field in which acceleration can bring a significant amount of available funds to the multinational company, lead to the optimum use of liquid assets, and thus increase potential profit.

11

Money Management and Control on an International Scale

ONCE the technical systems of international cash management discussed in Chapters 9 and 10 have been instituted, the international financial manager can apply himself to further IMM programs, including short-term borrowing and investment of funds. As has been pointed out, international money management emanates from a centralized control over the financial transactions of the multinational corporation; that control and its implications are discussed in the first section of this chapter. The section also describes three more sophisticated IMM programs—multilateral netting, pooling accounts, and accumulation-investment schemes—as examples of ways in which to rationalize the use of short-term funds or requirements on an international scale. They are but three of a number of techniques that have individual IMM application; others, including use of computer programs, are only briefly mentioned. IMM elements are further covered in Chapters 13 and 14, which deal with foreign exchange exposure and protection.

Centralized Control and Its Implications

The essence of international money management is centralized information and control. The problem of manipulating and rationalizing the liquid assets of the multinational corporation can best be solved by making an analysis of the underlying global position and problems of the group. Typically, that requires concise and frequent reporting from each group member, whether manufacturing, selling, or holding company, to a central coordination point.

It is the routine practice of the larger multinational companies to require several types of financial reports from foreign subsidiaries; they include balance sheets, income statements, and forecasts, often on a monthly basis. But for the rationalization of the use and movement of cash or its equivalent assets, for control over exchange exposure, and for short-term investment purposes, additional data are needed. For example, intercompany netting programs require definition of the exact intercompany position of each subsidiary in advance of a single clearing date. Service-oriented companies, such as airlines and shipping and insurance companies, may have cash-rich periods within a single month when agents submit payments or when premiums arrive; the funds are disbursed over a period of time. Forecasts of expected receipts and expenditures during a month would therefore allow the central coordinator to shift or invest surplus funds within the month, and that may be beyond the responsibility (or, indeed, capability) of the local manager.

Centralized reporting systems and resultant financial directives do result in a loss of autonomy for the local finance manager, which must be dealt with. The arguments for centralized control are strong ones:

1. Local executives can rarely know the liquidity position of the group.
2. Local executives cannot analyze the exchange exposure of the group in either its component parts or as consolidated entity.
3. The central financial office, no matter what shape it takes, draws on information from a wide number of financial institutions and so can formulate a better decision on the probable nature of financial events and a broader approach to protection against them.

Against those arguments can be weighed a lack of whole-hearted support for rationalizing systems if the local manager feels his sphere of influence is limited or his achievements are downgraded.

The answer to what is a discernible management problem—acceptance of new techniques directed from above—is to insure that the local finance manager will be judged by the new constraints imposed upon him and the management of assets entrusted to him. His input and raw data, as well as his judgments on local economic conditions, hedging, and marketing, continue to be determinant in analyzing the group's position. Furthermore, the fees, commissions, interest, or float saved by IMM systems accrue directly to the individual participating companies according to their own payment patterns. International money management can, however, distort the financial reporting from separate profit centers and thus require an internal allocation of profits and/or costs.

Most multinational corporations impose a direct and centralized control over their international affiliates for the reasons given in the preceding paragraphs. The location of centralized control is influenced by communications, time differences, and the depth of local financial institutions. Owing to the problem of day-to-day control of subsidiaries when the parent company is several thousand miles removed, recourse is often had to an international headquarters or several regional or continental offices. London has the largest number of international financial headquarters, owing to its historical role as a world financial center and the large number of financial and related institutions (brokerage, shipping, insurance) located there. As the center of the Euro-currency market, the only free and international money market and one that influences and connects the local financial markets of many countries, London has a paramount advantage. The lack of a language barrier also makes it popular with U.S. firms. Other centers for company international headquarters are Brussels, Geneva, Zurich, and, to a lesser extent, Paris.

Centralized control is less mandatory in international companies of such size and history that they have built up experienced managers in a number of countries. Decision making can then be based in a wider group, and operative constraints imposed on local managers can be broader and less direct. Even then, however, questions of foreign exchange exposure, borrowing policy, and the like are apt to be decided by the parent company. A corollary has been the closing of certain European headquarters of U.S. firms over which parent companies felt they had insufficient control or with which they had a lack of communication. The advent of jet travel and direct Telex links have reduced the need to have some executive functions abroad, but the time-lag problem continues.

The balance of this chapter describes three more advanced IMM systems in detail: bilateral and multilateral netting, pooling accounts, and accumulation-investment programs. All have a common basis in centralized reporting and control; each seeks to rationalize the use of cash resources or optimize the financial transactions within a group.

Bilateral Netting

A substantial number of international companies are multilayered; that is, they have manufacturing operations in both the parent country and a number of other countries that are often tied in with an additional structure of selling companies. It has been our experience that a sizable expense is incurred and time is unnecessarily consumed in the international transactions between the individual members of such groups. More specifically, payments may go back and forth between affiliates when actually only a net amount need be transferred. However, amounts must be relatively large in order to generate substantial savings by netting. Otherwise, the system changes and the cost of management time may not be offset by the savings on the transfers.

Bilateral netting arises when two affiliated companies have complementary or reciprocal sales. A number of industries, particularly in the automotive, electronics, and farm equipment fields, have a structure wherein subsidiary A buys components or materials from subsidiary B and assembles them for resale to subsidiary B and incorporation in a final product. Specialization by country and product also leads to bilateral sales, when one subsidiary buys from another for resale in its local market. Reciprocal invoicing ensues, and if no action is taken, there will be a two-way flow of funds and a double purchase of foreign exchange. Given the two-day value system and the transfer lags discussed in Chapter 9, the amount of time during which funds are unavailable to both companies is not negligible.

Most countries permit bilateral netting when it reflects actual trade transactions between a domestic company and a related foreign company. Fees, royalties, and dividends are not so readily included in bilateral or multilateral programs, because the possibility of income transfer or manipulation is more apparent. Bilateral netting does not affect the balance of payments of either country concerned, because the net recipient and payor of funds are in the same position as before.

Bilateral netting calls for the simple netting of amounts due and receivable between two affiliates at a fixed date. If subsidiary A owes affiliate B DM 500,000 and B owes A DM 1,000,000, only a net amount of DM 500,000 is sent from B to A at the due date. Any payment commission, the exchange spread, and other fees on DM 1,000,000 are saved in this example. In addition, value compensation can be used for the payment so that a same-day value transfer is accomplished. A qualification to this simple system is that intercompany transactions may not be expressed in a single currency. If they are not, it is necessary to convert them to a common currency denominator. That raises the question of how the ultimate exchange rate for the net transfer of deutsche marks is determined. If the prevailing IMF parity is used, it can have a quite different effect than if the daily spot rate between the deutsche mark and another currency is the basis. Depending upon whether the second currency's spot rate is above or below its parity, the net transfer may have a cost relatively less or more than its nominal balance sheet designation.

It may be necessary to have an entry of the amounts "paid" and "received" on the books of the bank in which the transaction is centered for compliance with foreign exchange regulations or for matching of recorded payments with documentation, but the integral element is that only a net transfer is made. Statistical reporting to the relevant central bank, when it is required, will remain; that may indicate on an accounting basis that gross amounts were paid, but it presents no problem.

Multilateral Netting

Multilateral netting follows the principle of bilateral netting in groups in which there is a more complex structure of internal sales. By comparing the intercompany positions of all members of the group, a scheme may be devised whereby payments flow only to net creditors within the group. The amount of actual transfers can often be reduced sharply and with a resultant saving of foreign exchange spreads, fees, and commissions. Again, value compensation techniques and cable transfers combined with netting can save a substantial amount of float. Aggregate savings can be of the order of $\frac{1}{4}$ to $\frac{1}{2}$ percent of the amount of foreign exchange not purchased. The mechanics of achieving the savings will next be described.

Collection of information. Central to any multilateral clearing scheme is detailed information on the intercompany accounts of each participating company at specified intervals, typically at month end. A centralized control point will record that information, make the necessary calculations arising from a matrix of payables and receivables, and instruct each payor and creditor company as to its net disposition at the date of clearing. Essential also is that there be a single fixed date for the payment of intercompany receivables. Since most multinational companies bill affiliates on a net 30-, 60-, or 90-day basis, it should be possible to reduce several payment dates per month to a single payment date at month end. That may lead to certain distortions in the cash flows of some affiliates from marginally extended credit terms, although not to increased working capital needs. The central control point will request complete data on intercompany payables due at month end by a certain date early in each month, perhaps the tenth. That will include the invoice amount and currency of each intercompany account payable and take the following form:

> To: Central clearing point
>
> From: Subsidiary *A*
>
> Re: Intercompany payable position for end
>   of _____

Due to	Currency and amount	U.S. $ equivalent
Subsidiary *B*	_____	_____
Subsidiary *C*	_____	_____
Subsidiary *D*	_____	_____

A cross-check can be obtained by asking participants to list month-end intercompany receivables as well. Subsidiaries may also be asked to list payments in or out that they are required to receive or make by the clearing date under exchange control regulations in their countries.

Determination of clearing payments. The central clearing point will prepare a summary matrix after tabulating replies; an example is Exhibit 5. The matrix compares all payables and receivables to and from the members of the group. The mathematical result of gross payments to be made and received is given on the bottom line, which shows the net intercompany position of each participant—the amount it will be asked to pay or receive.

In the example of Exhibit 5, *B* and *E* are net receiving companies and *A, C, D,* and *F* are net intercompany debtors. Assuming that each subsidiary participates in the multilateral scheme, the net payments within the group are reduced to $1,795,000 ($1,050,000 to *B* plus $745,000 to *E*) from $3,870,000, a saving of over half the foreign exchange conversion and transfer costs that would otherwise be incurred. The central clearing point then issues, on about the twentieth of the month, cable instructions to each participant to transfer or receive a net amount of currency, as determined by the matrix, to or from group members. The brief cables are followed by a detailed written description, also prepared by the central clearing entity, of the aggregate month-end receivable and payable amounts that the net clearing instructions represent. That allows proper registration and accounting for internal bookkeeping and documentation for foreign exchange control purposes. Invoice numbers to document the payments can be sent between companies at this point.

Instruction to local banks. As has been pointed out, bank mail transfers between related affiliates are highly inefficient. Intercompany netting payments should be made strictly by cable—not always standard practice for intercompany transfers. Delay of funds during mail transfer typically costs more in lost interest than cables cost. In addition, payments must also be made on a single prearranged date.

Local banks also should be given instructions to make month-end transfers by cable. From a global point of view, which entity bears the cable cost is immaterial, but for the sake of convenience, each remitter can absorb the cable charge. More importantly, payors should give instructions to their local banks with sufficient lead time to allow value compensation, that is, at least two days before the transfer date. That will insure same-day value of the net transfers when possible and minimize lost time.

Result. One day after the clearing date, at the latest, the net creditor companies will have received in good funds the amounts due them as suppliers to other affiliates. Exchange conversion costs and float will have been reduced to a minimum, and duplicate payments to and from affiliates will have been avoided.

The preceding account is a simplified description of the operational techniques needed to set up a multilateral clearing system. There are other factors that must be looked at closely, namely, relevant foreign exchange controls and the currency of invoices when it is different from

Exhibit 5. Typical summary matrix of one month's intercompany payments (in thousands of U.S. dollars).

Receiving Companies	Paying Companies						
	A	B	C	D	E	F	Receives
A	×	100		200	75	150	525
B	300	×	500		300	100	1,200
C	200		×	50	100	75	425
D	10	30	40	×	70	10	160
E	500		400	300	×	100	1,300
F	100	20	30	100	10	×	260
Pays	1,110	150	970	650	555	435	3,870
Receives	525	1,200	425	160	1,300	260	3,870
Net intercompany position (+) or (−)	−585	+1,050	−545	−490	+745	−175	

that of the clearing payment. The discounting of relevant trade receivables can also affect the system.

Other Aspects of Multilateral Netting

Exchange control. Multilateral netting requires express permission from the exchange control authorities in several European countries in which foreign transactions are officially regulated. The request for permission is usually accompanied by relevant data concerning amounts, currencies, and participants. Netting has no essential impact on the external position of the country involved, and if the underlying export or import transaction is acceptable or permissible, the exchange controls of such countries as the United Kingdom, Belgium, and Italy typically will not offer substantial objections. Latin American countries, on the other hand, rarely allow netting; in general, exchange controls are restrictive and must be seen as the most important difficulty in establishing any type of clearing.

Requests for exchange control approval of netting can be submitted with the help of house banks (foreign or U.S.) in the countries involved. Most European exchange control authorities look carefully at any netting proposal on a case-to-case basis; permission in France, for example, may take a number of months to obtain or indeed be refused. Even so, strict adherence to the formalities of documentation and centralization of documents and payments at a single bank, which prepares the gross and net entities, may permit participation. In any case, the usual export and import documents that substantiate foreign receipts and payments must be submitted regularly; the paperwork is not saved by netting, nor is it increased.

Flexibility. By requiring a tighter structure of reporting intercompany receivables, multilateral netting will increase management's flexibility in handling the liquidity position of the group. Group payment obligations are known in advance, and sometimes they can be delayed or accelerated, at the instigation of the central control entity, to provide temporary working capital (within the permitted range of the relevant exchange control regulations). That type of flexible control or manipulation becomes a related benefit of the netting system.

Borrowing. Also to be considered is local financing of trade receivables from affiliated companies. Actual discounting of trade drafts may preclude the participation of a discounting company to that extent, because the payment at maturity must go to the banks holding the discounted paper. Open account sales, even if finance is based on pledged receivables, do not create the same problem.

Costs. Few costs are involved in the establishment of the control system per se. Some additional personnel time will be required, but the costs are likely to be small relative to expected savings if the total volume of transfers is substantial. Increased communications may foster marginal extra costs.

Exchange exposure. When a number of currencies are used for internal invoicing, different exchange exposures may occur. For instance, a company that buys from the United Kingdom and is traditionally billed in pounds may be asked to pay dollars to a net recipient in the United States, which will significantly change its exchange exposure. A solution is to have all intercompany payments in a single currency, essentially that of the parent. In such cases, centralized control allows a better and more concise analysis of internal exchange exposures and possible anomalies.

Other types of clearing systems. The netting program presented in the preceding pages is a simple and rational one for the multinational company, but modifications of the system are found in practice. For example, further control can be exerted after the aggregate intercompany position is determined. Despite the book payables, the central control point may direct a subsidiary to pay only a certain part of its intercompany debt and thus manipulate the group's internal transactions for either liquidity or foreign exchange hedging or speculation purposes when that is permissible. A comparable effect may be obtained by having intercompany transactions pass through and be reinvoiced by an intermediary company, often in Switzerland. That gives a portion of the flow of funds within the group a nonresident status and thus greater capacity to be netted or manipulated without regulation.

A system used by some large U.S. corporations is an expanded form of bilateral netting. Each participant determines its intercompany position vis-à-vis each of the other group affiliates at a fixed date. A system of accounts in the names of the affiliates is maintained at a London bank. After the amounts owed are determined, a gross payment in each debtor's currency is made to the bank, which credits the proper amount to each creditor company in that company's currency. The pool of funds from debtor companies thus will typically be in currencies other than those owed to creditor companies, and the associated risk is accepted by the bank of account. The funds can be used for corporate purposes other than simple payments of net intercompany debts, such as short-term investments or short-term loans to cash-poor affiliates. The parent company also can be included for normal commercial transactions, but it does not use the clearing system for extraordinary purposes, such as capital transfers, because that might be construed as a constructive dividend under U.S. tax law.

Pooling Accounts

Pooling, or accumulation, accounts are an attempt to control and rationalize certain of the liquid assets of a group of related companies. A pool account is a way to visualize, or combine, the cash and equivalent assets of more than one company on an accounting or on an actual basis. In a pooling account, a central point will consolidate internally certain balance sheet items (cash and short-term investments, for example) of several subsidiaries in order to optimize their utilization and/or disbursement as if they belonged to a single company.

Ideally, pooling will allow cash-rich subsidiaries to finance cash-poor ones or permit a higher rate of return on short-term investment of larger amounts of surplus funds. Like netting programs, pooling requires a system of reporting cash positions and a centralized control point. Related advantages can be greater flexibility in shifting funds between subsidiaries and a better analysis of cash needs and surpluses.

One-country pool accounts. A simple type of pooling account consists of subsidiaries in one country that use a single domestic currency. Each subsidiary will typically be an independent entity with its own financial statements and bank relationships. Fundamental to single-country pools and other cash management programs is that, if possible, local bank relationships not be disturbed, lest credit and other needs fulfilled by local banks be endangered.

Detailed cash forecasts are the basis of pool accounts. They are sent to the central control point regularly and in advance of expected borrowing needs or cash surpluses. Conceivably, reports could be sent only when specific needs arise, but that would not permit optimum control.

The establishment of a local pool account can take different forms and is affected by local taxation and exchange control regulations. If, for example, four related subsidiaries in a country are to participate in a pooling account, the actual structure can take one of the following forms:

1. The pool account holder is one of the four affiliates; surplus funds flow to and borrowings flow from an established or new account in its name.

2. The pool account holder is a further related company (often an international finance subsidiary or other holding company). Funds transferred to and from actual account participants move over that separate account.

3. If, as is best, the pool account is centered at one bank, two further variations with bookkeeping accounts are possible:

(*a*) Four actual working accounts are established, and a hypothetical bookkeeping account combines their aggregate debit or credit balances. Principally, that allows the bank to offset credit balances against its own short-term loans to group members and may not result in less expensive credit on an interest rate basis.

(*b*) One actual account is held jointly by four companies, and surplus funds are placed in it or funds are borrowed from it. Four bookkeeping or hypothetical accounts show the net debit or credit position of the individual affiliate.

If the regulatory aspects permit, structure 2 is perhaps the optimal solution. Funds flow from an actual account of each subsidiary to an actual account of an independent control body, usually identical with the central control point. The control point will receive cash forecasts, direct payments, and identify the internal flows (and have to allocate interest costs or earnings among the participants). Drawbacks in the setup occur if the central account holder is a foreign company and exchange control regulations require extensive documentation for every transfer to or from the pool account.

To investigate the feasibility of a local pool account in a given country, local taxation, business, and banking regulations and foreign exchange control must be examined to see which intercompany transactions are permitted and which may have an adverse tax effect. If properly set up, a pool account system will not only maximize control over cash and certain equivalent holdings of a domestic group but also allow somewhat higher credit interest and lower debit interest when subsidiaries borrow from each other. Suppose, for example, that subsidiary *A* can expect to receive 7 percent per annum on its short-term time deposits in local currency and subsidiary *B* is borrowing at 9 percent per annum. An intercompany loan via the pool account from *A* to *B* may bear a rate of 8 percent per annum, which is favorable to both parties. Credit and debit interest calculations at the 8 percent rate can be carried out internally by the account manager, and interest can be paid via the account as well. Again, the problem of local autonomy versus central control may arise. In the transaction outlined, the local treasurer gives up some of his control over cash, and so also his protection against unexpected working capital needs. Therefore, he must have an immediate and unquestioned drawing right against the pool account.

Multicurrency pool accounts. The ultimate step in international money management is the multicurrency pool account, which combines part of the liquidity of several affiliates in different countries. The short-term investment of surplus cash held abroad is discussed in Chapter 12; in this section a description of the type of international money management toward which multinational companies should direct themselves is given.

A multicurrency pool account provides a means of controlling and investing the short-term surplus funds of international affiliated companies. As such, it is analogous to the domestic pool account, but it is complicated by the different currencies involved, local taxation, and local exchange controls. Furthermore, there do not always exist local money markets that offer short-term investment possibilities for tenors below one month. The following format for overcoming that problem is cast in very general terms; obviously, any individual company scheme must be developed uniquely.

As in a domestic pooling account, cash forecasts are requested from affiliates in a number of countries and directed to a central control point. The financial manager in charge of the pooling system makes an analysis of the periods in which certain currencies are available, what cash needs are forecast, and what exchange control constraints exist. Unlike the domestic cash manager, he will have to take into account the foreign exchange implications of the investment when it involves conversion into another currency. Investment alternatives will be in any or all of the following forms:

1. Investment in the same currency in the local money market.
2. Investment in the same currency in the Euro-currency market.
3. Conversion into and investment of Euro-dollars in a Euro-currency center and reconversion at the end of the period.
4. Conversion into and investment of another Euro-currency and reconversion at the end of the period.
5. Intercompany loans to cash-poor affiliates.

Alternatives 1 and 2 are simply formalizations of what is available to the local finance manager and do not entail exchange risk or conversion costs. Assuming, however, that there is no investment possibility in his own currency or that yields are negligible, the financial manager may wish to place funds in Euro-dollars or other Euro-currencies to obtain a better rate. He may establish a formal pool account in which short-term surplus funds of subsidiaries in a number of currencies are directed to a single international bank. The holders of the funds may remain the local subsidiaries, or, under certain company structures, the holder may become an affiliate.

Short-term funds will have to be held on a nonresident basis in most cases; for exchange control regulations often do not permit foreign short-term investment of local currencies or establishment of accounts abroad. An international bank that places the funds on deposit in the Euro-currency market may either passively accept instructions from the financial manager or actively recommend investment possibilities. It may even be willing to accept responsibility for investing independently or converting short-term funds of an international group following strict company guidelines, particularly regarding the foreign exchange risk.

The critical aspects of a short-term investment in a Euro-currency are the cost of conversion and the risk of rate movement. There will be a double exchange spread when a local currency is converted and reconverted and possibly also exchange commissions or brokerage. More importantly, the financial manager must decide whether to place his funds unhedged or via a swap transaction to insure the foreign exchange rate at which the funds will be reconverted into the original currency at the end of the period. As explained earlier, covering a short-term investment by means of a swap will typically eliminate the interest advantage gained by placing deposits in another currency. That is untrue only when speculative or central bank pressures have resulted in abnormal forward exchange markets and rates.

To place Euro-deposits unhedged involves the company in two risks, either of which may curtail the advantages of alternatives 3 and 4. There is the obvious risk of devaluation of the Euro-currency, revaluation of the original currency, or of either currency floating freely at a central bank's disposition. With the exception of floating rates, gross changes in currency rates would usually be predicted and anticipated beforehand. However, the movement of any currency within IMF bands can negate the interest rate advantage gained from investing in another currency.

Take the case of a German participating company that changes deutsche marks into dollars and places the dollars for three weeks in the Euro-dollar market through a London bank. If it does so when the mark stands at 3.295 per dollar (lower intervention point) and reconverts the Euro-dollars into marks at 3.265, it suffers a net loss in marks of 0.9 percent flat on the three-week deposit, or approximately 15 percent on a per annum basis. That cancels any conceivable interest rate yield on the Euro–deutsche mark deposit. Thus, the local treasurer will be more ready to convert a local currency into an unhedged Euro-currency for short-term investment when his currency is at or near its upper intervention point, or when one or the other of the two currencies is expected to change its parity or spot rate in his favor.

As has been shown, spot movements within the bands have a major impact on short-term investment in alternative currencies. Intraband movements can be forecast with some degree of accuracy by experienced traders, but the spot rate can also fluctuate widely because of unexpected or even irrational pressures. Broader bands complicate decision making, as do floating rates, which can unpredictably swing either up or down in a short period. The financial manager must weigh interest yields against the potential loss from either type of exchange movement to determine how far he is willing to speculate; here the use of computer formulation can greatly help his decision-making process.

Alternative 5—intercompany loans across country lines—is comparable with intercompany loans under domestic arrangements but is subject to other regulatory controls and tax measures. The loans can be an excellent use of international cash—since credit interest rates are higher than deposit rates, but the following must be considered before any commitment of funds between international affiliates:

Tax aspects. Withholding taxes on interest paid abroad. Taxes on loans from parents or affiliates that, in effect, replace capital increases.

Exposure aspects. Increased exchange exposure of borrower or lender. Chance of speculation via intercompany transactions.

Banking aspects. Alternative costs of finance. Alternative short-term investment possibilities. Maintenance of banking lines as backstop or as part of continuous relationship with house banks.

Regulatory aspects. Exchange control and balance of payments measures, particularly the OFDI program in the United States, which can make shifting of funds between affiliates difficult, disadvantageous, or impossible in certain cases.

Each intercompany lending scheme across national borders should be looked at on the basis of the preceding and other considerations. If certain factors weigh against intercompany loans, a counterpart solution may be found via the several branches of an international bank. The financial manager should investigate whether one branch of an international bank will offer a subsidiary a credit facility predicated upon deposits held at another office. In a less complex version, credit balances may act simply as collateral for loans to a financially weak subsidiary. In a true multioffice facility, however, the borrower might obtain an interest rate advantage in that the debit interest rate in one country can be determined in part by the negotiated credit interest rate on equivalent deposits abroad. For example, cash-rich subsidiary *A* may accept a lower interest rate on its deposit to insure a prime borrowing rate for affiliate *B* elsewhere. Basically, a bank with branches in both countries should be able to look at its net return on an aggregate basis and reconcile internally the varying interest rates in separate countries. Fiscal considerations have, of course, a limiting effect on such arrangements.

All three of the schemes discussed in this chapter—netting, domestic pooling, and multicurrency programs—aim at a more rational and optimum use of the liquid assets of the multinational company. The central coordinator may attempt to manipulate the cash and equivalent assets of his affiliated companies by using any or a combination of the cash management schemes. Formalization and rationalization of cash control and reporting systems will also allow the international corporation to respond more quickly to the continual changes in international finance and foreign exchange areas.

12

Further Considerations of International Money Management

SO far we have discussed the principles, practices, and techniques of foreign exchange. It is now desirable to consider some further ramifications of foreign exchange in regard to money management on an international scale.

Certain basic principles of money management must be expressed and then related to foreign exchange. The first principle is that the possible earnings or savings from money management must exceed the cost of the management. No matter how advantageous a particular system may be, it makes no sense to install it if the overall effect is to spend $20,000 to save $10,000. The key is volume. Potential savings as expressed in percents are always very small, so transactions must be substantial in both number and size to make proper money management worthwhile. The principal expense is in obtaining or developing an individual who is capable of handling the function. Alternatively, a number of banks offer services in the area. Application of foreign exchange techniques requires expert knowedge and judgment and is usually impossible on a routine basis.

Second, money has a time value; in fact, money is never idle and is always earning for someone somewhere. What the money manager aims at is to have funds available to earn interest as soon as possible as long as possible. To repeat a simple example, a check mailed to a debtor is not charged to the drawer's account until it is deposited by the payee and clears through the banking system. That may take several days, during which the drawer's bank earns interest on the funds, since the undrawn funds are included in the bank's position. Banks invest their excess funds on a day-to-day basis through various money market instruments and thus earn money on undrawn funds or adjust their reserve position. In a like manner funds used in foreign exchange earn interest daily for someone somewhere.

Availability of Funds

Principal considerations of the money manager. The decision having been made that there is enough money around to need managing and that the expense of managing it is warranted, the first consideration is to cut down or eliminate the time funds are in transit. The way in which that is done depends on whether the recipient or the payor controls the transaction. (See Chapters 9 and 10 for more detail.) What is most important is a thorough understanding of how the banking system of a particular country works and in what way the banks are compensated for their services. Deposit balances are not the rule in many countries abroad; instead, fees and commissions form the bulk of bank income. An examination of the system and, what is particularly important, its interaction with the system in the home country will indicate the best way to go about making collections. That, of course, will take time and expertise and a large amount of detailed information.

When both sides of the transaction are under common control, both the timing of the payments and the method of conversion can be arranged to maximize the advantages. As was pointed out earlier, it is essential to have a clear understanding of just how the banking systems in the countries involved work. That understanding must include a knowledge of facilities for short-term investment and borrowing and foreign exchange procedures.

Examples. A couple of examples will illustrate some of the considerations. In the United Kingdom, investment in hire purchase paper may yield 8 percent when finance company paper in the United States is yielding 7 percent. Leaving out the devaluation risk, it is advantageous to defer payments from the United Kingdom as long as possible or advance them from the United States. The matter can be further complicated by the degree of ownership, which could enrich one interest at the expense of another. Payment timing considerations can be factored down to a few days to maximize advantages. The comparison of cable charges with interest earnings given in Chapter 9 illustrates the point.

Another example is that, in certain European countries, facilities for investment of funds for periods of less than a month are available only at very low interest rates, whereas the rates for more than one month are normal. It therefore may be desirable to borrow for short periods of time on overdraft facilities to provide the funds for a portion of the payments due. Those facilities can then be paid down as receipts come in while the funds otherwise needed for payment earn interest at the monthly rate. This is a function of the amount of interest paid on borrowing as compared with the additional interest earned on funds invested.

Clearing systems. The exact method of payment used is also important, because moving funds into and out of the local banking system often incurs bank charges. These charges can sometimes be avoided by holding funds in interest-earning deposits at money market centers and using them to make payment. No currency risks need be involved, since deposits may often be made in the currency involved. The interest rate must be compared with that available locally to make sure the transaction is really worthwhile. The method of payment also may be arranged to avoid or minimize charges.

In Chapter 11 some aspects of clearing systems were considered. The systems can be bilateral or multilateral and in either event have the objective of reducing the amount of money that must be passed back and forth. The reduction results in two kinds of savings. First there is a differential between the buy and sell rates for a particular currency. When a conversion is made from francs to deutsche marks and then back to francs, there is a loss on the transaction in that fewer francs are received than were converted. The result is the same in going from francs to deutsche marks to lire and back to francs or in any other multicurrency transaction. Therefore, a clearing system that nets amounts due from against amounts due to results in the elimination or reduction of the amounts involved in conversions, with a consequent savings. The second source of saving is the elimination of any transit time, since, for the portion of funds offset by a clearing arrangement, receipt and payment are simultaneous on an agreed-upon date.

One difficulty with a clearing system is that payments are usually made at a particular moment in time. When there are interest rate differentials between countries, that may not be desirable on an overall basis. As discussed earlier, when there is an interest rate difference, it may be advantageous to delay payment from one country to another. A clearing system does not generally give that kind of flexibility. Of course, the very function of a bank is to provide a means of making payment and, in effect, act as a clearing agent for many customers. It is in avoiding the expenses inherent in the banking operation that a clearing system is advantageous.

Investment of Funds

Once it has been determined that funds are available for investment, the next consideration is how they should be invested on an international basis. Much of the theory of international monetary fluctuations is based on the concept that money will tend to flow where the interest rates are highest, taking into account the hedging cost. As has been explained in preceding chapters, the cost of buying or selling a particular currency for future settlement can be expressed as a percent per annum. If, therefore, three-month sterling short-term investments yield 8 percent and three-month dollar investments yield 6 percent it would be advantageous to invest dollars in the United Kingdom, provided the cost of selling pounds forward for three-month delivery was less than 2 percent per annum. According to monetary theory, the higher rates in the United Kingdom would attract funds from the United States. As the supply of funds offered in the United Kingdom increased, U.K. interest rates would tend to be reduced; and as the supply of funds in the United States decreased, U.S. interest rates would tend to increase. At the same time, sale of forward pounds would tend to increase the costs of forwards.

The flow of funds could also generate inflationary or deflationary effects in the countries concerned, and that is what might happen under a free market. However, governments wish to foster certain internal policies and have become aware that fiscal policy management can or should have internal effects. They therefore manipulate interest rates, the supply of funds, and, to some extent, foreign exchange rates in an effort to achieve the desired result.

The effect of government action can be continuing interest rate differentials after hedging costs are taken into account. To compensate for the flow of funds, the governments of a number of countries, including the United States, limit or prohibit monetary investments abroad. One way to get some advantage from the situation already referred to is to arrange the timing of payments to leave funds in countries with high interest rates as long as possible. There are a number of other reasons including liquidity needs and parochial attitudes, why funds do not flow freely.

If investments can be made abroad, there are ways to approach the hedging cost so as to maximize the yield. It is generally unsound not to hedge short-term investments, because the possible loss on any one transaction far exceeds the possible gain. The purpose of the transaction is to maximize the interest yield, not to make a foreign investment. That does not mean that some risk is not acceptable, particularly when there is no immediate pressure on the currency concerned. The way to maximize interest yield is to relate the hedge to the position, not to the specific transaction. For example, the hedge can be for a different time period and amount than the transaction. It may be desirable to cover principal only and not interest or to obtain a six-month hedge against a three-month investment, or vice versa. The aggressive company, however, can also undertake an unhedged investment in another currency.

When a foreign money market investment is made, liquidity must be considered because the different currencies make it much more difficult and expensive to undo such a transaction than a purely local investment. There is also the question of credit risk, which is much harder to evaluate in other countries. Other than for quasi-government securities, banks are often reluctant to give firm opinions on credit exposures. That reduces the criteria on which to base investment decisions and therefore considerably reduces investment possibilities.

Foreign Exchange Costs

In preceding chapters, reference has been made both to conversion of funds from one currency to another and to buying or selling foreign currencies forward. One aspect of international money management is to effect such transactions at minimum cost. As explained in Chapter 8, the conversion price is determined by getting quotes from buyers or sellers, and it can vary considerably, depending on the identity of the participant.

In most countries other than the United States, the banking system is so set up that the local bank expects to make a profit from its foreign exchange activities, and it factors that profit into considerations of the banking relationship with a particular customer. The possibilities for getting better rates that will be discussed in this section should therefore be weighed to determine whether or not a change would affect ability to get credit in one way or another or to continue other facilities. In addition, to repeat the caveat made at the beginning of this chapter, it is not advantageous to set up a foreign exchange system unless the possible savings or earnings exceed the estimated cost.

As has already been stated, the price of foreign exchange may vary at a particular moment, depending on the prospective buyer or seller. It is therefore easy to see that the way to get the best price is to get quotations from a number of sources at or as nearly at the same time as possible and take the best quotation. The techniques for doing so are similar to other trading techniques and can vary from company to company. The saving on any one transaction is generally not great; but if there are many transactions and they are large enough in size, the result can be significant. Chapter 8 also shows that the variance in rates quoted stems from the difference in bank position; each bank quotes according to its position and its feel for the market. If one bank is long and another is short of a currency, the first should quote a slightly better rate for a sale and the second for a purchase. A company can take advantage of that situation.

This best-quotation technique is applicable to spot transactions and to a certain extent to forward transactions, but forward rates are generally much more volatile. Rather than try to get competitive quotations at a particular instant for forward rates, it is often better to compare different market quotations and get an indication of rates. When the possible range has been determined, a firm order can be given at a particular figure or on a best-efforts basis, or action can be deferred until the situation improves. That approach will generally have best results, since if a firm quotation is requested and the market is fluctuating, either the price will be shaded to afford protection to the quoter or a quotation will be refused.

It is possible to operate in the suggested manner in the United States, Canada, and the United Kingdom. In most other countries, however, rates are either fixed or are not quoted on such a competitive basis. In addition, foreign currency conversion can involve a number of other costs that increase the total expense: transaction charges, brokerage commissions, fees, value dates, and minimum amounts. A comparison with rates quoted in the three countries referred to will generally show that conversion in one of those countries would have resulted in savings. Provided that conversions abroad are permissible under local exchange regulations and that the effect on local banking relations is not disadvantageous, the money manager will weigh the following steps.

There are two immediate possibilities. First, clearing arrangements discussed can result in net transfers in only one direction. By cutting down the amounts involved, expenses due to foreign exchange conversion cost can be reduced proportionately. Second, it is possible in a number of cases to convert foreign exchange in Canada, the United States, or the United Kingdom and thus realize the saving in the rate differential. It is not always possible to eliminate all local costs, but some savings can be realized.

Foreign exchange conversions can also be arranged outside a particular country for its own currency. As explained earlier, banks in each country have reciprocal accounts with banks in other countries. What actually happens in any foreign exchange transaction is that the account of the party entering into a purchase or sale with a bank is charged or credited in one country and the local bank instructs its correspondent in the other country to charge or credit its own account in the foreign bank and either pay the currency required to the recipient or payor or receive it from that party. Since the mechanics involve two parties and two banks, it is possible to arrange the transaction so that the relative amounts of the two currencies are determined in a competitive market and payment and receipt are then arranged accordingly. Two examples will illustrate the process.

Company A in the United States has an affiliate company B in Germany. Company B wants to pay company A $100,000 and advises company A accordingly. Company A gets quotations for the sale of deutsche marks in New York and picks the best rate, which might be $0.2750 per mark. That is equivalent to DM 363,636 for $100,000. The purchasing bank advises to what bank in Germany the deutsche marks should be transferred for its account. Company A then advises company B to pay DM 363,636 to bank X in Germany for account of bank Y in New York. On the date the deutsche marks are paid in Germany by company B, the dollars are credited or transferred to the account of company A in New York. This procedure results in use of the money in New York on the same day the funds are paid in Germany. It avoids as far as possible any charges in Germany. The expenses are the cost of communication with New York and the administrative cost of having a setup in New York to handle the transaction.

The procedure described can be expanded to third-party transactions. This time company B in Germany wants to pay company C in France FF 100,000 and advises company A in New York accordingly. Company A first obtains quotations for the purchase of FF 100,000 against the dollar. Let us say the lowest rate is $0.1810 per franc; this results in a cost of $18,100 for FF 100,000. Now company A obtains quotations for the sale of deutsche marks as before and picks FF 1.515 per mark as the best rate. This result in an equivalent of DM 65,818.

Company A instructs the bank from which it purchased the French francs to pay them to the account of company C with a bank in France by order of company B on the payment date. Company A, as before, then instructs company B to pay the DM 65,818 to the account of a New York bank with a German bank. On the payment date company A is credited with or receives payment of $18,100 from the New York bank that purchased the deutsche marks. Company A shows a transfer in of $18,100 and a transfer out of $18,100 on the same date. Funds are paid in Germany and received in France on the same day, and so the expenses can be kept to a minimum. The method can be used for payments to any number of countries from one country with only one sale of the paying country's currency once the total dollar equivalents have been determined. Often the result may be a better exchange rate on the sale than would be achieved from separate transactions on each currency.

It is perfectly feasible to obtain cross rates rather than buy and sell against the dollar, but because of the differential between buy and sell rates that often determines the cross rates, it is usually better to obtain separate rates. Both methods could, of course, be followed simultaneously and the one with the best result actually used for the transaction. Company A acts as agent for company B in a multilateral transaction. On its own books it shows a receipt of funds from one bank and the disbursement of a precisely similar amount from its account in the same or another bank on the same day. The transfer can thus be treated in the same manner as any other bank transfer. It is perfectly possible to add cable or other charges in; they can be added to the dollar cost of the transaction, and enough additional of the payment company's currency can be sold to meet the costs.

There are a number of other possibilities linked to the exchange system in various countries, the currencies in which billing or payments are made, and so forth. For example, in many South American countries European currencies are purchased by selling local currency for dollars and then buying the European currency concerned. The reason for that is lack of local exchange markets for European currencies. Since the buy and sell rates are usually wider, the cost can mount up. One way to avoid the high cost is to bill in dollars and convert the dollars, when received, in a more competitive market.

The preceding discussion has not touched on the matter of value dates. The difference between clearing funds in New York and Federal Reserve funds is generally one value day, and similar differences can exist in other countries. The difference in value dates can affect exchange rates, particularly over weekends. It is therefore important that the matter of value dates on all sides of the transaction be clearly understood so that the use of the funds is not lost for one or more days, which could change the specifics of the transaction.

Forward Coverage

In a number of chapters we have discussed the use of forward coverage and to some extent the way in which it should be purchased. When the coverage is for a specific transaction, there is little more that can be done except, as pointed out in Chapter 8, to consider the best market in which to purchase it.

When forward coverage is needed for an investment or other position in a particular currency, there are several possibilities because of the structure of the forward exchange market. Forward coverage for investment or position purposes is not obtained for a particular moment in time but rather to cover a time period. On the other hand, changes in currency equivalents through devaluation or revaluation do occur at one instant and do not generally change gradually over time. The method resulting in the least cost would be to take a forward position the day before a currency change and close it out the day after. That is not possible, so forwards must be obtained for longer periods.

Coverage beyond three months must generally be negotiated. There are two factors to be considered: the differential between months and the level of the spot rate. What that means is that if six times the one-month differential over spot is more or less than the six-month differential, it might be cheaper, if the spot rate does not move, to plan to have six consecutive one-month contracts instead of one six-month contract. If the currency is getting stronger and the spread is narrowing, then shorter contracts are to be preferred. The reverse is true when the spread is widening.

The position of the spot rate also is important. When the spot rate is near its upper limit, it is less costly to sell forward. Not only is the currency then exhibiting strength, but if it became weak, it would tend to fall toward its lower limit. That would reduce the cost of the forward coverage.

Since the objective is to provide continuing coverage, consideration should be given to settling outstanding contracts before their due dates and entering into new contracts at or about at the same time. That can reduce the expense of coverage when the short rates are more than pro rata to long rates. Suppose, as an example, that a six-month forward sale contract is entered into at a spread of 60 points. At the end of three months, the three-month spread is 35 points and the forward is still at 60. It is obviously advantageous to buy the original three-month contract in and enter into a new six-month contract. Changes in the spot rate on that kind of transaction make no difference, since a loss on one contract from that cause is exactly offset by a compensating change in the rate on the other contract.

There is one further forward coverage consideration. As has been pointed out, devaluations and revaluations occur at a particular instant that cannot usually be pinpointed in advance. In addition, forward rates are cheapest when there is no pressure on a currency, but that is the very time when coverage does not seem necessary. One way to cope with the situation is to enter into contracts on both sides but for different periods, so that one runs off and leaves the protection on the other side. For example, if sterling is strong today but it is anticipated that six months from today it will start to come under pressure, it is possible to sell one year forward and buy six months forward. If the calculation is right, six months from now there will be forward coverage at today's rates. An operation of that type can be utilized to provide facilities at minimum costs when rates are strong. Different time periods can be used to achieve the best results.

The following two chapters discuss the effect of changes in currency values on the transfer of funds and the translation of international accounts.

PART FIVE

Foreign Exchange Exposure and Protection

13

Changes in Currency Values
and the Transfer of Funds

IN preceding chapters it has been pointed out that changes in currency values have an immediate and measurable effect on the transfer of funds. Either the payor may pay more or he may pay less in terms of his own currency; alternatively, the payee may receive more or he may receive less in terms of his currency. That is true of all transactions in which payments are made, including exports, services, royalties, dividends, loans, and capital contributions.

General Considerations

The magnitude of changes in currency values can be divided into two categories: that due to devaluations or revaluations, when there is a change in the parity of a particular currency as related to other currencies, and that due to normal market fluctuations in a narrow band centered on parity or its equivalent. Between the floating of currencies in August 1971 and until the new parities were set in December, the market fluctuations of the major ones tended to remain within fairly narrow limits on a day-to-day basis, although the range was wider than before. This appears to result from the efforts of the central banks to maintain an orderly market. Generally, devaluations and revaluations occur infrequently. The factors that bring about those changes are discussed in Chapter 4. Market fluctuations are a function of supply and demand, and the way in which the foreign exchange market works is outlined in Chapter 6. The businessman who operates in more than one country, then, may be considered to have two different sorts of problems, one long range, the other short.

The simple solution to the currency value problem is to bill and receive all payments only in the currency of the originating country. But that is not really a solution. As pointed out in a preceding paragraph, what happens is that the payee or payor then has the problem of having to cope with the amounts of his own currency required to make payment or received in payment. Inevitably that is reflected in the business relationship involved. To take an ordinary example, an importer wishes to buy certain equipment. He is quoted prices by exporters in dollars, in deutsche marks, and in pounds. Assuming that the equipment offered is generally comparable, the importer must make an evaluation of what the probable cost to him will be in terms of his own currency. To the extent that his currency might be devalued in terms of dollars, that the deutsche mark might be revalued, or the pound devalued, some provision for the risk of changes in terms of his own currency must be made. Furthermore, there will surely be changes in the day-to-day spot values of the currencies that can significantly affect the desirability of a particular transaction at the time of payment. In summary, when a businessman does business in more than one currency, considerations of relative currency values affect the transaction whether or not one of the parties takes them into account.

The export-import transaction is relatively clear-cut, but the problem is much more complicated when other types of payments are considered. That is particularly true when both sides of the transaction are controlled by one organization, as in the case of payments between affiliates and parents.

Fluctuations in exchange have been shown to have a measurable effect on transfers of funds between countries. Furthermore, it has been shown that the effect always occurs when more than one currency is involved, since one party to the transaction has an exchange exposure so far as his currency is concerned.

The range of possible actions is great; it depends on the risk to be assumed, the facilities that exist for protection, exchange controls, and other factors that vary considerably with the country. Some of those factors will be referred to, but any proposed theoretical action must be evaluated against the practicalities in a particular country.

Direct Payments

To start with the simplest type of solution, a businessman enters into an agreement to receive or make payment in a currency other than his own on a predetermined future date. Let us assume that a U.S. exporter sells goods to an importer in the United Kingdom for £100,000 payable 90 days from date of sale. On the date of sale, spot sterling is selling at $2.40 per pound and forward sterling for delivery in 90 days is selling at $2.397 per pound. The U.S. exporter enters into a forward contract with a U.S. bank for the delivery of £100,000 in 90 days at $2.397 per pound. When the pounds are paid to him by the U.K. importer on the due date, they are paid to the account of the U.S. bank in London in settlement of the contract and the exporter's account in the United States is credited on the same day with $239,700. No matter what changes occur, either from market fluctuations or from devaluation or revaluation, the exporter receives a precise amount in dollars. The U.S. bank has assumed the exchange risk. How the bank handles foreign exchange transactions is explained in Chapter 8.

Now what has happened? Assuming that the exporter has not adjusted his price to compensate for a differential between the value of the currency he will receive and the value of the same currency at time of sale, he has paid $300 for insurance against any fluctuation in the value of the currency he is to receive. On a per annum basis, that could be figured as $300 × 4, or $1,200, in relation to $240,000, which is equivalent to ½ of 1 percent per annum. That would be included in the U.S. accounts of the exporter either as a cost or as a reduction of the sale price. The U.K. importer's pound costs are fixed.

To turn the transaction around, the U.S. exporter now bills the same sale to the U.K. importer in dollars for $240,000. The U.K. importer buys forward from his U.K. bank the dollars required at the same rate of $2.397 per pound. That means he must pay £100,125 to buy $240,000. When the forward contract comes due, he pays his bank the £100,125 for $240,000 and has the dollars paid to the U.S. exporter in the United States. On a per annum basis, the cost would be figured as 4 × £125, or £500, in relation to £100,000, which again is equivalent to ½ of 1 percent. The importer normally takes into his accounts the total pound cost as the cost of the goods purchased. Here again the importer has no risk. Regardless of what happens to the relationship of the pound to the dollar, the U.K. bank takes the exchange risk. That is a normal banking function.

When currencies sell at a premium forward, it is usually a reflection of relative strength, so that it is not necessary to sell forward to protect the spot rate. On the other hand, it may be advantageous to do so and base the price on the forward rate rather than the spot rate. If that is done, a forward sale must be entered into to protect the position. As an example, a U.S. exporter wishes to sell goods for deutsche marks to a German importer. The spot rate for deutsche marks is $0.2750 per mark, and the rate for six months sale is $0.2760. The exporter may base his deutsche mark price on the $0.2760 rate if delivery is to be made in about six months. That results in fewer deutsche marks being required. At the rates given, $100,000 is equivalent to DM 363,636 at $0.2760 and to DM 362,318 at $0.2760, a differential of DM 1,318. The result is the same if the price is quoted in dollars. In this case, the German importer requires fewer deutsche marks to buy the same number of dollars. Such considerations can and do affect international trade and are the rationale behind major currency changes through devaluation or revaluation. By changing in a major way, price relationships between countries change the flow of goods.

The examples given illustrate how a particular transaction that requires payment of funds between two countries can be protected. The reader may well ask why, if the mechanics are so simple, the procedure is not normal for all transactions involving two currencies. The fact is that a great many transactions are so handled and the importer or exporter treats the additional cost of the foreign exchange as an expense of doing business or factors it into his pricing determinations. However, the August 1971 change by the United States resulted in a substantial widening of the bands of fluctuation in currencies and a continuing possibility of change in relative values. This makes protection against changes in currency values both more expensive and more difficult.

Payments over Varying Periods

To see why the procedure of the examples is not always the way to handle the foreign currency problems or why it may not be practical, let us examine the assumptions, some expressed, some tacit, on which the transactions were based. To start with, it was assumed that the transaction was entered into at a particular moment in time. That is fine for an order received on a particular date to be filled out of inventory and delivered within a fixed period. But what about the situation in which it is necessary to quote prices in another currency subject to the customer's acceptance? Now there is no fixed starting date as far as the quotation is concerned, and a forward contract matching up the exact dates cannot be entered into.

As an example, a French customer requests a quotation in French francs for equipment in late July of 1969 from a U.S. exporter. The exporter quotes a price of FF 1,000,000, equivalent to approximately $200,000 at that time, without tying the quote to the existing U.S. dollar–French franc relationship. The franc is devalued on August 8, 1970. The French importer accepts the quotation, for delivery and payment in 90 days, but his acceptance is not received until August 10. The exporter now finds that he will receive approximately $180,000. That amount could be protected against changes for the 90-day period, but the loss has already occurred. The other side of this does not follow. If the French importer receives a quotation in dollars, his acceptance gives rise to his exchange exposure and at that time he enters into a forward exchange contract. After the devaluation of the franc, he has to reconsider the desirability of a specific purchase in terms of the additional cost in francs.

To examine the payment date assumption, a U.S. exporter again makes a sale for French francs calling for payment of FF 1,000,000 on July 31, 1969. The sale can be made on open account, or against a note due on July 31, or in a number of other ways. Payment is not received by the exporter on July 31, either because the customer delays or because of paperwork problems, and is not made until August 10. Assume the exporter has covered the transaction by selling the French francs forward for delivery July 31 at $0.199 per franc. The spot rate for value July 31 is $0.201 per franc. What happens? First of all, the exporter must buy spot francs to deliver on his forward sale. They cost him $201,000, and for them he receives $199,000. He has an immediate cost of $2,000. That should be in line with what he probably expected when he entered into the forward contract at the time of sale. Since payment is expected momentarily and the franc seems under no immediate pressure, entering into another foreign exchange contract does not seem necessary. The franc is devalued on August 8, and payment of francs 1,000,000 is received on August 15. The francs are sold at $0.18 per franc and the exporter realizes only $180,000 instead of the $199,000 that he had expected, a loss of $19,000. The payor pays only the agreed-upon FF 1,000,000.

It is clear from the examples given that, in general, the payor required to make payment in a foreign currency can cover the specific amount due by buying forward the currency required. There is no risk of variation in the time of payment, since in general that is determined by or can be met by the payor. The payee who receives funds in a foreign currency, on the other hand, has difficulty in covering specific transactions, since the date of receipt of payment is often imprecise.

Other Types of Payments

So far we have used export-import transactions as examples. In addition to those, there is a whole range of payments that are more variable in timing: service payments, royalties, dividends, capital investments, loans, loan repayments, and so forth. In all of these the timing of payment is much more flexible but the exchange risk still exists, and in terms of one currency or another it has an important bearing on the transaction.

Take as an example, a U.S. company that has an investment in a German affiliate. In July 1969 the German affiliate declares a dividend, of which the portion payable to the U.S. investor is DM 100,000. If payment is made in July, the U.S. investor receives $25,200; but if payment is delayed until November, the U.S. investor receives $27,100 because the deutsche mark has been revalued upward in the meantime. That is a difference of $1,900, as far as the U.S. investor is concerned. There is no impact on the German company, since the deutsche mark amount remains the same.

Now look at it the other way around. A German company has an investment in a U.S. company. In July 1969 the U.S. company declares a dividend of which the portion payable to the German investor is $100,000. Now, if the German investor receives payment in July, it receives DM 397,000, whereas if it receives payment in November, the amount is only DM 369,000, a difference of DM 28,000. In this case, there is no effect on the U.S. company, since the dollar amount remains the same.

The possible change in equivalent value of dividends is equally true of all the other types of payments referred to. Leaving aside for the moment the question of whether such payments can or should be covered by forward transactions, we may express a general rule: payments to be received that are denominated in stronger currencies should be deferred when there is a risk of change of one currency against the other. Payments to be made that are denominated in strong currencies should be expedited under the same circumstances. The converse is that payments to be received that are denominated in weak currencies should be expedited and payment to be made should be deferred.

It is generally not too difficult to make an evaluation of one currency against one other. A revaluation of the German mark had the same effect as a devaluation of all the other currencies, including the U.S. dollar against the mark. The devaluation of the French franc had the same effect as a revaluation of all the other currencies, so that consideration should be given to the relative currency value changes and not necessarily the type.

It is not, of course, possible to defer payments indefinitely or advance them at will. There are the usual business reasons why they may be required at a particular time. What is pointed out is that the timing of payment can have a substantial effect and that, if there is flexibility, consideration should be given to relative currency risks. The phenomenon involved is technically referred to as leads and lags.

Nonspecific Coverage

Earlier in this chapter the possibilities that exist for purchasing forward coverage for specific export-import transactions were pointed out. As was explained, it is easier for the payor to purchase coverage, since he can determine the timing of payment precisely. In addition to export-import transactions, we have discussed other types of payments in which the timing of payment may be even less precise. It is, in fact, not necessary that forward coverage be linked to specific transactions. A company that is involved in foreign business and has a good credit rating may generally arrange, through its normal banking courses, to buy or sell foreign currencies for future delivery in amounts related to its business needs. Banks may, however, frown on transactions entered into purely for speculative purposes not related to specific foreign operations.

The timing and extent of forward coverage that is obtained can be related to the probable exposures a business will have. For instance, a company wishes to make quotations in a foreign currency as in the example of the French importer. French francs can then be sold forward for the approximate period the quotation is expected to be outstanding; if the quotation is accepted, a new contract can be entered into for the approximate date by which payment might be expected. Alternatively, French francs might be sold forward in the beginning for the entire probable period of the transaction. If the quotation is not accepted, it is possible to purchase French francs forward for the same date as previously sold, which will result in a cost for the period of the quotation only.

Although the forward market in major currencies is quite flexible, it is usually easier for nonspecific transactions to deal in round 100,000 amounts of the currencies concerned. In a good many currencies, that is the equivalent of $25,000 to $30,000 more or less, and the quotations given by the banks are simpler.

Similar considerations affect payments such as royalties. Instead of expediting payments to be made that are denominated in a strong currency or payments to be received that are denominated in a weak currency, forward coverage to eliminate the exposure can be obtained. In the first case, the strong currency would be purchased forward and used when payments would normally be due. In the second, the weak currency would be sold forward and the actual currency received would be delivered when due. The amount of coverage should be related to the amounts involved. Determining the amount may not be simple, particularly when monthly or other regular payments are involved. For instance, should coverage be obtained on an annual basis equivalent to one month's royalty payments, one year's, or what amount? The decision should be based on the cost, the probable risks, and the loss a particular business is prepared to accept.

In this chapter we have not considered what happens to an investment in a foreign country when a currency change takes place. The timing of payments has an effect on the investment. The method used to evaluate and protect such an investment must be considered in making payment and forward coverage decisions. That will be explored in detail in the next chapter.

Cost of Coverage

So far we have not investigated the cost of foreign exchange coverage at any depth. Cost has an important bearing on both amount and period, particularly when nonspecific transactions are concerned. At times, the cost could exceed the possible loss, so that having protection would be more expensive than not having it.

Most of the examples that have been given have involved spot and forward rates at a moment in time and have shown what can happen when rate changes are caused by revaluation or devaluation. However, most such changes take place rarely and the vast majority of changes in rates in the past have occurred within narrow parity limits, as explained in Chapter 7. The cost then is related to two things: the difference in rates and the period of time. At a moment in time, it is possible to obtain quotations that give the spot rate and the difference between that rate and the forward premiums or discounts, usually for periods of 1, 2, 3,

6, and 12 months, as explained in Chapter 8. When he negotiates a particular transaction, the businessman can buy or sell a foreign currency forward at a fixed price, and that gives him, in terms of his own currency, a future determinable value. In that type of transaction, the cost is usually considered to be the differential between the spot rate and the forward rate.

The actual economic cost of any forward exchange transaction is the difference between the spot rate on the date of payment or receipt and the rate actually paid or received. The forward rate may be used to book the transaction, but that merely buries the real cost. All this becomes obvious when the foreign exchange for a particular forward contract is bought or sold on the delivery date in the open market rather than derived from the proceeds of a business transaction. The difference between the original forward rate and the spot rate used to settle the contract is the true cost or profit. The forward rate is derived from the spot rate at a moment in time plus or minus the forward differential, but that is not the cost. It is merely a conventional means of expressing the forward rate.

As example, the spot rate for sterling is $2.4050 per pound. Actually, a quotation may be $2.4049 to $2.4051, depending on whether sterling is bought or sold. The three-month forward rate is at a discount of $0.0060, or $2.3990. That is usually expressed as a percent per annum, in this case approximately 1 percent ($0.024 to $2.3990). Sterling is sold forward, and at the end of three months the seller has to deliver sterling he already has or buy sterling to deliver. Say he buys it in the open market at $2.3850. The seller has a profit of $0.0140 per pound on this particular transaction. Or to make a different assumption, spot sterling is at $2.41 on the delivery date. Now the cost of the transaction is $0.012 per pound or 2 percent per annum. Changes of that magnitude can take place very rapidly because of market forces, and that can quite violently influence the cost. Furthermore, when changes do occur, they tend to be reflected in equivalent or greater changes in the forward rates. As explained in Chapter 8, forward rates are theoretically free to fluctuate as widely as market forces dictate, although in practice they are often influenced by central banks.

Therefore, in trying to determine the probable cost of a particular transaction, the estimated spot rate at the future delivery date must be compared with the actual forward rate quoted. When the forward rate is outside the parity bands, the transaction is sure to result in a profit or loss, barring a revaluation or devaluation. In the example given, for instance, once the forward rate drops below $2.38, the seller of future sterling is certain to have a loss when the transaction is covered, unless there is a devaluation of sterling. When the spot rate approaches the lower parity limit, the protection purchased is against devaluation only, not against market changes, and should be evaluated on that basis. If sterling becomes stronger, there is no advantage in selling it forward.

The estimated cost expressed on an annual basis is important in evaluating continuing coverage for nonspecific transactions. Most major currency changes have been in the neighborhood of 15 percent. If, therefore, the cost approaches that figure over perhaps a two- to three-year period, the devaluation has been paid for whether it occurs or not. The cost must also be related to the risk one is prepared to undertake, particularly when infrequent transactions abroad are involved. Further considerations along these lines will be discussed in the next chapter in connection with protection of permanent investments.

The discussion has been based on the IMF parity limits. Up to August 1971 these were 1 percent on either side of parity, and subsequent to December 1971 they were $2\frac{1}{4}$ percent. Whether or not the parity system continues, currencies will fluctuate within reasonably determinable limits at a particular moment. Over time there will be larger fluctuations equivalent to mini-devaluations or mini-revaluations. The difference between normal fluctuations and actual currency value changes will be more difficult to determine and to protect against. The cost considerations can be worked out in the same manner as in the examples given, but there will no longer be absolute parity limits beyond which currency changes cannot go without a major change.

So far we have focused mainly on the possibility of devaluation or revaluation with a resulting major change in currency values, but the vast majority of short-term business transactions need be concerned only with changes in the spot rate.

Methods of Evaluating Cost of Coverage

To evaluate action required, it is necessary to understand how current spot rates relate to possible changes. Table 2 (Chapter 3) gives the par values of major currencies expressed in dollars. As has been explained, IMF rules permit members to let their currencies swing within a given percent on either side of parity.

Whether or not the IMF parities apply, currencies will tend to come into some kind of balance, one against the other, and, through central bank intervention, further international agreement, or normal market forces, the currencies will fluctuate within limits. These may be less definable and the risk of change greater. In evaluating the various courses of action set forth below, greater judgment may have to be exercised to determine what are upper or lower limits.

Let us examine what action should be considered in various situations but ignore the desirability of protecting against revaluation or devaluation. There are three broad categories and within each of them two subcategories. Spot rates may be at lower limits, upper limits, or between the limits. In each case, forward rates may be at premium or a discount.

Currency at lower limit, forwards at a discount. When currency is at its probable lower limit and forwards are at a discount, nothing can be gained by selling forward. Any increase in the spot rate will result in a higher equivalent, and the rate cannot drop lower. Of course, rates of that nature usually reflect a substantial risk of devaluation. If, as an example, spot sterling was at $2.38 and forwards were at a discount, sterling to be received in the future was sure to sell for at least $2.38, barring a devaluation, so there was nothing to be gained by a forward sale.

Currency at lower limit, forwards at a premium. For currency to be at its probable lower limit and forwards to be at a premium is a somewhat abnormal situation that usually reflects extraneous conditions. For example, deutsche marks were about $0.2710 in January and February of 1970 and three-month forwards were about $0.2718. That probably reflected an accumulation of deutsche marks prior to the fall of 1969 that had not yet been repatriated. In that case, the underlying strength of the mark clearly made the spot rate too low and the forward rate did not reflect the probable improvement. In March and April 1970, the mark advanced until it was around its ceiling of $0.2755 and forwards maintained about the same $0.0008 premium. Since the chance of improvement was great, it would not have been desirable to sell forward. If, however, forwards had been up around $0.2755, then nothing could have been lost by selling forward and something might have been gained if the spot rate had not advanced. Clearly, whenever forward rates are in excess of probable upper limits, it is advantageous to sell forward, barring the possibility of a revaluation.

The situation is more difficult when the forward rates are within the parity bands or other limits. Then the present forward premium must be weighed against a possibly more advantageous upward movement of spot rates. To repeat, for spot rates to be at lower limits and forward rates at premiums is an abnormal situation. The real question is how long it will last. As a possible rule of thumb for periods of three months or less, it might be advantageous to sell forward when the forward premium is more than half the differential between the spot rate and the upper limit of a particular currency. That approach is based on the old stock market adage that bulls can make money, bears can make money, but pigs always lose.

For periods beyond three months, the probability is that the factors that cause the distortion will probably be eliminated, which will allow the currency to rise to a more normal level.

Currency at upper limit, forwards at a discount. As when currency is at its lower limit and forwards are at a premium, it is an abnormal situation for currency to be at its upper limit and forwards to be at a discount. Probably some influence, such as central bank intervention to reduce arbitraged interest differentials and prevent an inflow of funds, is acting on the spot rates. If the strength of the currency is expected to continue, it would not be advantageous to sell forward. If the discounts are small, it might be wise to consider protecting the position.

Currency at upper limit, forwards at a premium. The situation when currency is at its upper limits and forwards are at a premium reflects some risk of a revaluation, but, barring that, it is advantageous to sell forward and take a reasonably sure profit. One can, of course, be greedy and wait for further widening, but that can work both ways.

We now come to the last two cases, which are the most common and which can be considered together.

Currency between the limits, forwards at a premium or a discount. Judgment and experience are called for when currency is between the limits and forwards are at either a premium or a discount. For instance, certain seasonal patterns based on trade and payment trends may be expected to influence rates. In Canada, delivery of the grain crop in the fall tends to strengthen the Canadian dollar, which then falls off in the winter and spring. In the United Kingdom, tourist expenditures during summer tend to strengthen the pound. In Switzerland and Germany, banks buy deposits on quarterly dates, particularly at year end. All those factors influence spot rates.

If the forward premium rates are close to or in excess of the upper limits, it is probably wisest to sell forward regardless of whether the spot rate is expected to improve. If the forward discount rates are close to or less than the lower limits, little or nothing can be gained by selling forward. If the forward rates are at a small premium or a small discount over spot and it is expected that the spot rate will improve, it is advantageous not to sell forward. If, however, it is expected that the spot rate may decline, then forward sale is probably desirable if the forward rate is at a premium. If it is at a discount, the probable decrease in spot rate should be weighed against the actual forward discount and the best position should be chosen.

All of the preceding considerations are based on the availability of the necessary expertise to make a continuing or periodic examination of the risks involved and adjust to forward positions when necessary. It is always possible at any time to close out open forward contracts, although that may involve additional costs. When transactions are limited in either size or number, it is probably cheaper and safer to cover all transactions and price accordingly.

14

Translation of Accounts

WE have seen in the preceding chapter how the actual transfer of funds in different currencies results in foreign exchange gains or losses and how the gains or losses can be handled. We come now to another type of exchange exposure: that which arises from having assets and liabilities in more than one currency.

Investment in Foreign Countries

When an initial investment is made in a foreign country, the transfer of funds results in an exact currency equivalent. The foreign currency funds are then used abroad to purchase assets, and liabilities are incurred; the resulting net worth has an exact equivalent in the original currency. As business operations are undertaken, changes occur in the assets and liabilities and therefore in the net worth of the business. The changes that occur in the foreign net worth have an effect on the value of the original investment, and they must be translated into a common currency equivalent for proper evaluation. If changes in the relative values of the currencies concerned also occur, they too must be reflected. The method used in translating the assets and liabilities affects the overall result.

At first sight, it would seem that the easiest way to translate assets and liabilities would be to translate the net worth and the underlying assets and liabilities at the current or spot rate of exchange at a moment in time. The difference between that value and the previous local currency equivalent would represent the profit or loss on the investment for the period. That might be appropriate for liquid assets or liabilities, but it is not generally appropriate for assets or liabilities that are realized over a longer period of time. The reason is that, as discussed in Chapter 4, changes in relative currency values are usually the result of inflationary forces. To protect against erosion of values, internal measures must be taken in the form of price adjustments.

To take a simple example, a machine is purchased in the United States in 1966 by a British businessman for $280,000, which is then equivalent to £100,000. The machine has a five-year life. In November 1967 the pound is devalued from $2.80 to $2.40 per pound. In 1971 the British businessman seeks to replace the machine, which is now fully depreciated. He has recouped the original cost of £100,000 through depreciation, but he now finds that sum equivalent to only $240,000. In other words, in terms of dollars he has not recovered his original cost; he has suffered a loss of $40,000 over the period. The same effect occurs when only one currency is involved, as when, because of inflation, the replacement cost in local currency is substantially higher. In either case, the businessman has suffered an economic loss. In the first illustration given, the businessman could have suffered a further loss if the replacement cost of the equipment in dollars had also increased owing to inflation in the United States.

In order to cope with inflation, the businessman must increase his prices sufficiently that the recovery from the customer covers the increased cost. In the example of machine replacement, the British businessman would have had to recover about £117,000 to equal the original $280,000 cost. He would have had to raise his prices to do so. That would have been further complicated by the additional £117,000 representing taxable income, some larger amount would have been required to offset the additional taxes.

It is essential that a businessman in an inflationary economy increase prices to at least compensate for erosion in the real values of long-term assets. If he does so, the assets do not lose their values with currency changes and may be maintained at constant values. If price adjustments are not made, an economic loss results.

Methods of Translation

A rule followed by many companies is to translate current assets and liabilities at the rate of exchange that obtains on the date on which valuation is being made. Capital assets and other long-term assets and liabilities are translated at the rate in existence when they were acquired or incurred. Two authoritative publications that outline translation methods in detail are *Accounting Research Bulletin 43* of the American Institute of Certified Public Accountants, Chapter 12, "Foreign Operations and Foreign Exchange," and Research Report 36 of the National Association of Accountants, *Management Accounting Problems in Foreign Operations.*

In theory, cash on hand could be converted into another currency at the current rate. Other current assets are equivalent to or realizable in cash and therefore follow the same rule. Since cash is used to pay current liabilities, they also follow the rule. Inventory may follow special rules when it is possible to adjust the price readily, since the realizable foreign currency equivalent may then be higher than the book value. Current assets and current liabilities stated in other currencies must be separately evaluated.

The rationale for keeping capital assets at a constant value has already been set forth. Long-term debt is generally considered to be used to acquire capital assets. It is therefore appropriate to take into account changes in the value of long-term debt only as they are realized by paying off the debt.

For the purpose of translating long-term debt, it makes no difference in what currency the debt is denominated until all or any part of the debt becomes short, if the rule is to keep the debt at a constant currency equivalent. To illustrate, a British company affiliated with a U.S. company borrows DM 1,000,000 in 1966 payable in 1973. In 1966 the sterling equivalent is £88,130 and the dollar equivalent is $250,000, and, in translating the accounts into dollars, $250,000 is used as the value. In 1967 the pound is devalued to $2.40. No adjustment to the dollar equivalent is made, although £104,170 will be required when payment is due.

In 1969 the mark is revalued upward. Now the dollar equivalent of DM 1,000,000 is $273,000 and the pound equivalent is £113,750, but again no change is made in the dollar equivalent. In 1972 the debt becomes short. At that time a loss of $23,000 will be picked up in the translation into dollars of the accounts and a sterling loss of £25,620 will be picked up by the British company in its accounts adjusted by changes in the values of the two currencies that have occurred since 1969. The actual bookkeeping of the British company will be governed by U.K. tax and legal considerations, so that the sterling loss may have been reflected earlier. That, however, will have been adjusted in translating the accounts, so that the effect is as given here.

The procedure described roughly brings in the gain as the capital assets are used up, and to some extent it offsets the economic loss referred to if price adjustments lag or are not made. Other long-term assets and liabilities are generally handled in the same way.

When the assets and liabilities of an enterprise have been translated as described, the resulting net worth as expressed in the currency into which they have been translated can be compared with the previous value of the investment. The change represents the profit or loss for the period of comparison. An illustration of what happens when there is a change in currency values is given in Table 7. Much of the detailed explanation is easier to follow if reference is made to the table.

There are separate rules for the translation of the profit and loss accounts. Generally, the figures for each month or other time period are translated at average exchange rates for the period. Depreciation and amortization are taken at their historical value regardless of the local currency figure, as are other accounts that have constant values. The resulting net profit or loss figure for the period is then compared with the change in the net worth derived from translating the assets and liabilities. The difference between the two figures is picked up in the profit and loss account as an exchange gain or loss.

The translation of profit and loss account for one year may, then, be seen to be composed of the 12 month-by-month translation figures. In Brazil, which has several devaluations in the course of a year, the gross income figure in cruzeiros translated at the year-end rate would be less than the sum of the monthly figures. The difference would represent the higher values earlier in the year. A series of upward price adjustments would have been required to protect the assets.

The preceding explanation of how accounts are translated is important for an understanding of the foreign exchange measures that may be taken in that connection. To some extent the mechanics bring about the result, and so it is necessary to know the reasons for the methods used.

Actual Exposure

From the preceding discussion it is apparent that, in general, it is the current assets and liabilities in foreign currency that are affected by

Table 7. Effect of change in currency values.

Account	Pounds	Dollars at 2.80	Dollars at 2.40
Current assets			
Cash	100	280	240
Cash in dollar account	20	56	56
Accounts receivable	400	1,120	960
Inventory	50	140	120
Prepaid expenses	20	56	48
	590	1,652	1,424
Current liabilities			
Loans payable	50	140	120
Accounts payable	250	700	600
Accounts payable in dollars	30	84	84
Accrued taxes and expenses	60	168	144
	390	1,092	948
Net working capital	200	560	476
Net capital assets	600	1,680	1,680
	800	2,240	2,156
Less			
Long-term debt	200	560	560
Long-term debt due in dollars	100	280	280
	300	840	840
Net assets	500	1,400	1,316
Stockholders' equity	500	1,400	1,400
Loss on devaluation			84
Net worth	500	1,400	1,316

changes in currency values. The net amount is defined as working capital. Two factors should be borne in mind. First, only current assets and current liabilities that are actually due or payable in the currency concerned should be taken into account. For example, a dollar cash account held by a U.K. company in a New York bank, even though expressed in sterling on the U.K. company's books, is not subject to changes as far as dollars are concerned. Similarly, a U.K. company may owe dollars to a U.S. exporter. Even though expressed in sterling, the payable has a constant value as far as dollars are concerned. The sterling value may, of course, vary. Second, the working capital position is fluid and changes from period to period. Protection is therefore required for average figures rather than for precise amounts.

As explained in Chapter 7, current or spot rates have, in the past, fluctuated within narrow bands around a preset parity. It is not generally desirable or necessary to try to protect working capital amounts against those changes, which, given no major currency value changes, tend to average out. What is required is consideration of the possible impact of major currency value changes. Furthermore, those changes have been related to a much longer time frame, generally years rather than days or months, although starting in August 1971, the time has shortened. There are three ways in which protection may be provided:

1. Purchase of forward coverage.
2. Management of the assets and liabilities concerned to reduce the amount exposed to possible currency change.
3. Flexible pricing and planning policies to compensate for actual or expected changes in currency values.

Purchase of Forward Coverage

Let us take the first protection possibility, purchase of forward coverage. The mechanics are explained in Chapter 8. The first step is to determine the working capital level or other net asset for which coverage might be desirable. As will be discussed later, the level may be managed to reduce the exposure. The determination should be in the local currency; the possible change in the value of local currency as against another currency can then be compared with the cost of obtaining forward coverage.

In Chapter 8 some of the considerations in determining cost were discussed. Basically, for a particular transaction, the possible future spot rate must be related to the present forward rate. Forward rates are normally quoted, in relation to the present spot rate, as so many points premium or discount or as x percent per annum. However, that is a valuation of the present spot rate in relation to the future spot rate. The relationship of the spot rates is not as significant for long-run as it is for short-run transactions, but it still is important in relation to the timing and amount of each transaction. The possible fluctuation has been between 1½ and 2 percent on a per annum basis in major currencies, but is now greater.

For example, spot sterling is $2.41 per pound and one-year-forward sterling is at a discount of 1 percent or $0.024 off the spot rate. That means that the one-year rate for selling sterling forward is $2.386 per pound. The reason for entering into a forward sale of sterling must be an appraisal that, within the next year, sterling will come under pressure and possibly be devalued. The exact timing is, of course, imprecise, and the businessman wants to insure his position against loss. Assume now that the analysis is correct and sterling does come under pressure but no devaluation takes place. At the end of the year, then, it is necessary to buy sterling to cover the forward sale. Since sterling has been under pressure, that will be reflected in a decline in the spot rate, which, let us assume, has dropped to $2.39 per pound. When the sterling is purchased, the net cost is $0.004 per pound rather than $0.024, the differential when the transaction was entered into.

The transaction may be evaluated in another way. Assume the appraisal is wrong and the pound strengthens instead of weakens. Under the IMF rules prior to August 1971, a currency could not fluctuate more than 1 percent on either side of parity and generally fluctuated about ¾ of 1 percent. Parity for the pound was $2.40 per pound, so the maximum upper limit was $2.424. If that limit were reached, the cost of the transaction would be $0.038 per pound rather than $0.024. On the two sets of assumptions, the possible swing in cost was from $0.004 to $0.038 per pound, or a difference of 0.17 to 1.6 percent per annum. That must be related to a possible devaluation of 15 percent in the next 10 years. Assuming a continuing cost of 1.6 percent, the possible protection cost would be 16 percent.

Before a decision is made to protect any net working capital position, further consideration is necessary. Although forward coverage may be obtained in sterling for one year, coverage for periods beyond one year is difficult to obtain, particularly as the period becomes longer. It cannot be assumed that one-year rates quoted today will continue at the same level. In fact, if sterling comes under pressure, the forward rates may widen out to 3, 4, or 5 percent per annum while the spot rate falls. The potential cost is then the actual forward percent related to the spot rate plus the possible change in the spot rate upward if the evaluation is incorrect; that is, the differential between the spot rate and the upper limit at which sterling might sell in the future, under the old IMF rules probably between $2.38 and $2.40. If that now comes to, say, 6 percent per annum as against a possible devaluation of 15 percent, the devaluation has been paid for whether it occurs or not in 2½ years. Thus, the consideration is not the simple one of buying insurance against currency changes at a continuing rate; it is the careful evaluating of the economic and political possibilities related to the cost and degree of risk to be assumed and the probable timing.

Adequate forward markets exist in deutsche marks, French francs,

Swiss francs, Japanese yen, Canadian dollars, and U.S. dollars and, in a more limited way, in certain other European currencies. In the past, the per annum percents when a currency is not experiencing difficulties have *generally* been in the neighborhood of 2 percent or less, so that, as long as the situation is not critical, coverage has been obtainable at reasonable cost. For most other currencies, particularly Latin American ones, forward coverage also may on occasion be obtained, but the probability of devaluation is so strong that the cost, if obtained on a continuing basis, is generally more than the eventual devaluation.

As pointed out earlier, the matter of timing has an important bearing on cost. As explained in Chapter 4, devaluations and revaluations are usually the result of internal economic factors that alter the relationship of the economy of one country to that of another. However, a change in the value of a particular currency is made by the government, which is influenced by political considerations. Devaluations especially may be considered to reflect unsuccessful fiscal action to restrain inflationary forces within reasonable limits. Governments tend to delay taking the step of a revaluation or devaluation until well after the time when it is apparent, from an economic standpoint, that action is required. In addition, as the economic factors become more and more evident, there is a flight out of or into a particular currency. That must be compensated for by the central bank of a particular country and, as explained in Chapter 4, it can eventually force devaluation or revaluation.

In the 1960s, there were four major European currency changes: revaluations of the German mark in 1961 and 1969, devaluation of the pound sterling in 1967, and devaluation of the French franc in 1969. It was clear six months to a year in advance of each of the changes that the currency was under pressure. During most of those periods, forward coverage could have been obtained at minimal cost—in the case of sterling almost to the last minute at less than 1 percent per annum—probably because of the involvement of the central banks. The early warning system in the shape of the lag in taking political action to cure economic distortions may not persist, but at least in each of the cases cited it would have been prudent to obtain coverage after the initial flurries had been dampened down.

The continued balance of payments deficits of the United States over the past ten years built up pressure against the dollar, which resulted first in Canada floating the Canadian dollar in 1970, second in Germany and certain other countries floating or revaluing their currencies in May 1971, then in the action of the United States in terminating gold convertibility of the dollar in August 1971, and finally in the setting of new parities in December 1971. This has resulted in a situation where there is much more possible change in relative currency value without the early warning signals. The potential political disadvantages in making permanent parity changes continue. It is therefore likely that currencies will continue to float. Changes will result from both internal and external forces rather than from specific government action.

In the discussion so far, we have considered the amount of forward coverage that should be obtained as related to the net working capital in a particular currency. We must also consider the tax effects of a transaction in foreign exchange. Translation of assets and liabilities from one currency to another results in a significant change when there has been a devaluation or revaluation. However, that does not represent a taxable gain or loss, since in the country of the first currency concerned there has been no change in assets and liabilities. There has been a change in the equivalents in another currency, but that has no tax effect until a transfer of assets has been made. If, however, the position is protected by forward coverage, the profit on the forward coverage becomes taxable at the time the forward contracts are closed out. The actual protection is the net amount received after taxes, and that amount must be compared with the working capital position exposed to currency changes.

As an example, a U.S. businessman has a wholly owned subsidiary in the United Kingdom with a working capital position in sterling running about £100,000. At the end of 1966 he sells £200,000 one year forward at a rate of $2.75 per pound. The pound is devalued in November 1967 to $2.40 per pound. In December 1967 the forward contract comes due and he purchases £200,000 at a rate of $2.40 per pound. He receives from his bank $70,000, the profit from the transaction. The profit may be subject to U.S. income tax at the rate of approximately 48 percent, so that after tax, the net amount he receives is approximately $36,000.

Now, what has happened overall? Assuming the businessman consolidates the accounts of the British subsidiary, the £100,000 working capital has declined from a dollar equivalent of $280,000 to $240,000. As explained, this difference would have been picked up through the consolidated profits and loss account as an exchange loss of $40,000. The gain on the sale of the forward contract of $70,000 would have been picked up in the same account, netting to $30,000 profiit. Taxes would have increased by $34,000, which would result in a net loss after taxes for both transactions of $4,000. To avoid an overall loss because of the tax consequences, substantially more coverage must be obtained than that required by the actual net working capital exposed to currency change. As a rule of thumb, about twice as much gives adequate protection.

One sidelight on the preceding example is that, since the gain or loss from the translation of the accounts is not taxable, the percent of taxes to the net income before taxes is distorted in presenting consolidated accounts.

To sum up: assets and liabilities in other countries, when translated into a second currency, change in value as the value of the currency changes. Because of the methods of translation used, the change is generally limited to the working capital position. Forward coverage to protect that position may be obtained in round amounts for periods of one year or longer. In deciding whether to purchase forward coverage, the probable cost must be compared with the estimated risk. There are tax effects that also must be considered.

Management of Assets and Liabilities

We come now to the management of assets and liabilities to minimize the amount exposed to a currency change in the case of a devaluation or maximize it in the case of a revaluation. As has been explained, what is usually exposed is the working capital position expressed in a currency that may change in value with reference to another currency. However, a net asset position may be determined in some other manner. In general, the type of action that may be taken involves the timing of purchase or purchases or payments and the utilization of credit by either the payor or the payee. We can examine the general types of current assets or liabilities and determine what action may be taken with regard to them. It might be simplest first to consider the possibility of a devaluation and then that of a revaluation.

To protect against a devaluation, the objective should be to reduce working capital to a minimum or make it negative. Since working capital consists of current assets less current liabilities, any action that reduces a current asset and at the same time reduces a current liability has no effect on the working capital position. In the same fashion, an action that increases both a current liability and a current asset has no effect as far as working capital is concerned. We must therefore consider actions that change only one or the other and not both.

Let us start with cash. The first measure of protection would be to turn cash into another currency not exposed to a possible devaluation. To some extent that can be done, but it is inhibited by several factors. The first factor is the operating needs of the business, which are difficult to cover by bank accounts outside the country. Second, frequent conversions are costly, since there is a differential between the buy and sell rates for a particular currency. Third, prior to a devaluation, exchange controls are often instituted, and they may prohibit bank accounts abroad. The effect of a cash account in another currency is to reduce the cash in local currency, and it will be remembered that only the working capital in local currency is exposed to devaluation.

What else can be done to reduce cash? As pointed out, there is no change in exposed assets if cash is used to pay off current liabilities or to purchase current assets with the possible exception of inventory. Therefore, cash must be used for purposes that do not reduce current liabilities. It follows also that cash must be in excess of the operating needs of the business so that it is actually available. First of all, excess cash may be used to reduce obligations in other than local currencies, since those obligations are excluded from the working capital calculation. Second, cash can be used to pay for the purchase of capital assets or other assets that have a constant value. That is not quite as simple as it seems, since there is generally a time lag between a decision to purchase a capital asset and the receipt and payment of the billing therefor. If the capital asset is translated at the value of the date of receipt, there is no protection until it is received. Third, cash may be used to repay long-term obligations. That does not give economic protection; but because of the usual translation procedures it does protect against an immediate loss from devaluation. Finally, cash may be used to repay capital as in a branch and for dividend and profit remittances. There are often legal formalities and exchange restrictions that may make it difficult to make such transfers readily, but to some extent they can be planned for if there is sufficient time.

Marketable securities are very similar to cash. If it is practical, they can be held in another currency. If they are in excess of the needs of the business, they can be turned into cash and the proceeds can be utilized as outlined under cash. Notes and accounts receivable should be held to minimum amounts and the cash generated by their reduction should be utilized as already outlined. Unfortunately, the inflationary forces that generate a devaluation are usually reflected in a slowdown in payments by customers who are meeting the increased needs of financing their own businesses by slowing down payments. Collections are a chronic problem for any business, and constant follow-up is required. In many cases, the old adage, "the squeaking wheel gets the grease," applies. For receivables, the measures to be taken are operational rather than financial.

Inventory is a more difficult item to manage. At first blush, it should be reduced to a minimum and then the excess cash should be appropriately utilized. However, that approach ignores general business considerations. Inventories should usually be managed to meet the operating needs of the business. With the advent of computers, much more sophisticated techniques have been developed to keep inventories in line. It follows that if inventories are being properly managed from a business point of view, adjustments to provide protection against devaluation by reduction might very well lose more than they could gain.

There is another dimension to inventory, and that is pricing policy to be followed in the event of a devaluation. As has been pointed out, if prices are not increased in an inflationary situation, a business suffers an economic loss. That applies to inventory, and it is more obvious when the change in values is translated into another currency. If the prices at which inventory is sold or utilized can be increased in the event of a devaluation to compensate in whole or in part for the loss in value, then in the long run inventory does not lose its value; the change in value is reflected in an increase in profits when sales are made. Under those circumstances, it could be advantageous to build up inventory rather than reduce it.

Prepaid expenses and deferred charges are another usual kind of current asset. In general, their nature is such that little can be done to reduce them, and, in effect, since they are expensed over future periods, those periods benefit by a lower expense equivalent. It should be observed in the event of a devaluation, such items as insurance should be reviewed to determine whether or not additional coverage is not required. All the preceding considerations apply to other types of current assets.

Liabilities. We turn now to the other side of the working capital equation: current liabilities. The intent should be to increase them as far as possible without increasing current assets at the same time. There is, for example, no point in not paying bills if the cash that would normally be used for payment simply builds up in a bank account.

Let us first look at short-term loans payable. In countries where inflation and devaluation is a way of life, it is very difficult to obtain long-term loans regardless of interest rates. In such countries, short-term loans are renewed or refinanced when due so that they remain outstanding. Essentially they represent permanent financing, and as such they may often be considered to be invested in the capital assets of the business. In countries where inflation and devaluation occur infrequently, it is usually considered imprudent to finance the long-term needs of the business with short-term debt. That is a normal business axiom. There is a certain amount of risk to short-term financing, and it could be dangerous to over-utilize that type of financing; but where a devaluation appears likely, the protection afforded may be more advantageous than the liquidity risk entailed. For it to be advantageous, the short-term debt incurred must be used for capital or other assets that do not lose their value. Bankers will generally not lend money that is expressly to be used for dividend or profit remittances, since that type of payment reduces their coverage. Of course, if profits are remitted and the remaining net earnings to be reinvested in the business are not sufficient for capital needs, then a loan is in order. The net result may be exactly the same, but it is important to observe the niceties.

That leads to a consideration of accounts payable. They are, of course, the other side of accounts receivable; that is, the payables of one company are the receivables of another. One of the common symptoms of inflationary problems is a slowdown in payments. That results in a need for increased working capital to meet payments if payments are continued at the same rate. A way to cope with the situation is to slow down payments of accounts payable. That frees additional funds for the business, which may be protected as described in connection with cash or used in lieu of additional borrowing. Flexibility of payments is a business decision that should be weighed against the possibility that the cost in lost discounts, deterioration of vendor relationships, and possible change in credit ratings will offset the advantages of protection against devaluation.

Accrued expenses are another type of current liabilities. To a large extent, they result from the accounting practice of matching expenses with income on a period basis before the expenses are actually payable. A typical example is income taxes, which are generally payable at particular times but should be accrued on a regular basis. An increase in accruals has the effect of reducing working capital at the expense of current income. Prudent management may decide to set up reserves to provide for future losses from devaluation, and that is where the reserves would be shown. A more detailed discussion of the reasons for and advantages of such a procedure is given later in connection with pricing and planning.

As explained previously, long-term debt generally keeps a constant value in terms of another currency until it becomes short; therefore, an increase in long-term debt in local currency does not offer immediate protection against devaluation. However, on a long-term basis, the increase is desirable, particularly as an alternative to additional outside capital or loans. The eventual effect is protection if proper pricing policies are followed to avoid a deterioration in the economic values of the capital assets.

Use of other long-term liabilities, such as pension fund reserves, to cope with inflationary influences often requires adjustment in the underlying agreements. It is preferable to hold those liabilities at constant values to avoid the additional charges to income that would be necessary if the plans were subsequently adjusted. Unless that is done, substantial additional past service costs might offset any temporary gain from translating those liabilities at a lower rate in the event of a devaluation.

Revaluations

We have now covered in some depth procedures to follow to protect assets in the case of a devaluation. Different procedures are desirable in the case of revaluation. Now the objective is to increase working capital in local currency. Again, any action that increases a current asset and at the same time increases a current liability has no effect. In general, the exact reverse of the procedures for a devaluation are desirable. However, it is worthwhile to go over some of them to point up the differences.

To start again, everything possible should be done to turn current assets in other currencies, including cash in another currency, into local currency cash. Even when rates appear advantageous, deposits or investments in other currencies should be avoided. Management of cash and short-term investments in different currencies is discussed more fully in other chapters. In the same way, obligations in foreign currencies should be incurred if possible, since they have the effect of increasing local currency working capital. In addition, long-term obligations could be incurred; because of the translation rules, they result in an immediate gain that is not offset until the obligations are repaid. When a revaluation may occur, there are generally no or few exchange restrictions. In fact, the central banks concerned generally try to promote outflows and inhibit inflows for the reasons explained in Chapter 8.

Notes and accounts receivable again should be managed on an operational rather than financial basis. When some of them represent obligations by foreigners, a further credit review should be made to insure that the debtor would not find it difficult to pay at a future date higher amounts in terms of his own currency. Furthermore, when billings are in one currency but are paid in another on the basis of a designated rate of exchange, consideration should be given to whether the provision is enforceable or whether, because of the customer problem, it should in fact be enforced for debts incurred prior to the revaluation.

The same kind of question is equally applicable when the currency in which payment is made is devalued, since that is equivalent to a revaluation of the currency in which the debt is incurred. If that seems complicated, two examples will clarify it. A German exporter bills customers in the United Kingdom in deutsche marks but regularly accepts payment in sterling at the current market rate to a bank account in London. The mark is revalued in September–October 1969. Although technically he should pay additional pounds at the new rate for outstanding debts, the customer could feel that only pounds at the old rate are really due, and some adjustment might be required.

Now take the same situation back to December 1967. The pound has been devalued, but again the customer may feel that payment should be made at the predevaluation rate. The reason for that point of view is that the revaluation or devaluation has the effect of a retroactive price rise and has to be considered for its effect on continuing customer relationships.

Inventory is not a problem in the case of a revaluation, since price adjustments downward do not occur right away. In fact, the business gets a windfall benefit when the accounts are translated.

Prepaid expenses and deferred charges increase expenses over succeeding periods. Here consideration might be given to reducing coverage such as insurance, particularly when capital assets purchased from abroad are involved.

On the other side, the intent should be to reduce current liabilities without at the same time reducing current assets. There are three areas of possible management. One that has already been referred to is replacing short-term debt with long-term debt. The second is the timing of purchase and payment for capital assets. If a capital asset is set up at a constant equivalent at the date of receipt but payment is delayed, the effect is to reduce working capital. It may therefore be desirable to reconsider the methods being used to avoid such a situation. The third area of possible management involves the accruals; decrease in accruals increases working capital and current income. Adjustments may depend on the management philosophy involved and the basis on which they are determined. Under usual accounting rules, it would not be proper to accrue for a possible profit from a revaluation, but the same result can be achieved by adjusting methods used for other accruals.

Relationships with Affiliated Companies

In this chapter we have been discussing the foreign exchange aspects of assets held abroad. In most cases, the assets result from inter- or intracompany transactions whereby accounts receivable on the one side and accounts payable on the other are incurred. Because timing the payment of those accounts is subject to some control owing to common ownership, it is possible to accelerate or delay payment and thereby obtain some degree of protection. An account is always payable in a particular currency. When entities in different countries are concerned, one of them has either a possible exposure or a possible advantage that depends on the relative strengths of the currencies.

To give two examples, suppose a U.S. importer in July 1969 owed, for goods shipped, a German exporter and a French exporter in deutsche marks and French francs, respectively. If the importer had delayed payment of the French francs until after August 8, approximately 15 percent fewer dollars would have been required. On the other hand, if the importer had not made payment of the deutsche marks until after the end of October, approximately 15 percent more dollars would have been required. Payment terms are generally agreed upon on an arm's-length basis, and normally the importer would not be able to change the timing. However, when an affiliation exists, it is possible to take advantage of the situation to achieve some measure of protection against a possible devaluation or revaluation. In the example given, payment to Germany could have been accelerated and payment to France delayed. The principle is simple: payments from countries with weaker currencies should be expedited and payments by countries with stronger currencies should be delayed. This is the phenomenon of leads and lags.

There are, however, a number of practical difficulties that restrict what can be done. First of all, nonpayment or prepayment may result in a financial burden in a particular country that arises from the availability of funds to finance continued normal operations and from the additional interest cost on funds borrowed or interest earnings lost on funds used. Second, government exchange regulations often require payment within a specified time. In the United States, for example, changes in accounts with affiliates are considered as changes in investment abroad and are covered by the Office of Foreign Direct Investments regulations. Finally, the effect of changing payments transfers the gains from possible protection to a different country. When profit centers are involved or there are other ownership interests, that can make for difficulties, even though there is an advantage for the group as a whole which arises from the fact that the country that delays payment has interest earnings or savings from the use of the funds and also benefits from any change in currency values. Of course, the country that does not receive payment does not have the use of the funds and does not receive the benefit of any change in currency values. That can in part be remedied by interest payments on overdue accounts, but such changes in payment terms may have other ramifications that make them undesirable.

Flexible Pricing Policies

The remaining area in which protection may be provided is flexible pricing and planning to compensate for actual or expected changes in currency values.

Basically, the methods we have discussed up to now are a cure for the symptoms and not the disease. Devaluations or revaluations occur at a moment in time, but they are the result of economic and political forces that extend over much longer periods. Those forces are discussed in some detail in Chapter 4. Since the forces exist, the prudent businessman should structure his business to take them into account properly. Principally, what are involved are inflationary influences that increase at different rates in different countries. Evaluation of results in terms of a common currency tends to highlight changes in value of other than the common currency. Forward coverage and management of assets protect against only the immediate change; other measures must be adopted to protect the business from the erosion of values by inflation.

Fundamentally, what is necessary is an increase in prices to offset the loss of values from inflation. Of course, that is what inflation in the broad sense is all about—an increase in prices on a wide scale that outruns any productivity benefits. Changes in prices are difficult. There is always the feeling that increases will result in a loss of sales, and there is, therefore, a considerable amount of management inertia to overcome. That is particularly true when the profit level of the business in terms of local currency continues to be good or even shows substantial improvement on a period-to-period basis. However, the improvement may actually include a return of capital in an economic sense when depreciation charges are inadequate to cover replacement costs. As has been previously explained, that is aggravated by taxes assessed on income.

Because of the inertia described, price increases almost inevitably lag behind inflationary changes. The proper time to change prices is well before currency value changes occur, not after they occur. Major changes in currency value are often coupled with various types of price and wage controls, which attempt to dampen down the inflationary forces that gave rise to the changes. It is much more difficult to increase prices at such times, and the result is to stretch the economic loss out over a period of time. To cope with the situation, a flexible pricing policy that permits and leads to price changes in line with the underlying inflationary forces should be adopted. It is a mistake to assume that price equivalence in terms of more than one currency is adequate protection, since that equivalence can change suddenly just when it is very difficult to bring prices back into line again. The preceding considerations apply equally to doing business in one country only, but the effect on one currency in terms of another is much easier to see.

Planning

It is most important that there be, coupled with a flexible pricing policy, a degree of financial planning in reporting and evaluating results in one currency in terms of another. Again, although devaluations and revaluations occur at particular moments, they reflect economic changes that have been going on for some time. Properly, the cost of the currency value changes should be applied to the period prior to the date of the change. For example, to show as a single figure a large loss in results for 1967 due to the devaluation of sterling essentially means that profits from sterling operations prior to that date were overstated. If the accounts were restated, the loss could with hindsight be spread back over an appropriate period of time.

There are two ways in which the situation can be taken care of. One is to use a rate other than the going one for the translation of some or all of the profit and loss accounts. As an example, we have explained that capital assets have a constant value in terms of translation into another currency and that depreciation retains the constant value. Other accounts might be treated in the same way. If one currency is weak in relation to another but its value has been supported by the central bank, it might be entirely appropriate to use a free market rate of some sort rather than the official market rate. Choice of the rate is particularly important in planning and budgeting for future periods. Use of a lower rate for later periods may clearly indicate that price changes must be instituted to maintain the level of results evaluated in terms of another currency.

The second area in which planning should be done is that of providing reserves from current income for future losses from expected currency value changes. Such reserves are generally not tax deductible, but changes in values that result from translation of assets and liabilities in foreign currencies also are not tax deductible, so that all that is changed is the timing of the deduction. Reserves may be provided on a general basis or against particular accounts. They can be provided by the local company in terms of local currency, by the affiliated company at the time the results are translated, or by the affiliated company on its own books.

The provision of reserves should be considered in conjunction with the possibility of forward coverage and the management of the net working capital exposed to currency changes. The costs of forward coverage should be evaluated against the probable exposure and self-insurance for the risk in the form of reserves considered as an alternative. Appropriate planning in that area and in the pricing area is essential to avoid losses and properly manage operations in other currencies.

A thorough understanding of the methods used in translating assets and liabilities is essential for a proper evaluation of operations in other countries. There are choices of methods, and the ones adopted should be suitable to the needs of a particular business. Once the methods are selected, the assets and liabilities and the business as a whole can be managed to minimize the effect of fluctuations in foreign exchange.

Glossary

Principal Technical Terms Used in Foreign Exchange

MANY professions, trades, and occupations develop terminologies of their own that may baffle the uninitiated and render communication with outsiders difficult. Foreign exchange is no exception; for it has an extensive and specialized vocabulary. Words and phrases that mean one thing in what might be called everyday English, for lack of a better term, often mean something quite different in the language of foreign exchange.

The following glossary of technical terms used in foreign exchange is designed to assist those who desire a greater understanding of foreign exchange and help lift the veil of mystery that all too often surrounds the subject. The list includes only the principal terms that are likely to be encountered and does not pretend to be complete.

accounts, foreign currency See *foreign currency accounts.*
active intervention. See *intervention, active.*
appreciation, exchange An increase in the value of a given currency in terms of other currencies and especially the dollar.
arbitrage, exchange, cross-rate, or space The simultaneous purchase or sale of a foreign currency in two or more centers to take advantage of differing rates in the centers and make a profit from those differentials.
arbitrage, interest The act of borrowing in one country and lending or investing in another to take advantage of differing rates of interest in the two countries.

arbitrage points or *arbitrage support points* The rate of spot exchange above or below parity at which a government intervenes in the exchange market to maintain the rate within the limits set by the IMF or EMA Agreements.

arbitrageur or *arbitrager* A person who engages in arbitrage operations.

at best Instruction to a bank to buy or sell foreign exchange at the best or most favorable rate available instead of at a specified rate.

authorized dealer A bank in the United Kingdom or other country with exchange controls that is authorized to engage in certain specified exchange transactions.

balance of payments A statistical tabulation of the economic transactions between the residents of one country and another country, region or a group of countries, the rest of the world, or international institutions.

bear One who sells foreign exchange spot or for future delivery (forward) in the expectation of purchasing it later at a lower rate or with a devalued par.

bills, foreign See *foreign bills.*

blocked account Currency that is owned by nonresidents of an exchange control country and cannot be freely transferred.

Bretton Woods system The international payments system that was utilized by the members of the International Monetary Fund and that functioned under the rules set forth in the IMF Agreement.

broker A person who arranges for the purchase or sale of foreign exchange between banks but is not a principal to the transaction.

brokerage Charges made by a broker for his services in arranging for the purchase or sale of foreign exchange between banks.

brokers, foreign exchange See *foreign exchange brokers.*

bull One who buys foreign exchange for delivery in the future (forward) in the expectation of selling it then at a higher price or who buys spot exchange in the hope of selling it later at a higher price.

business days See *clear days.*

buying rate Rate of exchange at which a bank or dealer will purchase a given foreign currency.

cable or *telegraphic transfers, TT* Foreign exchange transactions carried out by use of cable or telegraph.

certain, direct, or *fixed quotation* A quotation of fixed units of foreign exchange in terms of variable units of the domestic currency.

clear, business, or *market days* Days on which markets involved in a foreign exchange transaction are open for business and that are used in determining the value dates on which foreign exchange or Euro-dollar transactions must be consummated.

clearing house funds Funds transferred between banks in New York with good value the next business day.

covering The purchase or sale of forward exchange to parry the risk of fluctuations in a rate of exchange, devaluation, and revaluation when payments are to be made or received in a foreign currency in the future.

cross-rate arbitrage See *arbitrage, exchange, cross-rate, or space.*

currency, foreign accounts See *foreign currency accounts.*

currency, intervention See *intervention currency.*

deposit and swap See *swap and deposit.*

direct quotation See *certain quotation.*

discount That at which forward exchange is said to be when it is cheaper than spot and of spot exchange when it is lower than parity.

equilibrium rate For spot exchange, the rate that precisely balances the demand and supply of a currency; also, the rate that enables a country to balance its external accounts. For forward exchange, the rate that conforms to the interest parities.

escudo area A group of countries that transact their international business in terms of escudos, maintain their international reserves in escudos in Lisbon, and subscribe to international monetary regulations, chiefly exchange controls, established by Lisbon.

Euro-currencies Deposits of foreign currencies, denominated in terms of the foreign currency, in domestic banks. Also, lending and borrowing transactions in those currencies.

Euro-dollars Deposits of U.S. dollars in foreign banks denominated in dollars.

Euro-dollar market A group of markets outside the United States, principally in London, that deals in dollar and other currency deposits denominated in dollars and those other currencies as well as transactions in those currencies.

Euro-dollar or Euro-currency standard rates See *standard Euro-dollar or Euro-currency rates.*

Euro-sterling Deposits of sterling denominated in sterling in banks in non-sterling countries. Also, transactions in those sterling deposits.

exchange arbitrage See *arbitrage, exchange, cross-rate, or space.*

exchange clearing An arrangement between two countries to establish an account into which export earnings of exchange are credited or deposited and against which import payments are debited or charged. The net credit or debit balance of the account is periodically settled between the two countries.

exchange controls or *exchange restrictions* Limitations of free dealings in foreign exchange or restrictions on the free transfer of domestic currency into foreign currencies and vice versa.

exchange control risk The risk of defaulting on a foreign exchange obligation owing to the imposition of exchange controls that prevent the consummation of the transaction.

exchange rate The price of one currency in terms of another at a given moment of time. Also, the middle rates for telegraphic transfers of spot exchange between banks.

exchange rate risk The risk taken by a party who must make or receive payment in a foreign currency. The risk occurs by reason of fluctuations in the rates of exchange or devaluations or revaluations of the currencies to be received or paid out.

exchange rates, overvalued See *overvalued exchange rates* or *overvaluation.*

exchanged rates, undervalued See *undervalued exchange rates* or *undervaluation.*

exchange restrictions See *exchange controls.*

exchange risk The possibility of loss arising from an uncovered (open) position when the exchange rate rises or falls or the parity is devalued or revalued.

federal funds Literally, balances of U.S. commercial banks in the Federal Reserve banks. Used also to designate funds transferred with immediate good (available) value.

firm exchange Exchange rates that are either stable or appreciating.

firm quotation A quotation of a foreign exchange rate that is binding if immediately accepted for either the specified amount or the customary minimum transaction between banks.

fixed exchanges A system of relatively fixed parities in which exchange rate fluctuations are confined to a specified spread above and below par.

fixed quotations See *certain quotation.*

flexible exchange rates or *flexible exchanges* A system in which wide exchange rate fluctuations are permitted above and below par or in which the parities are frequently adjusted. Government intervention often is used to limit or stabilize flexible exchange rate movements.

floating exchange rates or *floating exchanges* A system in which either there are no parities or the parities are not enforced and the rate of exchange is allowed to fluctuate freely, although subject to occasional government intervention to influence its movement.

fluctuations of exchange rates or *exchange fluctuations* Movement of exchange rates either without limits or within the official support points.

foreign balances Credit balances in accounts abroad held by domestic residents and denominated in foreign currencies. In a broader sense, all liquid foreign short-term assets.

foreign bills Bills of exchange drawn on a foreign resident and denominated in a foreign currency.

foreign currency accounts Deposit or current accounts denominated in a foreign currency and held in foreign countries.

foreign exchange The procedure, methods, and institutions utilized in transferring the money of one country into that of another. In a wider sense, all the procedures, documents, and institutions involved in transactions between two or more currencies.

foreign exchange brokers Individuals or firms who act as intermediaries—not principals—between banks for foreign exchange or Euro-dollar transactions and who operate on a local market.

foreign exchange market See *international foreign exchange market.*

foreign notes Bank, corporation, or government short-term notes bought, held, and sold by residents of countries other than the country of issue.

Forex Club An association of foreign exchange dealers, with chapters in the more important foreign exchange markets, to promote the professional and social interests of the members.

forward exchange The procedures involved in buying or selling foreign exchange for future delivery. Also, foreign currencies bought or sold for future delivery against payment on delivery.

forward margin, swap margin, or *swap rate* The discount or premium on forward exchange with reference to the spot rate.

franc area or zone A group of countries that transact their international business in terms of French francs, maintain their international reserves in francs in Paris, and subscribe to the regulations, chiefly exchange controls, established by Paris. The members consist chiefly of some former French colonies.

gold bullion standard A previously existing monetary standard under which gold bars, but not gold coin, of a stipulated minimum amount were convertible against domestic money for use in foreign, but usually not domestic, payments.

gold coin standard A previously existing monetary system under which gold was the standard money and all money in any amount was convertible into gold coins on demand.

gold exchange standard An international monetary standard under which a country maintains its reserves in another country whose currency is directly or indirectly convertible into gold, maintains its currency on a par with that of the other country, and finances its international transactions with that currency.

gold points The limits, under the gold coin and gold bullion standards, to exchange rate fluctuations above and below mint parity as determined by the cost of exporting and importing gold.

gold price, free The price at which gold may be bought and sold on the free gold markets.

gold price, official Formerly the official U.S. buying and selling price of gold. Since 1934 and until 1971, it has been fixed at $35 per fine troy ounce.

gold withdrawals Formerly the conversion of dollars held by foreign monetary authorities into gold at the official price of $35 per fine troy ounce.

hedging The purchase or sale of exchange, spot or forward, to meet the exchange risks (rates, devaluations, or revaluations) that affect the values of foreign-currency-denominated assets and liabilities. Also, the taking of an exchange risk to offset a larger risk in the opposite sense.

hot money Foreign funds temporarily transferred abroad to avoid inflation or monetary instability at home or to avoid exchange controls, taxation, or other regulations.

inconvertible currencies Currencies that are not freely convertible into other currencies for current account transactions by either resident or non-resident holders.

indirect quotation The quotation of the value of a unit of domestic currency in variable amounts of a foreign currency.

interbank sterling Funds loaned between London banks in round amounts and without security.

interest arbitrage, inward Transfer of short-term funds from foreign into domestic currency loans or deposits to take advantage of interest rate differentials.

interest arbitrage, outward Transfer of short-term funds from domestic to foreign currency loans or deposits to take advantage of interest differentials.

interest parities A theory that attempts to explain the differential between spot and forward rates of exchange. It holds that the differential is conditioned by the amount that will equalize the interest rates between any two countries.

international brokers Individuals or firms who act as intermediaries between banks and non-bank parties in consummating transactions on the Eurodollar market.

international foreign exchange market An informal market that constitutes the focus of a communications network and is located in a principal financial center of an international trading country and in which foreign exchange is bought and sold and related transactions are carried out. Also, the sum of such individual markets.

intervention, active Actual government or official financial agency operation on the foreign exchange market to prevent, to limit, or to cause changes in rates of exchange.

intervention currency A foreign currency utilized by a nation to intervene in a foreign exchange market to limit, control, stabilize, or cause changes in the exchange value of its currency.

intervention, passive The sum of government or official financial operations to counter excess, or deficient, supply and demand for the government's currency.

investment currencies Foreign currency proceeds that are realized from the sale of foreign investments in the United Kingdom and that can be used for other foreign investments.

investment dollars Dollars that are realized by U.K. residents from the sale of dollar investments and that are usable for other dollar or foreign currency investments.

leads and lags Respectively the advance in and delay of payment of sums due in a foreign currency in anticipation of a rise or fall in its rate of exchange or devaluation or revaluation.

limits Specifically, the maximum amount that a party, usually a bank, will accept from another party, usually also a bank, for forward or Euro-dollar transactions or for payments arising from foreign exchange transactions on the same day. Generally, any limit placed on foreign exchange transactions.

long forward exchange Forward transactions having maturities usually in excess of 90 days.

long position   A situation in which a party, usually a bank, has an excess of short-term balances, spot exchanges or forward claims in a foreign currency.

loro accounts   The current accounts of domestic banks with foreign banks held in a foreign currency for the benefit of domestic customers.

mail transfers   Transactions in foreign exchange executed by airmail.

market days   See *clear days.*

market, foreign exchange   See *international foreign exchange market.*

market, official   In continental Europe, a designated and officially recognized place where traders meet to execute foreign exchange transactions or to fix rates of exchange applicable to certain specified purposes.

marrying foreign exchange transactions   The counterbalancing of exchange commitment or position that arises from a transaction with one client by a transaction for the same amount and maturity and in the same currency but in the opposite sense with another client.

maturities, odd   The dates for maturities other than those regarded as standard for forward and Euro-dollar business.

minimum amount   The smallest amount of a foreign exchange transaction acceptable for dealing in the market.

nonresident accounts   Accounts or balances owned by others than the residents of a country or monetary area.

nostro accounts   The current or deposit accounts of domestic banks with their branches and correspondents abroad. They are denominated in the currencies of those branches and correspondents and are generally used for current requirements.

open position   The difference between long and short positions in a given foreign currency. Also, the difference between the grand totals of all long and short positions.

optional forward contracts   Forward exchange contracts that give one of the parties a choice of delivery dates.

outright forward exchange   Buying or selling of forward exchange without a simultaneous cover in the form of spot exchange.

overvalued exchange rates or *overvaluation*   A situation in which the rate of exchange rises, or the par is set, above its equilibrium or purchasing power parity rate. Also, a situation in which forward premiums over spot are wider or forward discounts are lower than the interest parities between the two currencies.

pars or *parities*   The official rate of exchange established by a government with the agreement of the IMF in the case of a member or simply by fiat in the case of a nonmember of the IMF.

pegged rates of exchange   Rates of exchange maintained at a given level or within a band of fluctuations by government purchase or sale of its own currency or other operations.

pegging   Operations on the foreign exchange market designed to maintain a country's rate of exchange at a given level.

position sheet or book   A sheet or book that lists all of a bank's transactions at given date in all foreign currencies. The transactions are so arranged as to enable the traders to ascertain whether they have a long or short position, forward and spot, in any given currency or in all currencies. Also, the bank's position for a given currency, or for all currencies, at various dates.

premium   The amount paid for spot exchange in excess of par or for forward exchange above the spot rate.

quotations   Rates at which banks or dealers are prepared to buy or sell foreign currencies in limited amounts.

quotation, uncertain   See *indirect quotation.*

renewing commitments   The extending for an additional period of forward contracts that are about to expire, usually by means of a swap transaction.

resident accounts   Deposit or current accounts denominated in a domestic currency and owned by the residents of the country or monetary area in which that currency is the official one.

revaluation   An increase in the official parity whereby fewer units of the currency revalued are required to purchase other currencies than formerly.

risk, credit   A risk of default on international payments obligations due to the inability or the unwillingness of the debtor to remit.

risk, delivery   The possibility that a seller of foreign exchange may fail to deliver the foreign currency he has sold after he has collected payment for it in terms of the local currency.

risk, forward position   The possibility of a loss, due to a change in the swap margin, on a covered exchange transaction.

scheduled territories   Countries and territories that are members of the sterling area and that include, principally but not exclusively, former members of the British Empire. The list changes from time to time, but the larger banks in financial centers usually have an up-to-date list.

security currencies   See *investment currencies.*

selling rate   The rate of exchange asked by banks and dealers for a given foreign currency, usually in terms of the local or domestic currency.

short forward rate   The rate asked for forward exchange of relatively short maturities, usually of one month or less.

short position   A situation in which a bank's or a dealer's short-term net liabilities in a foreign currency exceed the respective short-term holdings or assets denominated in that currency.

space arbitrage   See *arbitrage, exchange, cross-rate, or space.*

specified currencies   Currencies of countries outside the sterling area held by U.K. residents who are under an obligation to sell them to authorized banks within a stipulated period after acquisition.

speculation, foreign exchange   The taking or maintaining of a spot position or an uncovered forward commitment in foreign exchange in the hope of making a profit by the future sale of the spot or the liquidation of the forward transaction.

spot exchange The purchase and sale of a foreign currency for immediate delivery (usually for two clear or value days) and paid for upon delivery.

spread (1) The difference between the selling and buying rates for a given currency. (2) The difference between the support points, or the arbitrage support points, for a nation's currency. (3) The difference between spot and forward rates for a given currency. (4) In general, any price differential for a given currency.

standard amounts The usual round amounts in which foreign exchange or Euro-dollar transactions take place between banks.

standard Euro-dollar or Euro-currency rates The going rates of interest applicable to Euro-dollar or Euro-currency loans to prime names.

steady exchange A situation in which there are relatively limited fluctuations in the several rates of exchange or in which exchange rates may be said to be firm.

sterling area A group of countries that transact their international business in sterling, maintain their international reserves in sterling in London, and apply exchange controls similar to those of the United Kingdom. The member countries, which change from time to time, consist of some former British colonies and some other countries that have traditionally employed sterling for international transactions.

swap (1) The purchase of spot against the sale of exchange forward. (2) The sale of spot against the purchase of exchange forward. (3) The purchase or sale of short against long forward exchange. (4) The exchange, between government central banks, of deposits to each other's accounts usually to provide foreign exchange to enable each to protect its rates of exchange.

swap and deposit An arrangement that combines a forward swap transaction with the borrowing of the currency involved by one of the parties from the other, who then has the use of both currencies for the life of the transaction.

swap arrangements, reciprocal See *swap (4)*.

swap margin See *forward margin*.

swap rate See *forward margin*.

switch currencies or dollars See *investment currencies*.

telegraphic transfers, TT See *cable or telegraphic transfers, TT*.

time arbitrage The use of forward exchange to take advantage of the price differentials between various forward maturity dates.

transfers, telegraphic, TT or cable See *cable or telegraphic transfers, TT*.

two-way quotations (1) The simultaneous quotation of both a buying and selling rate for a given currency. (2) For Euro-dollars, the simultaneous quotation of rates of interest for both lending and borrowing. In the case of a bank, a two-way quotation implies a willingness to trade either way.

ultimo The last business day of the current month. The term has reference to the Continental practice of timing transactions to fall on the last business day of the month.

uncertain quotation   See *indirect quotation.*

undervalued exchange rates or *undervaluation*   A situation in which the rate of exchange falls, or the parity is set, below its equilibrium or purchasing power parity rate. Also, the situation in which forward premiums are narrower or forward discounts wider than the interest differentials between the two currencies.

undoing cover or hedge   The creating of an open, uncovered, or unhedged transaction by the elimination of the forward transaction that formerly covered or hedged it.

valeur compensée (compensated value) or *here and there*   An arrangement whereby payments that arise from foreign exchange transactions are to be made on the same day in the two markets involved.

value date   The day or date on which foreign exchange transactions are to be settled by delivery and payment.

value today   The specification that spot transactions are to be settled on the day they are entered into instead of the usual two clear days later.

value tomorrow   The specification that spot exchange transactions are to be settled on the first clear day after the day on which they are entered into.

very long forward exchange   Forward exchange transactions that usually have a maturity of over 12 months.

vostro accounts   The accounts of foreign banks with domestic correspondents or branches denominated in the domestic currency. The vostro account of one bank is the nostro account of the other.

weak exchange   Exchange that is falling in relation to other currencies.

weekend influences   Technical influences on foreign exchange rates at the beginning of a weekend, that are due to rearrangements of foreign exchange positions.

window dressing   The repatriation by banks of funds held abroad to increase the proportion of liquid, as against other, assets in an effort to improve the appearance of their balance sheets or quarterly or monthly returns.

Bibliography

The Framework of International Business

Dunning, John H., *Studies in International Investment.* London: George Allen & Unwin, Ltd., 1970.

Fayerweather, John, *Facts and Fallacies of International Business.* New York: Holt, Rinehart and Winston, Inc., 1962.

The Growth and Spread of Multinational Companies. London: Economist Intelligence Unit, October 1969.

Kindleberger, Charles P., *The International Corporation.* Cambridge, Mass.: The M.I.T. Press, 1970.

Kolde, Endel J., *International Business Enterprise.* Englewood Cliffs, N.J.: Prentice-Hall, Inc., 1968.

Madeheim, Huxley, Mazzi, Edward Mark, and Stein, Charles S. (Eds.), *International Business: Articles and Essays.* New York: Holt, Rinehart and Winston, Inc., 1963.

Polk, Judd, "The Rise of World Corporations," *Saturday Review,* September 22, 1969, pp. 32ff.

Robinson, Richard D., *International Business Policy.* New York: Holt, Rinehart and Winston, Inc., 1964.

Rolfe, Sidney E., *The International Corporation.* Istanbul: International Chamber of Commerce, 1969.

———, and Damm, Walter, (Eds.), *The Multinational Corporation in the World Economy.* New York: Frederick A. Praeger, Inc., 1970.

Rose, Sanford, "The Rewarding Strategies of Multinationalism," *Fortune,* September 15, 1968, pp. 100–105, 180–182.

Servan-Schreiber, Jean-Jacques, *The American Challenge.* London: Hamish-Hamilton, 1968.

Smith, Dan Throop, "Financial Variables in International Business," *Harvard Business Review,* January-February 1966, pp. 93–104.

Tugendhat, Christopher, "A New Way of Looking at the International Company," *Financial Times,* August 12, 1968.

———, *The Multinationals.* London: Eyre & Spottiswoode, 1971.

Zenoff, David B., and Zwick, Jack, *International Financial Management.* Englewood Cliffs, N.J.: Prentice-Hall, Inc., 1969.

History of Foreign Exchange

Cassel, Gustav, *Money and Foreign Exchange After 1914.* New York: The Macmillan Company, 1923.

Einzig, Paul, *The History of Foreign Exchange.* London: Macmillan & Co., Ltd., 1962.

Mikesell, Raymond F., *Foreign Exchange in the Post-War World.* New York: Twentieth Century Fund, 1954.

Roover, Raymond de (Ed.), *Gresham on Foreign Exchange.* Cambridge, Mass.: Harvard University Press, 1949.

The International Monetary System

Horsefield, J. Keith, *The International Monetary Fund, 1945–1965,* Vol. I, *Chronicle.* Washington: International Monetary Fund, 1969.

Kindleberger, Charles P., *International Economics,* 4th ed. Homewood, Ill.: Richard D. Irwin, Inc., 1968.

League of Nations, *International Currency Experience.* New York: Columbia University Press, 1944.

Snider, Delbert A., *Introduction to International Economics,* 5th ed. Homewood, Ill.: Richard D. Irwin, Inc., 1971.

Tew, Brian, *International Monetary Cooperation, 1945–70,* 10th ed. London: Hutchinson & Co. Publishers, Ltd., 1970.

Triffin, Robert, "The Evolution of the International Monetary System: Historical Reappraisal and Future Perspectives," *Princeton Studies in International Finance,* No. 12. Princeton, N.J.: Princeton University, International Finance Section, 1964.

———, *The World Money Maze.* New Haven, Conn.: Yale University Press, 1966.

Wasserman, Max J., Hultman, Charles W., and Ware, Ray M., *Modern International Economics,* 2nd rev. ed. Cambridge, Mass.: Schenkman Publishing Co., Inc., 1971.

———, ———, and Zsoldos, Lazlo, *International Finance.* Boston: D.C. Heath & Company, 1963.

Balance of Payments Theory

Badger, Donald C., "The Balance of Payments: A Tool of Economic Analyses," *Staff Papers,* International Monetary Fund, Vol. II, No. 1 (September 1951), pp. 86–197.

Lary, Hal B., *Problems of the United States as World Trader and Banker.* New York: National Bureau of Economic Research, 1963.

Machlup, Fritz, "Three Concepts of the Balance of Payments and the So-called Dollar Shortage," *Economic Journal,* March 1950, pp. 46–68.

Meade, J.E., *The Balance of Payments.* London: Oxford University Press, 1966.

Wasserman, Max J., and Ware, Ray M., *The Balance of Payments.* Cambridge, Mass.: Schenkman Publishing Co., Inc., 1965.

Parity Changes

de Vries, Margaret G., "Twenty Years of Par Values," *Finance and Development,* Vol. 3, No. 4 (December 1965), pp. 283–289.

———, "The Magnitudes of Exchange Devaluation," *Finance and Development,* Vol. 5, No. 2 (June 1968), pp. 8–12.

Einzig, Paul, *Leads and Lags: The Main Cause of Devaluation.* London: Macmillan & Co., Ltd., 1968.

Thirlwall, A. P., "Another Autopsy on Britain's Balance of Payments: 1958–1967," *Quarterly Review of the Banca Nazionale del Lavoro,* September 1970, pp. 308–325.

International Monetary Problems and Proposed Solutions

Aliber, Robert Z., *Choices for the Dollar.* Washington: National Planning Association, 1969.

Halm, George N., "Toward Limited Exchange Rate Flexibility," *Essays in International Finance,* No. 73. Princeton, N.J.: Princeton University, International Finance Section, 1969.

Hawkins, Robert G., and Rolfe, Sidney E., "A Compendium of Plans for International Monetary Reform" and "A Critical Survey of Plans for International Monetary Reform," *The Bulletin,* C. J. Devine Institute of International Finance, New York University, 1965.

Machlup, Fritz, *Plans for Reform of the International Monetary System.* Princeton, N.J.: Princeton University, International Finance Section, 1962.

———, *Remaking the International Monetary System.* Baltimore: The Johns Hopkins Press, 1968.

———, and Malkiel, Burton G. (Eds.), *International Monetary Arrangements: The Problem of Choice.* Princeton, N.J.: Princeton University, International Finance Section, 1964.

Marris, Stephen, "The Bürgenstock Communiqué: A Critical Examination of the Case for Limited Flexibility of Exchange Rates," *Essays in International Finance,* No. 80. Princeton, N.J.: Princeton University, International Finance Section, 1970.

Melish, G. Hartley, and Hawkins, Robert G., "The Stability of Flexible Exchange Rates—The Canadian Experience," *The Bulletin,* C. J. Devine Institute of Finance, New York University, 1968.

Sohmen, Egon, *Flexible Exchange Rates.* Chicago: The University of Chicago Press, 1969.

Williamson, John H. "The Crawling Peg," *Essays in International Finance,* No. 50. Princeton, N.J.: Princeton University, International Finance Section, 1965.

Foreign Exchange Markets and Institutions

Bagehot, Walter, *Lombard Street: A Description of the Money Market,* new ed. Homewood, Ill.: Richard D. Irwin, Inc., 1962.

Chittenden, George H., *The New York Foreign Exchange Market.* New York: J. P. Morgan & Co., 1957.

Crump, Norman, *The ABC of the Foreign Exchanges,* 13th ed. London: Macmillan & Co., Ltd., 1965.

Einzig, Paul, *A Textbook on Foreign Exchange,* 2nd ed. London: Macmillan & Co., Ltd., 1969.

Evitt, H. E., *A Manual of Foreign Exchange.* London: Sir Isaac Pitman & Sons, Ltd., 1967.

Goschen, G. J., *The Theory of the Foreign Exchanges.* London: Sir Isaac Pitman & Sons, Ltd., 1932.

Hirsch, Fred, *Money International.* London: Allen Lane, 1967.

Holmes, Alan R., and Schott, Francis H., *The New York Foreign Exchange Market.* New York: Federal Reserve Bank of New York, 1965.

Lall, Sanjaya, "The Forward Exchange Market," *Finance and Development,* September 1967, pp. 187–194.

Schilling, Don, "Forward Exchange and Currency Position," *Journal of Finance,* December 1969, pp. 875–885.

Stein, Jerome L., *The Nature and Efficiency of the Foreign Exchange Market.* Princeton, N.J.: Princeton University, International Finance Section, 1962.

Swiss Bank Corporation, *Foreign Exchange.* Basle, 1968.

Walton, L. E., *Foreign Trade and Foreign Exchange.* London: MacDonald & Evans Ltd., 1958.

Whiting, D. P., *Finance of Foreign Trade and Foreign Exchange.* London: MacDonald & Evans Ltd., 1968.

Rates of Exchange and Their Determination

Einzig, Paul, *A Dynamic Theory of Forward Exchange.* London: Macmillan & Co., Ltd., 1967.

Feldstein, Martin S., "Uncertainty and Forward Exchange Speculation," *Review of Economics and Statistics,* May 1968, pp. 182–192.

Houthakker, H. S., "Exchange Rate Adjustment," *Factors Affecting the United States Balance of Payments,* Joint Economic Committee, Congress of the United States, 87th Congress, 2nd session. Washington, D.C.: Government Printing Office, 1962.

Machlup, Fritz, *International Monetary Economics.* London: George Allen & Unwin, Ltd., 1966. (Published in the United States by Charles Scribner's Sons under the title *International Payments, Debts and Gold.*)

————, "The Theory of Foreign Exchanges," *Economica VI,* new series, November 1939, pp. 375–397, and February 1940, pp. 23–49.

Metzler, Lloyd A., "Exchange Rates and the International Monetary Fund," *International Monetary Policies.* Postwar Economic Studies No. 7. Washington, D.C.: Board of Governors of the Federal Reserve System, 1947, pp. 1–45.

Ozga, S. A., *The Rate of Exchange and the Terms of Trade.* London: Weidenfeld and Nicholson, 1967.

International Money Management

"Are Currency Exchange Costs Nibbling at Your Overseas Profits?" *Business Abroad*, February 1970, pp. 14–15.

Prindl, Andreas R., "International Money Management: I—The Environmental Framework," *Euromoney*, September 1971; "II—Systems and Techniques," ibid., October 1971; "III—The Effects of International Money Management," ibid., November 1971.

Shulman, Jones, "When the Price Is Wrong—by Design," *Columbia Journal of World Business*, May-June 1971, pp. 69–76.

Stonehill, Arthur I., *Readings in Financial Management*. Pacific Palisades, Calif.: Goodyear Publishing Co. Inc., 1970.

Moore, Russell F., (Ed.), *AMA Management Handbook*, Section 8, "International Management." New York: AMA, 1970.

Zenoff, David B., "Remitting Funds from Foreign Affiliates," *Financial Executive*, March 1968, pp. 46–63.

Translation of Accounts and Exchange Risk

"The Accounting Treatment of Major Changes in the Sterling Parity of Overseas Currencies," Council of the Institute of Chartered Accountants, Recommendation 25, February 1968.

Burge, Marianne, "Devaluation and Its Tax Consequences," *Price Waterhouse Review*, Summer 1968, pp. 3–13.

"Foreign Operations and Foreign Exchange," *Accounting Research Bulletin*, No. 43, Chapter 12, American Institute of Certified Public Accountants, September 1953.

Lietaer, B., "Managing Risks in Foreign Exchange," *Harvard Business Review*, March–April 1970, pp. 127–138.

————, *Financial Management of Foreign Exchange*. Cambridge, Mass.: M.I.T. Press, 1971.

"Management Accounting Problems in Foreign Operations," National Association of Accountants, Research Report 36, March 1, 1960.

Scottish Institute Research Study, "The Treatment in Company Accounts of Changes in the Exchange Rates of International Currencies," *The Accountant's Magazine*, September 1970, pp. 415–423.

Verroen, J., "How I.T.T. Manages Its Foreign Exchange," *Management Services*, January–February 1965, pp. 27–33.

Index